Java Programming 10-Minute Solutions

Java™ Programming 10-Minute Solutions

Mark Watson

San Francisco · London

Associate Publisher: Joel Fugazzotto
Acquisitions Editor: Tom Cirtin
Developmental Editor: Tom Cirtin
Production Editor: Liz Burke
Technical Editor: Chris N. Crane
Copyeditor: Sally Engelfried
Compositor: Happenstance Type-O-Rama
Graphic Illustrator: Happenstance Type-O-Rama
Proofreaders: Laurie O'Connell, Darcy Maurer, Nancy Riddiough, Amy Rasmusen
Indexer: Ted Laux
Book Designer: Maureen Forys, Happenstance Type-O-Rama
Cover Illustrator/Photographer: John Nedwidek, Emdesign

Library of Congress Card Number: 2003115440

ISBN: 0-7821-4285-0

Manufactured in the United States of America

10 9 8 7 6 5 4 3 2 1

SOFTWARE LICENSE AGREEMENT: TERMS AND CONDITIONS

The media and/or any online materials accompanying this book that are available now or in the future contain programs and/or text files (the "Software") to be used in connection with the book. SYBEX hereby grants to you a license to use the Software, subject to the terms that follow. Your purchase, acceptance, or use of the Software will constitute your acceptance of such terms.

The Software compilation is the property of SYBEX unless otherwise indicated and is protected by copyright to SYBEX or other copyright owner(s) as indicated in the media files (the "Owner(s)"). You are hereby granted a single-user license to use the Software for your personal, noncommercial use only. You may not reproduce, sell, distribute, publish, circulate, or commercially exploit the Software, or any portion thereof, without the written consent of SYBEX and the specific copyright owner(s) of any component software included on this media.

In the event that the Software or components include specific license requirements or end-user agreements, statements of condition, disclaimers, limitations or warranties ("End-User License"), those End-User Licenses supersede the terms and conditions herein as to that particular Software component. Your purchase, acceptance, or use of the Software will constitute your acceptance of such End-User Licenses.

By purchase, use or acceptance of the Software you further agree to comply with all export laws and regulations of the United States as such laws and regulations may exist from time to time.

Reusable Code in This Book

The author(s) created reusable code in this publication expressly for reuse by readers. Sybex grants readers limited permission to reuse the code found in this publication, its accompanying CD-ROM or available for download from our website so long as the author(s) are attributed in any application containing the reusable code and the code itself is never distributed, posted online by electronic transmission, sold, or commercially exploited as a stand-alone product.

Software Support

Components of the supplemental Software and any offers associated with them may be supported by the specific Owner(s) of that material, but they are not supported by SYBEX. Information regarding any available support may be obtained from the Owner(s) using the information provided in the appropriate read.me files or listed elsewhere on the media.

Should the manufacturer(s) or other Owner(s) cease to offer support or decline to honor any offer, SYBEX bears no responsibility. This notice concerning support for the Software is provided for your information only. SYBEX is not the agent or principal of the Owner(s), and SYBEX is in no way responsible for providing any support for the Software, nor is it liable or responsible for any support provided, or not provided, by the Owner(s).

Warranty

SYBEX warrants the enclosed media to be free of physical defects for a period of ninety (90) days after purchase. The Software is not available from SYBEX in any other form or media than that enclosed herein or posted to www.sybex.com. If you discover a defect in the media during this warranty period, you may obtain a replacement of identical format at no charge by sending the defective media, postage prepaid, with proof of purchase to:

SYBEX Inc.
Product Support Department
1151 Marina Village Parkway
Alameda, CA 94501
Web: `http://www.sybex.com`

After the 90-day period, you can obtain replacement media of identical format by sending us the defective disk, proof of purchase, and a check or money order for $10, payable to SYBEX.

Disclaimer

SYBEX makes no warranty or representation, either expressed or implied, with respect to the Software or its contents, quality, performance, merchantability, or fitness for a particular purpose. In no event will SYBEX, its distributors, or dealers be liable to you or any other party for direct, indirect, special, incidental, consequential, or other damages arising out of the use of or inability to use the Software or its contents even if advised of the possibility of such damage. In the event that the Software includes an online update feature, SYBEX further disclaims any obligation to provide this feature for any specific duration other than the initial posting.

The exclusion of implied warranties is not permitted by some states. Therefore, the above exclusion may not apply to you. This warranty provides you with specific legal rights; there may be other rights that you may have that vary from state to state. The pricing of the book with the Software by SYBEX reflects the allocation of risk and limitations on liability contained in this agreement of Terms and Conditions.

Shareware Distribution

This Software may contain various programs that are distributed as shareware. Copyright laws apply to both shareware and ordinary commercial software, and the copyright Owner(s) retains all rights. If you try a shareware program and continue using it, you are expected to register it. Individual programs differ on details of trial periods, registration, and payment. Please observe the requirements stated in appropriate files.

Copy Protection

The Software in whole or in part may or may not be copy-protected or encrypted. However, in all cases, reselling or redistributing these files without authorization is expressly forbidden except as specifically provided for by the Owner(s) therein.

I dedicate this book to my customers:
we learn from each other.

— Mark Watson

Acknowledgments

I would like to thank my acquisitions and developmental editor Tom Cirtin, my technical editor Chris N. Crane, my production editor Liz Burke, and my copy editor Sally Engelfried for all their help in producing this book. I wish to express my appreciation to my wife Carol for both encouraging me to write and acting as my "first line" proofreader.

Contents

Introduction

This book was designed and written to provide professional Java programmers with short code examples for the most common Java programming problems encountered in day-to-day work. I wrote this book to save you time when working on Java programming projects. I have attempted to compress into one short book most of the low-and mid-level Java programming techniques that I use in my own Java consulting business.

I expect you to use this book to look up solutions to current programming problems that you encounter, but I hope that you also enjoy reading through the entire book to learn new Java programming techniques. I cover low-level techniques such as file I/O, string handling, XML processing, searching and sorting, network programming (using sockets, RMI, CORBA, SOAP, and XML-RPC), and JDBC database programming. I also cover higher-level techniques for server-side programming and web services like servlets and JSPs (including struts) and Enterprise Java Beans (EJBs).

The Java language and platform are proven technologies and, arguably, more new software development uses Java than any other programming language. The advantages of the Java platform include runtime error detection, rich class libraries, and solid support for web service applications. Still, the Java class libraries and available third-party libraries and tools are not a complete solution. This book is intended to be both a handy reference for frequently used Java programming idioms and an addition to your arsenal in your daily work.

Although I also use Common Lisp, Smalltalk, Prolog, and Python in my own work, Java is my preferred language for the vast majority of my own projects. The advantages of Java are clear: portable code, ease of maintenance, many qualified Java programmers for code modification and maintenance, and a great wealth of free infrastructure tools (many of which are used in this book).

Obtaining the Source Code for the Examples

If you have not already done so, you should get the ZIP files from the website for this book, which you can find at the main Sybex website: `www.sybex.com`. The following ZIP files are available:

Java_10_minute_solutions.zip Contains the code for Solutions 1 through 39. For example, the code for Solution 1 is in the subdirectory `S01` and the Java classes are in package `S01`.

part10.zip Contains the code for the servlet Solutions 40 through 44 in Part 10.

part11.zip Contains the code for the JSP and struts Solutions 45 through 49 in Part 11.

parts_12_13.zip Contains the EJB code for Solutions 50 through 53 in Part 12 and the ant, XDoclet, and JUnit files from Solutions 54 through 58 in Part 13.

ant_demos.zip Contains a few standalone ant project demos.

ant_jsp_struts.zip Contains a complete struts demo project, including ant build files.

junit_demos.zip Contains JUnit examples with ant build files.

part14.zip Contains the Hibernate JDO files for Solutions 59 and 60.

I have tried to minimize long program listings in this book since you have the source code available for download from the Web. Still, it is useful to have example code snippets in the text so I often intersperse code and text. One problem that authors of computer books always have is formatting program listings and code snippets on a page with a limited number of columns. You will notice that the code snippets are occasionally formatted strangely in order to get them to fit in the available page width. The code in the ZIP files for this book is formatted "normally."

NOTE In addition to the Sybex's website to support this book, you can always find current information and a link to the publisher's site for this book at `www.markwatson.com/books`.

File I/O

SOLUTION 1

Copying and Deleting Directories and Files

PROBLEM Your Java application needs to be able to copy and delete individual files and entire directories. You also want the option of copying and deleting nested file directories. You need to get lists of files in directories.

SOLUTION I will present a Java utility class *FileUtils* that you can use in your Java programs to copy and delete files and nested directories and also get directory listings.

One of the advantages of the Java platform is that once you know a technique like opening and reading files, that technique works on all computing platforms that support Java. In this solution you will build on the inherent portability of Java with a Java class library for general file manipulations that will solve most of your file handling problems on any platform. We will start by discussing the API of the class *FileUtils* in order to get you started quickly. Later, we will look at the implementation details.

It will be helpful if you open the file `FileUtils.java` in the directory `S01` in your favorite text editor or Java IDE while reading this section. This class has five static methods:

- The method `getNonDirFiles(String path)` returns all files in a specified directory path that are not subdirectory files:

```
static public Vector getNonDirFiles(String path)
     throws IOException;
```

- The method `getFiles(StringPath, String[] extensions)` returns all files in a directory path that end in file extensions that are passed to the method in an array of strings:

```
static public Vector getFiles(String path, String[] extensions)
     throws IOException;
```

- The method `getFiles(String path)` returns a vector of all files in the directory path. The elements of the returned vector are strings that include the full path to each file:

```
public static Vector getFiles(String path) throws IOException
```

- The method *copyFilePath* will copy either single files or entire directories, depending on if the first argument is a file path or a directory path name:

```
public static final void copyFilePath (File sourceFilePath,
                                       File destinationFilePath)
     throws IOException;
```

- The method *deleteFilePath* deletes both single files and recursively deletes entire directories:

```
public static final boolean deleteFilePath(File filePath);
```

All five methods are public static. Since this class has no instance data, the class never maintains state. It makes sense to make the methods static so that you do not need to create a class instance in order to use these utility methods. Here is an example for calling the first three methods for listings files:

```
Vector non_dir_files = FileUtils.getNonDirFiles("./S01");
Vector txt_java_files = FileUtils.getFiles("./S01",
       new String[]{".txt", ".java"});
Vector all_files = FileUtils.getFiles("./S01");
```

In all cases, the returned vectors contain strings that are complete path names for the listed files. When calling `getFiles(StringPath, String[] extensions)`, you build an array of strings containing file extensions that you want to use for fetching files.

The method *copyFilePath* copies either a single file or a complete directory (including recursive copying of subdirectories), depending on whether the first argument, *sourceFilePath*, is a path to a file or a path to a directory. If the first argument is a path to an individual file, then the second argument, *destinationFilePath*, must also be a path to an individual file. If the first argument is a path to a directory, then the second argument, `destinationFilePath`, must also be a path to a directory. Here is an example of copying the contents of the directory `./temp123` to `./temp234` and then deleting the original directory `./temp123`:

```
FileUtils.copyFilePath(new File("./temp123"),
                       new File("./temp234"));
FileUtils.deleteFilePath(new File("./temp123"));
```

The method *deleteFilePath* takes a file argument that can be either an individual file or a directory.

Implementation Details

Using the `java.io` package classes, it is fairly simple get the contents of a file directory, as shown in the following example:

```
String path = "./S01"; // must be a directory
File dir = new File(path);
// create a custom file filter to
// accept all non-directory files:
AllNonDirFileFilter filter = new AllNonDirFileFilter();
String[] ss = dir.list(filter);
```

The method `list()` either takes no arguments, in which case all files are returned in the specified directory, or it takes one argument that is an instance of a class implementing the `java.io.FilenameFilter` interface. Classes implementing this interface must define the following method:

```
public boolean accept (File dir, String name)
```

The file `FileUtil.java` includes three inner classes that all implement the *`FilenameFilter`* interface: *`LocalFileFilter`* (constructor takes an array of strings defining allowed file extensions), *`AllNonDirFileFilter`* (empty constructor, accepts all files that are not directory files), and *`AllDirFileFilter`* (empty constructor, accepts all files that are directory files).

Using the `java.io` package classes, it is simple to copy and delete single files, but there is no support for copying and deleting entire nested directories. The class *`FileUtils`* methods *`copyFilePath`* and *`deleteFilePath`* use recursion to process nested directories. The processing steps used by the method *`copyFilePath`* are

1. Check that both input arguments (source and target files) are either both single files or both file directories.
2. If you are copying directories, get all files in the source directory: for each file, if it is a single file, copy it; if it is a directory file, recursively call `copyFilePath` on the subdirectory.

The processing steps used by the method *`deleteFilePath`* are

1. If the input file path is a directory, get all files in the directory and recursively call deleteFilePath on each file.
2. If the input file path is a single file, delete it.

You can refer to the source file `FileUtils.java` for coding details.

SOLUTION 2

Reading and Writing JAR/ZIP Files

PROBLEM You want to be able to write data out in a compressed format (JAR, ZIP, and GZIP) and later read this data. You want to store different data entries in a single ZIP or JAR file.

SOLUTION You will use the standard utility classes in the packages `java.util.zip` (for both ZIP and GZIP support) and `java.util.jar` (for JAR support) to create and read compressed ZIP and JAR files and to create compressed GZIP streams.

The APIs for handling ZIP and JAR files are almost identical. In fact, the internal formats of ZIP and JAR files *are* identical except that a separate manifest file can be optionally added to a JAR file (actually, you could create a manifest file and add it to a ZIP file also).

I will cover examples of writing and reading ZIP files and JAR files; the JAR example program in directory `S02` is identical to the ZIP example program except I use `JarOutputStream` instead of `ZipOutputStream`, `JarInputStream` instead of `ZipInputStream`, *and* `JarEntry` *instead of* `ZipEntry`. The GNU ZIP format is popular on Unix, Linux, and Mac OS X; the classes `GZipOutputStream` and `GZipInputStream` can be used if you prefer the GNU ZIP format to compress a stream of data.

ZIP and JAR files contain zero or more entries. An entry contains the path of the original file and a stream of data for reading the original file's contents. The GZIP classes do not support archiving a collection of named data items like the ZIP and JAR utility classes. GZIP is used only for compressing and decompressing streams of data. The directory `S02` contains three sample programs:

ReadWriteZipFiles Demonstrates writing a ZIP file, closing it, and then reading it

ReadWriteJarFiles Demonstrates writing a JAR file, closing it, and then reading it

GZIPexample Demonstrates compressing a stream and then decompressing it

After you run the `ReadWriteZipFiles` example, the file `test.zip` will be created. Here is a list of this ZIP archive file:

```
markw% unzip -l test.zip
Archive:  test.zip
 Length    Date     Time    Name
 ------    ----     ----    ----
     66  05-18-03  11:31   test.txt
     19  05-18-03  11:31   string-entry
 ------                    -------
     85                    2 files
```

The entry named `test.txt` was created from the contents of the file `test.txt`. The entry named `string-entry` was created from the data in a Java string.

NOTE If you are extracting the files from a ZIP file containing nested directories, you will see entry names that include the full file path for the included files. If you are saving files stored in a ZIP archive, you need to create the full directory path for the files that you are extracting. `ZipEntry` objects that contain only a directory entry can be determined by using the method `isDirectory()`. You can create a new file directory for every directory `ZipEntry` object. Alternatively, you can discard the directory path information in the ZIP entry names and extract the files to the current directory.

After you run the `ReadWriteJarFiles` example, the file `test.jar` will be created. Here is a list of this JAR archive file:

```
markw% jar tvf test.jar
    66 Mon May 19 14:40:26 MST 2003 test.txt
    19 Mon May 19 14:40:26 MST 2003 string-entry
```

The entry named `test.txt` was created from the contents of the file `test.txt`. The entry named `string-entry` was created from the data in a Java string.

The *GZIPexample* program demonstrates compressing a file stream that is written to disk creating a file named `test.gz`.

NOTE The GZIP utility classes are also useful for compressing data streams transferred, for example, via network sockets (which are covered in Solutions 29 and 30). You will also look at Java streams in more detail in Solution 5 when you write a custom stream class.

Implementation Details

We will look at the ZIP example program in some detail; the JAR example program is identical except for the class substitutions mentioned earlier. Java allows I/O streams to be nested, so you can create a standard file output stream, then "wrap" it in a *ZipOutputStream*:

```
FileOutputStream fStream = new FileOutputStream("test.zip");
ZipOutputStream zStream = new ZipOutputStream(fStream);
```

The data that you write to a ZIP stream includes instances of the class *ZipEntry*:

```
ZipEntry stringEntry = new ZipEntry("string-entry");
zStream.putNextEntry(stringEntry);
String s = "This is\ntest data.\n";
zStream.write(s.getBytes(), 0, s.length());
zStream.closeEntry();  // close this ZIP entry
zStream.close();  // close the ZIP output stream
```

NOTE In this example, I simply wrote the contents of a string to the output stream associated with the ZIP entry; a more common use would be to open a local file, read the file's contents, and write the contents to the ZIP entry output stream.

The instance of class *ZipEntry* labels data written to the ZIP output stream. You can then write any data as bytes to ZIP output stream for this entry. After you close the ZIP entry, you can either add additional ZIP entries (and the data for those entries) or, as I do here, immediately close the ZIP output stream (which also closes the file output stream). The example program `ReadWriteZipFiles.java` writes two ZIP entries to the ZIP output stream.

To read a ZIP file, you first get a `java.util.Enumeration` object containing all the ZIP entries in the file:

```
ZipFile zipFile = new ZipFile("test.zip");
Enumeration entries = zipFile.entries();
```

The example program loops over this enumeration; here I will just show the code for reading a single ZIP entry:

```
ZipEntry entry = (ZipEntry) entries.nextElement();
InputStream is = zipFile.getInputStream(entry);
int count;
while (true) {
 count = is.read(buf);
 if (count < 1) break; // break: no more data is available
    // add your code here to process 'count' bytes of data:
}
is.close();
```

After reading each ZIP entry and processing the data in the entry, close the input stream for the entry.

The GZIP example program is very short, so I will list most of the code here:

```
// write a GZIP stream to a file:
String s = "test data\nfor GZIP demo.\n";
FileOutputStream fout = new FileOutputStream("test.gz");
GZIPOutputStream out = new GZIPOutputStream(fout);
out.write(s.getBytes());
out.close();
// read the data from a GZIP stream:
FileInputStream fin = new FileInputStream("test.gz");
GZIPInputStream in = new GZIPInputStream(fin);
byte[] bytes = new byte[2048];
while (true) {
     int count = in.read(bytes, 0, 2048);
     if (count < 1) break;
     String s2 = new String(bytes, 0, count);
     System.out.println(s2);
}
in.close();
```

You see again the utility of being able to wrap one input or output stream inside another stream. When you wrap a standard file output stream inside a GZIP output stream, you can still use the methods for the file output stream, but the data written will be compressed using the GZIP algorithm.

SOLUTION 3

Java Object Persistence with Serialization

PROBLEM You create Java objects in your programs that you would like to be able to save to disk and then later read them back into different programs.

SOLUTION You will use Java serialization to write objects to an object output stream and later read them back in from an object input stream.

The Java package `java.io` contains two stream classes that are able to respectively write and read Java objects that implement the `java.io.Serializable` interface: *`ObjectOutputStream`* and *`ObjectInputStream`*. Most Java standard library classes implement the *`Serializable`* interface, and it is simple to write your own Java classes so that they also implement the *`Serializable`* interface. The *`Serializable`* interface is a marker interface that contains no method signatures that require implementation: its purpose is to allow Java's persistence mechanism to determine which classes are intended to be serializable.

NOTE In addition to using Java object serialization as a lightweight and simple-to-use object persistence mechanism, it is also widely used in Remote Method Invocation (RMI), which I will cover in Solutions 30 and 31.

The file `SerializationTest.java` in the directory *S03* provides a complete example of defining a Java class that can be serialized, writing instances of this class and other standard Java classes to an output stream, then reading the objects back into the test program. While saving standard Java objects is simple, I will first cover the details of making your own Java classes implement the *`Serializable`* interface. Consider the nonpublic class *`DemoClass`* that is included at the bottom of the file `SerializationTest.java`:

```
class DemoClass implements Serializable {
    private String name = "";
    private transient Hashtable aHashtable = new Hashtable();

    public String getName() { return name; }

    public void setName(String name) { this.name = name; }

    public Hashtable getAHashtable() {return aHashtable; }
```

```
        public void setAHashtable(Hashtable aHashtable) {
            this.aHashtable = (Hashtable)aHashtable.clone();
        }
    }
```

There are two aspects to this class definition that deal specifically with object serialization issues: the class implements the *Serializable* interface and the use of the keyword *transient* to prevent the serialization process from trying to save the hash table to the output stream during serialization and to prevent the deserialization process from trying to read input data to reconstruct the hash table. If you do not use the keyword *transient* when defining your Java classes, then all class variables are saved during serialization. All of a class's variables must also belong to classes that implement the *Serializable* interface or be marked with the *transient* keyword. The following code creates test data to be serialized:

```
// define some test data to be serialized:
Hashtable testHash = new Hashtable();
Vector testVector = new Vector();
testHash.put("cat", "dog");
testVector.add(new Float(3.14159f));
DemoClass demoClass = new DemoClass();
demoClass.setName("Mark");
Hashtable hash = demoClass.getAHashtable();
hash.put("cat", "dog");
```

The following code serializes this data:

```
// now, serialize the test data:
FileOutputStream ostream = new FileOutputStream("test.ser");
ObjectOutputStream p = new ObjectOutputStream(ostream);
p.writeObject(testHash);
p.writeObject(testVector);
p.writeObject(demoClass);
p.close();
```

The standard Java container classes `Hashtable` and `Vector` can be serialized if all the objects that they contain can also be serialized. If you try to serialize any object (including objects contained inside other objects) that cannot be serialized, then a `java.io.NotSerializableException` will be thrown. When you write the Java objects to a disk file `test.ser` in the test program, you'll once again wrap a file output stream inside another stream, this time an instance of class *ObjectOutputStream*. The class *ObjectOutputStream* adds an additional method that can be used on the output stream: *writeObject*.

It is also simple to read serialized objects from an input stream; in this case, I use a file input stream (wrapped in *ObjectInputStream*) to read the `test.ser` file:

```
InputStream ins = new java.io.FileInputStream("test.ser");
ObjectInputStream p = new ObjectInputStream(ins);
Hashtable h = (Hashtable)p.readObject();
```

The example program `SerializationTest.java` in the directory *S03* contains additional code demonstrating how to test the class type of objects as they are deserialized; here, you know that the first object that was written to the file was a hash table. Similarly, you can read the other two objects in the same order that they were written to the file `test.ser`:

```
Vector v = (Vector)p.readObject();
DemoClass demo = (DemoClass)p.readObject();
```

The object `demo` (class `DemoClass`) will not have the instance variable *aHashtable* defined. It has a null value because it was declared transient in the class definition.

NOTE No class constructor is called during deserialization. In the example program, the nonpublic class *DemoClass* has a default constructor (no arguments) that prints a message. When you run the example program, please note that this message is printed when an instance of *DemoClass* is constructed for serialization, but this message is not printed during deserialization.

Changing Java's Default Persistence Mechanism

The `SerializationTest.java` example program uses Java's default persistence mechanism with the modification of the class *DemoClass* using the *transient* keyword to avoid persisting one of the class variables. In general, you use the *transient* keyword for class data that either cannot be serialized or makes no sense to serialize (e.g., socket and thread objects). You can also customize Java's persistence mechanism. There are three ways to customize persistence:

- Implement custom protocol by defining the methods *writeObject* and *readObject*.
- Implement the *Externalizable* interface instead of the *Serializable* interface.
- Override default version control.

If you chose to customize the protocol for saving instances of one of your classes, then you must define two private methods:

```
private void writeObject(ObjectOutputStream outStream) throws IOException
private void readObject(ObjectInputStream inStream) throws IOException,
ClassNotFoundException
```

When you implement these methods, you will usually use two helper methods: *defaultWriteObject* in class *ObjectOutputStream* and *defaultReadObject* in class *ObjectInputStream*; for example:

```
private void readObject(ObjectInputStream inStream) throws IOException,
ClassNotFoundException {
    inStream.defaultReadObject();
    // place any custom initialization here
}
```

```
private void writeObject(ObjectOutputStream outStream) throws IOException {
    outStream.defaultWriteObject();
    // place any custom code here (not usually done)
}
```

You can alternatively create a new protocol for serializing your classes by not implementing the *Serializable* interface and instead implementing the *Externalizable* interface. To do this you must define two methods:

```
public void writeExternal(ObjectOutput out) throws IOException
public void readExternal(ObjectInput in)
    throws IOException, ClassNotFoundException
```

ObjectOutput is an interface that extends the *DataOutput* interface and adds methods for writing objects. *ObjectInput* is an interface that extends the *DataInput* interface and adds methods for reading objects.

NOTE Regardless of whether you use default serialization, write your own *readObject* and *writeObject* methods, or implement the *Externalizable* interface, you simply call the methods *readObject* and *writeObject* in your programs and the Java Virtual Machine (JVM) will automatically handle serialization correctly.

You might be wondering what happens if you change your class definitions after saving application objects to a disk file using serialization. Unfortunately, in the default case, you will not be able to read the serialized objects back because Java's default class version control mechanism will detect that the serialized objects were created from a different version of the class. However, there is a mechanism you can use to insure that serialized objects for a class are still valid for deserialization: overriding the default static class variable *serialVersionID*. For example, for the class `MyDemoClass`, use the Java toolkit utility program `serialver`:

```
> serialver MyDemoClass
MyDemoClass: static final long serialVersionID = 1274998123888721L
```

Then copy this generated code into your class definition:

```
public class MyDemoClass implements java.io.Serializable {
    static final long serialVersionID = 1274998123888721L;
    // … rest of class definition:
}
```

For example, if you now add a class variable, the deserialization process will continue without error, but the new variable will not have a defined value.

SOLUTION 4

Using Random Access File I/O

PROBLEM You need to randomly access data in a file.

SOLUTION Use the class *RandomAccessFile* to open a file for random access.

The class *RandomAccessFile* implements the *DataInput* and *DataOutput* interfaces, but it is not derived from the base classes *InputStream* and *OutputStream*. As a result, you cannot use the typical Java I/O stream functionality on instances of class *RandomAccessFile*. Think of a random access file as a randomly addressable array of bytes stored in a disk file. The file pointer acts like an index of this array of bytes. The class *RandomAccessFile* has three methods for accessing the file pointer of an open random access file:

void seek(long newFilePointer) Positions the file pointer to a new value.

int skipBytes(int bytesToSkip) Skips a specified number of bytes by moving the file pointer.

long getFilePointer() Returns the current value of the file pointer.

The example program `RandomAccessTest.java` in the directory `S04` opens a random access file for reading and writing and writes 50 bytes of data:

```
RandomAccessFile raf = new RandomAccessFile("test.random", "rw");
// define some data to write to the file:
byte[] data = new byte[50];
for (int i = 0; i < 50; i++) data[i] = (byte) i;
// by default, a random access file opens at the beginning,
// so just write the data:
raf.write(data, 0, 50);
```

The following code reads this data back in reverse order, which is inefficient but serves as an example. Here you are reading one byte of data at a time, starting at the end of the file and moving to the beginning of the file using the method *seek*:

```
// read back the data backwards (not efficient):
int count;
for (int i=49; i>=0; i--) {
```

```
        raf.seek(i);
        byte[] littleBuf = new byte[1];
        count = raf.read(littleBuf, 0, 1);
        if (count != 1) {
            System.out.println("error reading file at i="+i);
            break;
        }
        System.out.println("at i=" + i + ", byte read from file=" +
                           littleBuf[0]);
    }
    raf.close();
```

The constructors of class *RandomAccessFile* takes two arguments. The first argument can be either a string file path or an instance of class `java.io.File`. The second argument is always a string with one of these values:

"r" Opens file as read-only.

"rw" Opens file for reading and writing.

"rws" Opens the file for reading and writing and guarantees that both the file contents and file maintenance metadata are updated to disk before returning from any write operations.

"rwd" Opens the file for reading and writing and guarantees that the file contents are updated to disk before returning from any write operations.

The options `"rws"` and `"rwd"` are useful to guarantee that application-critical data is immediately saved to disk. There are several different methods for reading and writing byte data; in this example, I use the most general purpose read and write methods that take three arguments: an array of bytes, the starting index to use in the array of bytes, and the number of bytes to read or write. Although the logical model for random access files is an array of bytes, the class *RandomAccessFile* also has convenient methods for reading and writing Boolean, short, integer, long, and strings from a file, starting at the current file pointer position.

NOTE While there are legitimate uses for random access files, you should keep in mind the inefficiency of managing the storage of an array of bytes in a disk file. In some ways, random access files are a legacy from the times when random access memory (RAM) was expensive and it was important to reduce memory use whenever possible. For most Java applications, it is far more efficient to store data in memory and periodically serialize it to disk as required. A good alternative is to use a relational database to store persistent data using the JDBC portable database APIs (see Solutions 34–39).

SOLUTION 5

Writing Text Filters

PROBLEM You need a framework for processing text files.

SOLUTION You will use a custom Java I/O stream class to perform text filtering by applying a sequence of filtering operations on input stream opened on the text data.

Before I get into implementing custom streams for supporting custom text filtering, we will take a brief overview of stream classes in the Java package `java.io`. The abstract base classes *`InputStream`* and *`OutputStream`* form the basis for byte handling streams. Streams for handling character data are derived from the base classes *`Reader`* and *`Writer`*. Since you are interested in processing text, in this solution we will only deal with character streams that are derived from the class *`Reader`*. The following illustration is a UML class diagram for the standard Java I/O classes *`Reader`* and *`InputStreamReader`*: the example class *`WordCountStreamReader`*, its base class *`InputStreamReader`*, and *`InputStreamReader's`* base class *`Reader`*.

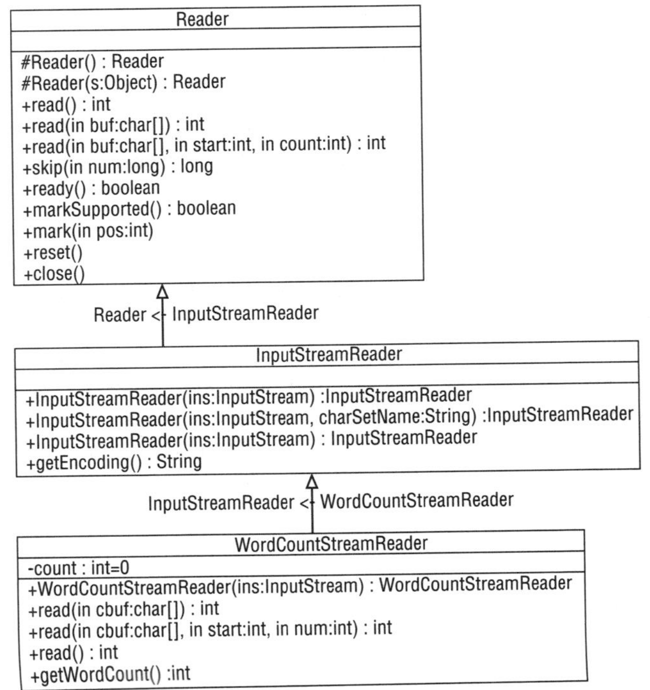

Indirectly, the example class *WordCountStreamReader* inherits the methods of class *Reader* that are actually used to read from an input stream. You override these methods by calling the super class method and then performing application-specific filtering operations (in this case, counting the words in the character stream). In addition to defining a class constructor (which simply calls its super class constructor), the example class defines the method *getWordCount* that can be called at any time to get the number of space-delimited words read from the input stream.

The example stream class overrides all three read methods that are indirectly inherited from the class *Reader*. In each case, the read methods call the inherited read method with the same signature to actually read from the input stream, then look for word breaks:

```
public class WordCountStreamReader extends InputStreamReader {
    public WordCountStreamReader(InputStream ins) {
        super(ins);
    }
    public int read(char[] cbuf) throws IOException {
        int count =  super.read(cbuf);
        for (int i=0; i<count; i++) {
            if (cbuf[i] == ' ')  this.count++;
        }
        return count;
    }
    public int read(char[] cbuf, int start, int num)
                                          throws IOException {
        int count =  super.read(cbuf, start, num);
        for (int i=0; i<count; i++) {
            if (cbuf[i] == ' ')  this.count++;
        }
        return count;
    }
     public int read() throws IOException {
        int character =  super.read();
        if (character == ' ')  this.count++;
        return character;
    }
    public int getWordCount() {
        return count+1;
}
    private int count = 0;
}
```

NOTE In this example, you are simply counting spaces between words. In most real applications, you would use the `java.util.StringTokenizer` class to separate a string into individual words.

This is a simple class, but it demonstrates the basic strategy for defining new stream classes to act as text filters: use inherited methods to actually perform stream read operations while adding desired filtering behavior.

NOTE There are many applications that can use custom text filtering stream classes. For example, translating the input stream from English to German using the BabelFish web services, removing HTML markup from an HTML input stream (that is, leaving only plain text), and performing spelling correction.

The ability to wrap Java streams inside other Java streams is a powerful technique that is greatly enhanced by writing custom stream classes to perform application-specific filtering and information extraction operations.

TIP Remember: you can nest streams inside each other to any reasonable depth. For example, if you implemented a custom stream for translating English to German and another custom stream for stripping HTML tags, then your application might wrap (or nest) streams like this: `new WordCountStreamReader(new EnglishToGermanStreamReader (new StripHtmlTagsStreamReader(new InputStream(…))))`. This would allow you to count the translated German words without counting HTML tags.

String Handling

SOLUTION 6

Efficiently Performing Multiple Replacements

PROBLEM You need to efficiently perform multiple replacements in a Java string either ignoring differences in upper- and lowercase or using case-sensitive matches.

SOLUTION I will present the Java utility class `StringUtils` that you can use in your Java programs to efficiently perform multiple replacements.

It will be helpful if you open the file `StringUtils.java` in the directory `S06` in your favorite text editor or Java IDE while reading this section. There are three public static methods in class `Stringutils`:

```
public static int countStrings(String sourceString,
                               String targetString,
                               int start, boolean ignoreCase)
public static int indexOf(String sourceString,
                          String targetString, int start,
                          boolean ignoreCase)
public static String replace(String sourceString,
                             String oldString,
                             String  replacementString,
                             int start, boolean ignoreCase)
```

The method `countStrings` is used to determine how many instances of a target string are in the source string (starting at a specified index). The method `indexOf()` in the `StringUtils` class is used to find the first instance of a target string in a source string (starting at a specified index). The method `replace()` in the `StringUtils` class replaces all instances of an old string with a new string (starting at a specified index in the original source string). The last argument in all three methods is a Boolean flag that allows the string matching operation to be done in a case-insensitive mode.

The following examples show how to use the public static methods in the `StringUtils` class:

```
String s = "The bad dog ran down the street after the black cat";
int num1 = StringUtils.countStrings(s, "dog", 0, false);
int num2 = StringUtils.countStrings(s, "Dog", 0, true);
int index1 = StringUtils.indexOf(s, "the", 0, false);
```

```
int index2 = StringUtils.indexOf(s, "the", 0, true);
String s2 = StringUtils.replace(s, "the", "THE", 0, true);
```

The use of this utility class is simple. In this example, `num1` and `num2` are both 1, `index1` is 21, `index2` is 0, and `s2` is "`THE bad dog ran down THE street after THE black cat`".

Java strings are immutable in order to allow the compiler to optimize string operations. The `StringBuffer` class is not immutable and in general should be used to dynamically build long strings by adding smaller strings together. The `StringBuffer` class does have a method called `replace()` that will replace any substring with a new string using case-sensitive matching; for example:

```
StringBuffer sb = new StringBuffer("01234567890");
sb.replace(1,5, "A");
```

Here, the string content of the variable `sb` has been replaced with the value "`0A567890`". The `StringBuffer` method `replace` is useful, and if the authors of the Java string classes had included a `replaceAll()` style method in the `StringBuffer` class, there would be less need for the `StringUtils` utility class. (There is a `replaceAll()` method in the standard String class.) However, the `StringUtils` class also allows case-insensitive matching and I use this class frequently in my own programs.

Implementing the *StringUtils* Class

The `StringUtils` public static method `indexOf` has a different argument list than the `String` class method `indexOf`:

```
public static final int indexOf(String sourceString,
                                String targetString,
                                int start, boolean ignoreCase)
```

If the last argument, `ignoreCase`, is false, then this method simply uses the standard `String` class `indexOf()` method. If the argument `ignoreCase` is true, then this method makes use of the `String` class method `regionMatches()` that allows for case-insensitive matching; the method signature for `regionMatches()` is:

```
boolean regionMatches(boolean ignoreCase, int startIndex,
                      String subString, int subStringStartIndex,
                      int numCharsToCompare)
```

The entire method `StringUtils.indexOf` is short enough to list here:

```
public static final int indexOf(String sourceString,
                                String targetString,
                                int start, boolean ignoreCase) {
```

```
    if (ignoreCase == false) {
        return sourceString.indexOf(targetString, start);
    } else {
      int sourceStringLength = sourceString.length();
      int targetStringLength = targetString.length();
      int stringLengthDifference =
               sourceStringLength - targetStringLength;
      while (start < stringLengthDifference) {
        if (sourceString.regionMatches(ignoreCase, start,
                                       targetString, 0,
                                       targetStringLength)) {
            return start;
        }
        start++;
      }
      return -1;
    }
  }
```

The standard method `regionMatches()` in the `String` class is final, so the JIT compiler will generate inline code for the repetitive calls to `regionMatches` in the while loop, so this is not as inefficient as it might look. The implement method `replace()`, calculates an upper bound on how large the resulting string will be. The `variable occurenceCount` is used for counting the number of occurrences of the target string in the source string. This method is fairly simple, using the case-insensitive `indexOf()` method to do most of the work:

```
  public static final int countStrings(String sourceString,
                                       String targetString,
                                       int start,
                                       boolean ignoreCase) {
      int targetStringLength = targetString.length();
      int occurenceCount = 0;
      if (targetStringLength > 0) {
          while (true) {
              int i = indexOf(sourceString, targetString,
                              start, ignoreCase);
              if (i == -1) break;
              occurenceCount++;
              start = i + targetStringLength;
          }
      }
      return occurenceCount;
  }
```

The input argument `start` defines the starting point in the source string where you start counting. The local value of the argument `start` is incremented by the length of the target string whenever a match is found. It would be incorrect to simply add 1 to the value of `start`; for example, if you were counting the number of occurrences of the target string “aaa” in the source string “aaaaaa”, you would expect the occurrence count to be 2, not 4.

The method `replace()` is too long to list here, but we will look at some implementation details. For reference, here is the method signature:

```
public static String replace(String s, String oldString,
                             String replacementString, int start,
                             boolean ignoreCase)
```

The first step in implementing this method is to count the number of occurrences of `oldString` in the source string `s`. If there is no occurrence, return the value of the source string `s`. If there is at least one occurrence, then you calculate an upper bound on the size of the new string and allocate working storage for it:

```
char[] buf = new char[newStringLengthCount];
```

Now, you simply have to loop, finding the indices of occurrences of string `oldString` and copying both changed and original (as appropriate) characters into the array `buf`:

```
while (true) {
    int nextMatchIndex = indexOf(s, oldString, lastPos,
                                 ignoreCase);
    if (nextMatchIndex == -1) break;
    s.getChars(lastPos, nextMatchIndex, buf, lastDest);
    lastDest += nextMatchIndex - lastPos;
    replacementString.getChars(0, replacementStringLength,
                               buf, lastDest);
    lastPos = nextMatchIndex + oldStringLength;
    lastDest += replacementStringLength;
}
```

When the last occurrence of string `oldString` has been found, break out of this loop without copying the remaining characters from the source string `s`; next, copy these remaining characters in the array `buf` after the while loop ends:

```
s.getChars(lastPos, sourceStringLength, buf, lastDest);
```

In the general case, the array `buf` will be larger than the new string, so copy only the characters used in this array into a new string and return this new string as the value of this method:

```
return new String(buf, 0, lastDest-lastPos + sourceStringLength);
```

SOLUTION 7

Using Regular Expressions for Information Extraction

PROBLEM You need to match patterns in Java strings.

SOLUTION You will look at Java code examples of using the new standard regular expression library and also review example regular expressions to solve common text extraction problems.

This solution uses the standard Java regular expression libraries that are available for Java versions 1.4 and later. The example program `RegularExpressionDemo.java` contains a method *`test`* that demonstrates the use of the new regular expression API that is defined in the `java.util.regex` package.

Introduction to Regular Expressions

The Java standard regular expression library supports the following metacharacters: `([{\^$|)?*+..`

I will cover the meaning of the most commonly used metacharacters by looking at a few short examples that were generated by the test program `RegularExpressionDemo.java` in the directory `S07`.

NOTE Sun Microsystems has a very good Java regular expression tutorial at `http://java.sun.com/docs/books/tutorial/extra/regex/intro.html`. (In case this URL changes, you can find the site by searching the Web for "Sun Java regular expression tutorial.")

Using a regular expression pattern that contains no metacharacters allows you to find all occurrences of that pattern string in input text. Here is example printout from the demo program that shows this:

```
regular expression: dog
input text: The big dog was off the leash and bit the little dog.

matching text: 'dog' starting index=8,ending index=11
matching text: 'dog' starting index=49,ending index=52
```

The metacharacter asterisk (*) will match zero or more occurrences of any character:

```
regular expression: do*
input text: The big dog was off the leash and bit the little dog.

matching text: 'do' starting index=8,ending index=10
matching text: 'd' starting index=32,ending index=33
matching text: 'do' starting index=49,ending index=51
```

The metacharacter period (.) will match any single character:

```
regular expression: do.
input text: The big dog was off the leash and bit the little dog.

matching text: 'dog' starting index=8,ending index=11
matching text: 'dog' starting index=49,ending index=52
```

You can also use negation. The following example will match any token in the input text that starts with the letter "t" and has a second character not equal to "b" (note that you place the negation in `[ ]` brackets and use the caret (^) character to indicate negation for the following pattern):

```
regular expression: t[^b]
input text: ta tb tc td

matching text: 'ta' starting index=0,ending index=2
matching text: 'tc' starting index=6,ending index=8
matching text: 'td' starting index=9,ending index=11
```

You can also exclude multiple characters from matching, in this case, discarding any potential matches where the second character is either "b" or "c":

```
regular expression: t[^bc]
input text: ta tb tc td

matching text: 'ta' starting index=0,ending index=2
matching text: 'td' starting index=9,ending index=11
```

You can also match ranges of characters. The following example matches "a" through "z" and "A" through "Z":

```
regular expression: t[a-zA-Z]
input text: ta tb tC td

matching text: 'ta' starting index=0,ending index=2
matching text: 'tb' starting index=3,ending index=5
matching text: 'tC' starting index=6,ending index=8
matching text: 'td' starting index=9,ending index=11
```

You can also combine matching a range of characters with negation by using the "&&" and operator; in this case, matching the characters "a" through "z", except for "b":

```
regular expression: t[a-z&&[^b]]
input text: ta tb tC td

matching text: 'ta' starting index=0,ending index=2
matching text: 'td' starting index=9,ending index=11
```

The following regular expression extracts e-mail addresses:

```
regular expression: [a-zA-Z]*@[a-zA-Z]*\.[a-zA-Z]*
input text: email is markw@markwatson.com now

matching text: 'markw@markwatson.com' starting index=9,ending index=29
```

In this example, because the period (.) character is a metacharacter, you have to "escape" it by preceding it with a backslash character. Here is an example of extracting simple URLs from text (there are more URL examples in the demo program):

```
regular expression: http://[a-zA-Z]*\.[a-zA-Z]*\.[a-zA-Z]*
input text: web is http://www.markwatson.com now

matching text: 'http://www.markwatson.com' starting index=7,ending index=32
```

Using the Java Regular Expression Libraries

The Java code for using the regular expression libraries is fairly simple—most of the work is in formulating regular expressions that will extract the data that you are interested in. The example program `RegularExpressionDemo` produced the sample output seen in the last section; this class contains a test method that shows how to apply regular expressions to text:

```
private static void test(String regularExpressionPattern,
                         String inputText) {
    System.out.println("\n  regular expression: " +
    regularExpressionPattern +
                      "\n  input text: " + inputText + "\n");
    Pattern pattern =
        Pattern.compile(regularExpressionPattern);
    Matcher matcher = pattern.matcher(inputText);
    while(matcher.find()) {
        System.out.println("matching text: '" +
                           matcher.group() +
                           "' starting index=" +
                           matcher.start() +
                           ",ending index=" + matcher.end());

    }
}
```

Here, I am using two classes in package `java.util.regex`: `Pattern` and `Matcher`. You saw examples of regular expression patterns in the last section. The public static method `Pattern.compile` accepts a string argument that contains a regular expression pattern and returns an instance of the class `Pattern`. There is some overhead to creating this instance of class `Pattern`, so for applications that require repetitive regular expression matching operations, you should cache patterns and reuse them (this is not done in the demo program).

An instance of the class `Matcher` acts like an enumeration object: an instance of class `Matcher` is created by the `Pattern` class method matcher and then method *`find`* is used to enumerate all matches for the pattern in the input text string.

SOLUTION 8

Using Java Properties to Configure Applications

PROBLEM You want to be able to configure your Java applications by setting properties and use Internationalization to support multiple languages.

SOLUTION You will use both properties set as command-line arguments and in property files. You will also use property resource bundles for supporting multiple languages.

The following table shows commonly used system properties. The example program `PropertyDemo.java` prints all system properties; the following single line of code shows you how to do this:

```
System.getProperties().list(System.out);
```

The static method `System.getProperties()` returns an instance of the class `java.util.Properties` that contains all property values currently set in the current Java Virtual Machine (JVM).

Property Key	Property Value
"file.separator"	File separator
"java.class.path"	Java classpath
"java.home"	Java home directory
"java.vendor.url"	Java vendor URL

Property Key	**Property Value**
"java.version"	Java version number
"line.separator"	Line separation character
"os.name"	Operating system name
"path.separator"	Path separator (";" for Windows, ":" for Unix, Linux, and Mac OS X)
"user.dir"	Current working directory
"user.home"	Logged in user's home directory
"user.name"	Logged in user's account name

It is simple to set new properties from inside a Java program; for example:

```
Properties p = new Properties(System.getProperties());
p.setProperty("weight", "185");
System.setProperties(p);
```

You can fetch properties by name:

```
String prop2 = System.getProperty("weight");
String prop2 = System.getProperty("weight", "192");
```

In the second example, you specify a default value for the property `"weight"` that will be returned from `System.getProperty` if there is currently no property named `"weight"` defined in the JVM.

While it is sometimes useful to be able to set and change property values inside a Java program, properties are usually used to specify configuration parameters for a Java program. You will see how to specify configuration data using both command-line arguments and also property files. If you want to set a property `"weight"` on the command line, use the –D command line option:

```
java -Dweight=182 S08.PropertyDemo
```

This will set the property `"weight"` to the value `"182"`; this property value can be accessed in a program using:

```
String weight_value = System.getProperty("weight");
```

The Java system properties are set in property files located in the `JAVAHOME/jre/lib` directory. Some example Java system properties are

```
java.util.logging.FileHandler.count = 1
serif.0=-b&h-lucidabright-medium-r-normal--*-%d-*-*-p-*-iso8859-1
security.provider.1=sun.security.provider.Sun
```

The common format is *<property name>=<property value>*. The following code can be used to read the property file `MarkDemo.property` in directory `S08`:

```
Properties properties = new Properties();
try {
  properties.load(new FileInputStream("S08/MarkDemo.properties"));
} catch (IOException ioe) {
  ioe.printStackTrace();
}
Enumeration enum = properties.propertyNames();
while (enum.hasMoreElements()) {
  String resource_name = (String) enum.nextElement();
  String resource_value = properties.getProperty(resource_name);
  System.out.println(" property:  name: " + resource_name +
                     " value: " + resource_value);
}
```

Internationalization Using Property Bundles

The class `PropertyResourceBundle` is a nonabstract derived class of `ResourceBundle`. This class can be used to fetch different properties files depending on a specific locale. In the Java system, different locales can represent combinations of different human languages, different countries, and different operating systems. Here, we will only look at an example that uses the default locale (for me, that is English) and a locale for the French language. Here is sample code for obtaining both the default locale and a local based on human language for French:

```
Locale locale1 = Locale.getDefault();
Locale locale2 = new Locale("fr", ""); // French language,
                                       // any country.
```

The directory `S08` contains two sample property files. The contents of the file `MarkDemo.properties` is

```
last_name=Watson
first_name=Mark
```

The contents of the file `MarkDemo_fr.properties` is

```
last_name=Sartre
first_name=John Paul
```

Now, when you fetch bundle properties, you can specify different locales and then use different property values based on locale. Here is the code for fetching two different bundles based on local (assuming locale1 and locale2 are as just defined):

```
ResourceBundle bundle1 =
        ResourceBundle.getBundle("S08.MarkDemo", locale1);
ResourceBundle bundle2 =
        ResourceBundle.getBundle("S08.MarkDemo", locale2);
```

Now, calling `bundle1.getString("last_name")` returns `"Watson"` while calling `bundle2.getString("last_name")` returns `"Sartre"`. The example program `PropertyDemo.java` contains example code for using property bundles.

NOTE Property bundles can also be specified using Java class files.

XML Processing

SOLUTION 9

Using DOM to Manipulate XML Documents in Memory

PROBLEM Data in an XML document is tree structured. You want to be able to easily manipulate this tree data structure in memory.

SOLUTION You will use the dom4j library to read XML documents from an input stream into memory, manipulate them, and save them back out to an output stream.

NOTE The formats of XML documents can be checked against formatting templates expressed as DTD documents or XML Schema. In Solutions 9, 10, and 11, I will use legal XML formats that are not checked against a DTD or XML Schema. I will use both DTDs and XML Schemas in Solution 12.

XML is a great technology. I use XML for archiving important information in a file format that I know that I will always be able to read; for messaging using SOAP, XML-RPC and as Java Message Service (JMS) payloads; and for program configuration files. In this chapter, I will cover programming techniques that facilitate the use of XML. XML processing with Java is a huge topic, so I'll cover the important programming techniques in this chapter and provide references.

While there is an open-source Java XML Document Object Model (JDOM) library that is often used, I will stay with the standard DOM APIs in this solution. You can download an implementation of JDOM from `www.jdom.org`, but you will not use JDOM here. Instead, you'll use the dom4j package that includes an implementation of the XPATH search functionality using the Open Source Jaxen project. The example code for this solution uses dom4j version 1.4, which is available from `www.dom4j.org`. You will also be using dom4j in Solution 11, when you transform XML documents with Extensible Stylesheet Language Transformations (`XSLT`).

One common problem in dealing with XML is finding specific elements (or nodes in DOM). It is simple to find all elements with a given name using either DOM or SAX (see Solution 10). The problem is that in many XML documents, element names are used in multiple contexts. For example, you might have elements `name` inside containing elements `company` and `employee`. Enumerating all elements with the name `name` will get both company and employee names. You will see examples in this solution (and Solution 10) for dealing with this problem, but there are two techniques that I use when designing XML applications (that is, when I design the format of XML documents for a specific application) that minimize this name conflict problem: using attributes instead of contained elements whenever possible, and uniquely naming elements. Instead of nesting elements like this:

```
<company>
   <name>ABC Corporation</name>
</company>
```

you can use an attribute:

```
<company name="ABC Corporation" />
```

The directory S09 contains a short XML test file test.xml:

```
<?xml version="1.0" encoding="UTF-8"?>
<company name="KnowledgeBooks">
  <employee first_name="Mark" last_name="Watson" />
  <employee first_name="Carol" last_name="Watson" />
</company>
```

The code examples in this solution are all contained in the Java source file TestDOM.java. It is simple to read an XML file from any input stream into a memory resident DOM tree; here I define a utility method that you can use to read the file S09/test.xml:

```
public Document parse(String fileName) throws DocumentException {
    SAXReader reader = new SAXReader();
    Document document = reader.read(fileName);
    return document;
}
```

See the example file TestDOM.java for required import statements for using dom4j. Every DOM Document class instance contains a top-level tree node (referred to as the root element) that implements the interface org.dom4j.Element. You will usually get this top-level element and use it to read and modify a DOM:

```
Document document = test.parse("S09/test.xml");
Element element = document.getRootElement();
test.searchTree(element, 0);
```

Once you have the top-level element, you can either recursively traverse the tree as I do here with the TestDOM method searchTree(), or as you will see later, you can use XPATH to find parts of the DOM tree that interest you. Here is the implementation of the searchTree() method:

```
public void searchTree(Element element, int depth) {
    System.out.println("parent node: depth=" + depth +
                       ", element=" + element);
    for (int i=0, size=element.nodeCount(); i<size; i++) {
        Node node = element.node(i);
        if (node instanceof Element) {
```

```
                System.out.println("non-leaf child node: depth=" +
                                   depth + ", element=" + element);
                searchTree((Element) node, depth + 1);
            } else {
                System.out.println("leaf child node: depth=" +
                                   depth + ", element=" + element);
            }
        }
    }
```

This demo method does not perform any interesting work; it simply recursively traverses the DOM tree printing out node (element) data as it goes. You will see shortly how to get attribute data from elements. In this method, the second argument depth is used to show you how far "down" in the DOM tree each call to the `searchTree()` method is. There are a few ways to find the child elements of a specific element. In the last code snippet, I first used the `Element` class method `nodeCount()` to get the number of child nodes (elements) and then in a loop used the `Element` class method *node*. As an alternative, given an element, you can create a Java `Iterator` to iterate over child nodes (assuming that you have set the variable element):

```
for (Iterator iter = element.elementIterator();
     iter.hasNext();) {
    Element childElement = (Element)iter.next();
    System.out.println("Iterator demo: childElement =" +
                       childElement);
}
```

While it is possible to perform any DOM manipulation using the techniques seen in this section, there is a better way to access portions of a DOM tree: use XPATH.

Using XPATH

You can simplify searching DOM trees by using an XPATH implementation. The dom4j library contains the open source Jaxen XPATH implementation. The demo file `TestDOM.java` also shows the use of XPATH. I will again be using the short example XML file `test.xml`:

```
<?xml version="1.0" encoding="UTF-8"?>
<company name="KnowledgeBooks">
  <employee first_name="Mark" last_name="Watson" />
  <employee first_name="Carol" last_name="Watson" />
</company>
```

If, for example, you wanted to find all elements matching the pattern `/company/employee` (that is, `employee` elements that are contained directly in `company` elements), you could use the XPATH APIs:

```
List list = document.selectNodes("//company/employee");
for (Iterator iter = list.iterator();
```

```
         iter.hasNext();) {
        Element element = (Element) iter.next();
        System.out.println("XPATH demo: element=" + element);
}
```

This not only finds employee elements that are contained inside company elements, but it will ignore other elements named employee that are not directly contained inside a company element. Note that in the file test.xml the employee elements have two attributes: first_name and last_name. If, for example, you were interested in extracting just the first names from employee elements contained in company elements, you could also use XPATH matching to do this:

```
List list=document.selectNodes("//company/employee/@first_name");
for (Iterator iter = list.iterator();
       iter.hasNext();) {
    Attribute attribute = (Attribute)iter.next();
    System.out.println("Found //company/employee/@first_name : " +
                       attribute);
}
```

That is great—much easier than using either direct DOM APIs or the SAX APIs (to be covered in Solution 10). Now, suppose that you want to search for the existence of a specific attribute value. Again, XPATH pattern matching does the job:

```
List list =
 document.selectNodes("//company/employee/@first_name=\"Mark\"");
for (Iterator iter = list.iterator();
       iter.hasNext();) {
    Boolean obj = (Boolean)iter.next();
System.out.println(
     "Found //company/employee/@first_name='Mark' : " + obj);
}
```

Here, if XPATH finds an attribute first_name with the value "Mark" inside an element named employee that in turn is contained inside an element company, then the printout will be "true", otherwise "false". Here the return value of iter.next() is of type Boolean.

A common problem in dealing with DOM trees is inserting new nodes in a specific location in the tree. You do this by finding the node that represents the parent of the new node that you are inserting. As you may have guessed, I will use XPATH to find the parent node, and then insert a new node:

```
List list = document.selectNodes("//company/employee");
for (Iterator iter = list.iterator();
       iter.hasNext();) {
    Element element = (Element) iter.next();
    Attribute attribute = element.attribute("first_name");
```

```
    System.out.println(" ** attribute value= " +
                       attribute.getValue());
    if (attribute.getValue().equals("Mark")) {
      // add a new child node:
      element.addElement("programming_language").
             addAttribute("favorite", "Java").
             addAttribute("least_favorite", "Basic");
  }
  }
```

Here I used the fact that the `addElement()` and `addAttribute()` methods return as their value the element operated on—this allows cascading these method calls in one statement.

After modifying the in-memory DOM tree, it is simple to write it out to an output stream; here I write the DOM to a new file, `S09/test2.xml`:

```
OutputFormat format = OutputFormat.createPrettyPrint();
XMLWriter writer = new XMLWriter(new FileWriter("test2.xml"), format);
writer.write(document);
```

This code must catch `IOException` errors (see the `TestDOM.java` file). Here are the contents of the file `test2.xml`, with the new element added:

```
<?xml version="1.0" encoding="UTF-8"?>
<company name="KnowledgeBooks">
  <employee first_name="Mark" last_name="Watson">
      <programming_language favorite="Java"
                            least_favorite="Basic"/>
  </employee>
  <employee first_name="Carol" last_name="Watson"/>
</company>
```

It is also simple to delete an element in a DOM tree. Here is an example showing the removal of an `employee` element with the attribute `"first_name"` equal to `"Mark"`:

```
list = document.selectNodes("//company/employee");
for (Iterator iter = list.iterator();
     iter.hasNext();) {
    Element element = (Element) iter.next();
    Attribute attribute = element.attribute("first_name");
    if (attribute.getValue().equals("Mark")) {
        boolean status = element.getParent().remove(element);
        System.out.println("status from removing element="
                           +status);
    }
}
```

When I found the matching attribute, I used the `getParent()` method to get the `parent` element of the element that I wanted to remove, and then I used the `remove()` method.

SOLUTION 10

Using SAX to Efficiently Parse XML

PROBLEM You need to efficiently process large XML input streams without using a DOM-based parser that requires an entire XML document to be stored in memory.

SOLUTION You will use an "event-based" SAX XML parser to efficiently process XML input streams.

While DOM and XPATH are useful, I find myself using event-driven SAX XML parsers for most of my XML applications. SAX processing is very lightweight: the parser makes a single pass through an XML input stream and notifies your program when certain events occur, including (this is not an exhaustive list):

- Start of a new XML document
- End of a document
- Warnings for bad syntax
- Errors for illegal syntax
- Notification for ignorable characters
- Start of a new element
- End of an element
- Character data for an element

For my SAX applications, I usually process the last three events in this list. It is fairly simple to handle SAX parsing events. There is a utility class `org.xml.sax.helpers.DefaultHandler` that defines stub ("do nothing") methods for all SAX parsing events. You simply derive your own class from this default handler class and implement the methods corresponding to the SAX events that you care about in your application. This default event-handler base class provides stub methods for handling parsing errors that I usually do not override, so any parsing errors simply throw appropriate exceptions that Java applications can catch.

I frequently use a design pattern in my own applications that is implemented in the example program `S10/TestSAX.java`: a Java class that I want to be able to save to XML to and from which I can later create new class instances from saved XML files. In this design pattern, I include an inner class that is derived from the default SAX event handler class. In the class

TestSAX, the class constructor for inner class TestSAXHandler requires an instance of the outer class TestSAX; this reference to the parent class is used to set data in the instance of the TestSAX class. You will only see short code snippets here so you should have the source code to TestSAX.java available as you read this solution.

Before you look at the example program implementation, it helps to look at the example input file S10/test.xml that I use for this demo:

```
<?xml version="1.0" encoding="UTF-8"?>
<TestSAX name="Mark Watson" weight="192">
    <hobby>hiking</hobby>
    <hobby>music</hobby>
</TestSAX>
```

You will want to refer to this file as I go through the code for handling SAX parsing events. We will look at the implementation of the inner class to handle SAX parsing events:

```
static class TestSAXHandler extends org.xml.sax.helpers.DefaultHandler {
        public TestSAXHandler(TestSAX parent) {
            this.parent = parent;
        }
        private TestSAX parent;
        private String lastElementName = "";
```

The first thing to notice is that this inner class has been declared static so that the class TestSAX can have a static "factory method" that uses this inner class. The private variable lastElementName will be used to store the last element name processed by the start element event handler method. The sequence of SAX parsing events is generally:

1. Process start of element event
2. Process and store character data for the element
3. Process end of element event

When you process character data, you will need to know which element the character data is for. The start of element event handling method is passed four arguments:

- URI for namespace definition
- Local name of the element (for example, template)
- Fully name space qualified name (qName) of the element (for example, xsl:template)
- Attribute data for the element

Here is the implementation of the start of the element event handler used in the example program:

```
public void startElement(String uri, String localName,
                         String qName,
```

```
                                 Attributes attributes)
            throws SAXException {
        lastElementName = qName;
        if (qName.equals("TestSAX")) {
            String w = attributes.getValue("weight");
            try {
                parent.setWeight(Integer.parseInt(w));
            } catch (Exception ee) {
            }
            parent.setName(attributes.getValue("name"));
        }
    }
```

I used public methods `setWeight()` and `setName()` of the class `TestSAX` to save element `TestSAX` (same name as the demo class name, but here it refers to an XML element name) attributes weight and name in the parent class instance. Notice that I also saved the current element name. In the example XML input file, I nest `hobby` elements that contain character data. When the SAX parser encounters the start of a `hobby` element, it calls the `startElement()` method that stores the `hobby` element name in the `lastElementName` private instance variable. Now, when the SAX parser encounters the character data for a `hobby` element, the character handling method "knows" that it is processing data for a `hobby` element and saves the character data in the parent class instance:

```
public void characters(char ch[], int start, int length)
        throws SAXException {
    if (lastElementName.equals("hobby")) {
        String s = new String(ch, start, length).trim();
        if (s.length() > 0) {
            parent.addHobby(s);
        }
    }
}
```

In general, it is necessary to both "trim" leading and trailing spaces from character data and to check for a string length greater than zero before processing character data. For valid character data, I use the public `TestSAX` method `addHobby()` to add the character data of a hobby element in the parent `TestSAX` instance.

In the `TestSAX.java` demo program, I did not need to handle end of element events, but it is often useful to be able to process all element data after the entire element has been processed. In these cases, I use private instance data for my application-specific inner SAX event handling class to store element data and process this data in the end of element handler method.

The `TestSAX.java` demo program contains a static "factory" *method* for creating new class instances from an XML input stream. Here is this method (with exception handling code removed for brevity):

```
static public TestSAX fromXML(String xmlInputFile) {
    TestSAX test = new TestSAX();
    SAXParserFactory f = SAXParserFactory.newInstance();
    SAXParser p = f.newSAXParser();
    InputSource is =
        new InputSource(new FileReader(xmlInputFile));
    p.parse(is, new TestSAXHandler(test));
    return s;
}
```

You'll want to be able to construct new class instances from any XML input stream. This example is less general: the static method `fromXML()` requires a path name to an XML file that is expected to be in the correct format for this application (for example, this file might have been created from the output of the `toXML()` method that you will see later). When this method creates a new `TestSAX` instance, the default class constructor is called and the instance variables are not set to useful values. However, when you create a parser and parse the XML input source you also pass an instance of this "empty" TestSAX instance to the (inner) class `TestSAXHandler`. When the SAX parser processes new elements and character data for any element, then the `TestSAXHandler` methods `startElement()` and `characters()` are called—these methods will set data in the "empty" `TestSAX` instance. When the parser is finished processing the XML input source, the `TestSAX` instance referenced by the variable `test` will be set from data contained in the XML input file.

It is also useful, given an instance of class `TestSAX`, to be able to write an XML file that can later be reloaded using the static `fromXML()` method. The method `toXML` performs this simple task:

```
public String toXML() {
    StringBuffer sb = new StringBuffer("<TestSAX name=\"" +
                    name + "\" weight=\"" + weight + "\">\n");
    for (int i = 0, size = hobbies.size(); i < size; i++) {
        sb.append("  <hobby>" + hobbies.get(i) + "</hobby>\n");
    }
    sb.append("</TestXML>\n");
    return sb.toString();
}
```

From reading Solution 9, you know how simple it is to write a DOM tree to an output stream. However, while the SAX libraries do not have a similar facility, it is usually easy to write output

XML files from any structured data. As a test, you can read the XML written by the `toXML` method back using the static `fromXML()` method.

Using the *ConfigFile* Utility Class

The Java class in `S10/ConfigFile.java` is intended to be a reusable utility and serves as a second example of using SAX event-driven parsers. The class constructor requires a path to an XML file that is parsed and the top-level elements (that is, the elements directly contained by the top root element) each have their data stored as in a list:

- Element name
- Character data for the element
- A hash table containing attribute name/value pairs (or null if no attributes for the element)

We will first look at an example of using this class and later we will look at its implementation. The file `S10/config.xml` contains some test data:

```
<?xml version="1.0" encoding="UTF-8"?>
<company name="KnowledgeBooks">
  <employee first_name="Mark" last_name="Watson">
     character data for Mark
  </employee>
  <employee first_name="Carol" last_name="Watson">
     character data for Carol
  </employee>
</company>
```

The `ConfigFile` class will ignore the root document element and collect element names, attribute values, and any character data for the elements directly contained in the root document element. Here is an example showing how to use this utility class:

```
ConfigFile config = new ConfigFile("S10/config.xml");
int num = config.getNumberOfElements();
for (int i=0; i<num; i++) {
    String elementName = config.getElementName(i);
    String characterData = config.getCharacterData(i);
    Hashtable h = config.getAttributes(i);
}
```

There is a more complete example in the method `main()` in the file `ConfigFile.java`. The `ConfigFile` class provides simple functionality, but I often use it in my own work when program configuration data is either too complex or too structured to easily express as Java properties.

TIP To save and maintain data (for my work, this is frequently natural language processing data like lexicons, word frequency tables, and text categorization data), I prefer permanently archiving data as XML documents along with Java utility code for reading the data into Java objects and inserting it into relational databases using JDBC (see Solutions 34 through 39). A classic problem is storing data in a proprietary data format and later not having an application that can read the data. Using self-describing XML avoids this problem.

ConfigFile Class Implementation

The implementation of the `ConfigFile` class is similar to the example class `TestSAX` seen earlier in Solution 10, so you will just take a brief look at the implementation of `ConfigFile`. The class constructor uses an inner SAX event handler class `ConfigFileSaxHandler` to process SAX parsing events and record element data form the XML input stream:

```
public ConfigFile(String xmlPath) {
    try {
        SAXParserFactory f = SAXParserFactory.newInstance();
        f.setNamespaceAware(true);
        SAXParser p = f.newSAXParser();
        InputSource is =
             new InputSource(new FileReader(xmlPath));
        p.parse(is, new ConfigFileSaxHandler(this));
    } catch (Exception e) {
        e.printStackTrace();
    }
}
```

Here, you pass a reference to the `ConfigFile` instance (that is, the variable `this`) to the `ConfigFileSaxHandler` inner class. As you saw earlier in Solution 10, the order of event processing for an XML element will be:

Process start of element You capture the element name and the attributes (if any) and store this data in `ConfigFileSaxHandler` instance variables `currentElementName` and `currentAttributes`. Increment the counter `depth` (`ConfigFileSaxHandler` instance variable).

Process character data The character data for elements often has extra white space characters so you use the Java String trim method to eliminate extra white space characters at the beginning and end of the character data.

Process end of element You decrement the element depth counter and then use this depth counter to make sure that the current element is a top-level element (that is, directly contained by the document root element). Save all data collected by this element in the parent `ConfigFile` instance that was passed to the inner class `ConfigFileSaxHandler` class constructor.

TIP

I prefer using SAX XML parsers for XML documents without deeply nested elements because of the requirement to maintain state information where SAX parsing events occur in the document. In the `ConfigFile` class, this state information is the XML element depth and the name of the current element. For complex XML documents, I prefer using DOM, as in the example in Solution 9.

Because of the similarity to the `TestSAX` example, we will look at just a few implementation issues. The inner class `ConfigFileSaxHandler` contains instance data for storing element data:

```
private String currentElementName = "";
private Hashtable currentAttributes = null;
private String characterData = "";
```

In the `ConfigFileSaxHandler` method `startElement()`, we set this instance data:

```
currentElementName = qName;
if (attributes.getLength() < 1) {
    currentAttributes = null;
} else {
    currentAttributes = new Hashtable();
    for (int i=0, size=attributes.getLength(); i<size; i++) {
       currentAttributes.put(attributes.getLocalName(i),
                             attributes.getValue(i));
    }
}
```

The main class `ConfigFile` contains an `ArrayList` instance data element named `allElements` that is used to hold the element data extracted by the `ConfigFileSaxHandler` inner class. Here, the `ConfigFileSaxHandler` method `endElement()` contains code to copy the extracted element data back into the top-level class:

```
ArrayList al = new ArrayList();
al.add(currentElementName);
al.add(characterData);
al.add(currentAttributes);
parent.allElements.add(al);
```

The parent class `ConfigFile` provides public access methods for using the element data extracted from an XML file:

```
public int getNumberOfElements()
public String getElementName(int index)
public String getCharacterData(int index)
public Hashtable getAttributes(int index)
```

NOTE In general, writing application code that uses SAX is not quite as easy as using DOM and XPATH, but SAX is lighter weight and avoids having to store a complete DOM in memory. This can be an issue with very large XML files.

One of the advantages of SAX parsing is avoiding having to store the entire DOM tree in memory. However, you see in this example that some storage is required for storing data during the SAX event handling methods in an `ArrayList` instance. An alternative design for a configuration file utility would be to simply to use an in-memory DOM object and XPATH. Most applications that use SAX event-based parsing store at most a subset of the data in the original XML input stream.

SOLUTION 11

Transforming XML with XSLT

PROBLEM You want to maintain structured data in XML and then generate HTML for display.

SOLUTION You will use a combination of XPATH and XSLT transformations to separate XML content from XML formatting information.

The good news is that the dom4j library simplifies using XSLT formatting objects to transform XML content objects into XHTML. XHTML is well-formed HTML; that is, it's HTML that is legal XML. The bad news is that the learning curve for writing XML XSLT formatting objects is a bit steep. I will start out with the easy part of this solution, the Java application that uses dom4j to apply XSLT to XML documents. I will then present a short tutorial on XSLT, and the interested reader is encouraged to read one of more of the excellent XSLT tutorials on the Web.

NOTE I recommend the XSLT tutorial on the ZVON website, `www.zvon.org/xxl/XSLTutorial`, or Chuck White's book *Mastering XSLT* (Sybex, 2002).

The Java example program `S11/TestXSLT.java` is less than 50 lines of code. The `TestXSLT` class constructor requires the path name of an XSLT formatting file and generates a transform object that can be reused any number of times to use the XSLT transformations in the XSLT formatting file:

```
public TestXSLT(String xsltFile)
    throws javax.xml.transform.TransformerConfigurationException,
           java.io.FileNotFoundException {
  StreamSource xslt = new StreamSource(new FileReader(xsltFile));
  TransformerFactory factory = TransformerFactory.newInstance();
  xsltTransform = factory.newTransformer(xslt);
}
private Transformer xsltTransform;
```

The method *`transform`* takes a DOM tree as an argument and, using the XSLT transforms set in the class constructor, creates a new DOM object that is the input DOM with the XSLT transforms applied:

```
public Document transform(Document doc) throws
javax.xml.transform.TransformerException {
  DocumentSource source = new DocumentSource(doc);
  DocumentResult result = new DocumentResult();
  xsltTransform.transform(source, result);
  return result.getDocument();
}
```

The constructor and transform method is all there is for writing application-level XSLT translators. Here is some test code (without exception handling) for using the `TestXSLT` class:

```
TestXSLT test = new TestXSLT("S11/xslt.xml");
SAXReader reader = new SAXReader();
Document document = reader.read("S11/test.xml");
Document doc = test.transform(document);
// now, write out the DOM for the generated XHTML to a new file:
OutputFormat format = OutputFormat.createPrettyPrint();
XMLWriter writer =
  new XMLWriter(new FileWriter("S11/xslt_output.xml"), format);
writer.write(doc);
writer.close();
```

You will start the next section by looking at the input files used in this example (`xslt.xml` and `test.xml`) and the generated file `xslt_output.xml`.

A Brief XSLT Tutorial

You saw in the last section that it is very simple to use the dom4j library to write applications for transforming XML documents using XSLT. Here we will look at a simple example and then discuss a few XSLT techniques. I will start by showing you the example XML input file `test.xml`. This file contains the "content":

```
<?xml version="1.0" encoding="UTF-8"?>
<company name="KnowledgeBooks">
    <employee first_name="Mark" last_name="Watson" />
    <employee first_name="Carol" last_name="Watson" />
</company>
```

This is the same example XML file that I used in Solution 9 and earlier in Solution 10. The file `xslt.xml` contains example XSLT transformations. This file contains the "formatting information":

```
<?xml version="1.0" encoding="UTF-8"?>
<xsl:stylesheet version="1.0"
                xmlns:xsl="http://www.w3.org/1999/XSL/Transform">
  <xsl:template match="/">
    <html>
     <body>
      <xsl:for-each select="//company">
        <h1>
          <xsl:value-of select="@name" />
        </h1>
         <xsl:for-each select="//company/employee">
          <h2>
            <xsl:value-of select="@first_name" />
            <xsl:text> </xsl:text>
            <xsl:value-of select="@last_name" />
          </h2>
         </xsl:for-each>
      </xsl:for-each>
     </body>
    </html>
  </xsl:template>
</xsl:stylesheet>
```

The first element in the `xsl:stylesheet` element is the `xsl:template` element. Notice that the match attribute of the `xsl:template` element uses XPATH matching syntax. Here, you are matching the entire input XML document; if, for example, you had an `xsl:template` element that had an opening tag like this:

```
<xsl:template match="company">
```

then any matches inside this `xsl:template` element would only work for `company` elements or elements contained inside `company` elements. Notice that immediately inside the `xsl:template` element that I placed two standard HTML elements, `<html>` and `<body>`. The XSLT processor will simply copy these non-XSLT elements to the output XML document, regardless of whether of not any of them are contained inside an `xsl:for-each` element.

As an example, if you changed the element:

```
<xsl:for-each select="//company">
```

to:

```
<xsl:for-each select="//companyXXXX">
```

then there would be no matches to elements in the input DOM (or input XML document) and the output XML document would look like this:

```
<?xml version="1.0" encoding="UTF-8"?>
<html>
  <body/>
</html>
```

However, with the original `xsl:for-each` match pattern `//company`, then the generated XML (XHTML) is:

```
<?xml version="1.0" encoding="UTF-8"?>
<html>
  <body>
    <h1>KnowledgeBooks</h1>
    <h2>Mark Watson</h2>
    <h2>Carol Watson</h2>
  </body>
</html>
```

Here, after the XSLT transformer found a match for a `//company` element, it also found two matches for the inner element:

```
<xsl:for-each select="//company/employee">
```

The matching of `employee` elements and the generation of XHTML to represent these elements deserves a closer look; here are the relevant XSLT elements:

```
<xsl:for-each select="//company/employee">
    <h2>
      <xsl:value-of select="@first_name" />
      <xsl:text> </xsl:text>
      <xsl:value-of select="@last_name" />
    </h2>
</xsl:for-each>
```

For each match against the `//company/employee` XPATH pattern, the XSLT transformer will write an opening and closing `h2` tag with the values of the attributes `first_name` and `last_name`. The `xsl:text` element is used to define any text that you want "passed through" to the output XML document; in this case I wanted to add a space character between the first and last names.

XSLT is a great technology, but the learning curve for effectively using XSLT is steep. You have only looked at a few examples here; the interested reader is encouraged to work through a complete XSLT tutorial.

NOTE Using XSLT to transform "content" in XML files to HTML or XHTML is a powerful technique. You might have a large investment in XML data files; using XSLT allows you to reuse this "content" in flexible ways. If you want to convert XML "content" documents to PDF, you can use the Apache Jakarta FOP project.

SOLUTION 12

Using Java XML Binding

PROBLEM You work with complex XML documents and you do not want to have to manually write code to read and manipulate these XML documents.

SOLUTION You will use Java XML Bindings to generate code automatically for reading and writing XML documents.

Sun Microsystems recently released the final specification for JAXB, the Java XML Binding. Fully covering Sun's JAXB reference implementation is well beyond the cope of a Solution section, but we will look at a very simple example of using JAXB and leave it to the interested reader to read Sun's JAXB tutorial for more information. If you use the Apache Jakarta ant build tool, the JAXB reference implementation integrates well with the ant build process. Java files generated by JAXB require a runtime library that is distributed with JAXB.

NOTE Sun's JAXB reference implementation is available in their web services development kit available at `java.sun.com`. Sun also provides a detailed tutorial on the use of JAXB written by Scott Fordin.

I also use and recommend a very much simpler Java XML Binding toolkit called Zeus. You can download Zeus from `zeus.enhydra.org`. Zeus works by processing an XML DTD file and then automatically generating Java source files for reading, accessing, and writing out XML files that conform to the DTD used to generate the Java source files. The generated Java classes are self contained—no Zeus libraries are required at runtime. Zeus is lightweight; I like it and I think that you also will find it to be a useful tool. Zeus also integrates well with the Apache Jakarta ant build tool.

NOTE Do you use the ant build tool? If not, I strongly recommend that you start using ant to automate building Java programs, automatically run `JUnit` (a testing tool) tests, build deployable JAR files, and so on. Search the Web for "Apache ant tutorial".

Using Zeus Tools for Java XML Bindings

To use Zeus, you should download the latest version of it from `zeus.enhydra.org` and install it in a convenient place. You will need to have the directory `$ZEUS/bin` in your path. Start by running the Zeus tool to generate Java access files from an XML DTD. Starting in the top-level source directory for the examples in this book (that is, the directory that contains the subdirectories `S01`, `S02`, etc.), enter the following command (I am assuming that the Zeus bin directory is in your path):

```
zeus -constraints=S12/company.dtd -javaPackage=S12.zeus_generated
```

It is important that you not run this from the S12 directory—you must be in the parent directory of `S12` when you run this command. This command generates six Java source files in the package `S12.zeus_generated`. These files are generated using the information in the DTD file `S12/company.dtd`:

```
<!ELEMENT company (#PCDATA | employee )* >
<!ATTLIST company
          name CDATA #REQUIRED
>
<!ELEMENT employee (#PCDATA)>
<!ATTLIST employee
          last_name CDATA #REQUIRED
          first_name CDATA #REQUIRED
>
```

The example program `ZeusTest.java` imports the package `S12.zeus_generated`. There is no reason that you ever need to read the Java source code generated by Zeus, unless you are curious. All you need to do is write code that uses this generated code. The example file `ZeusTest.java` shows how simple it is to read in the contents of the XML file `S12/company.xml`:

```
<?xml version="1.0" encoding="UTF-8"?>
<company name="KnowledgeBooks">
  <employee first_name="Mark" last_name="Watson">
      character data for Mark
  </employee>
  <employee first_name="Carol" last_name="Watson">
      character data for Carol
  </employee>
</company>
```

Here, you read in the company.xml file, examine the element data, add a new employee element, and then write a new XML file S12/company2.xml:

```
// unmarshalling from the XML file S12/company.xml:
boolean xmlValidation = false;
Company company = CompanyUnmarshaller.unmarshal(
                    new File("S12/company.xml"), xmlValidation);
String companyName = company.getName();
List employees = company.getEmployeeList();
System.out.println("Company name: " + companyName);
for (Iterator iter = employees.iterator();
     iter.hasNext();) {
    Employee employee = (Employee)iter.next();
    String last_name = employee.getLast_name();
    String first_name = employee.getFirst_name();
    System.out.println("  employee: " + first_name + " " + last_name);
}
// add a new employee:
Employee employee3 = new EmployeeImpl();
employee3.setFirst_name("John Paul");
employee3.setLast_name("Sartre");
company.addEmployee(employee3);
// Marshal to a new XML file S12/company2.xml:
company.marshal(new FileOutputStream(
                   new File("S12/company2.xml")));
```

The automatically generated Company class provides utility methods for getting the name of the company in the input XML file and for getting a list of employees in the XML input file. The Company method getEmployeeList() returns a Java List whose elements are instances of class Employee (another class automatically generated by Zeus from the DTD). When you add a new employee, you use the method addEmployee(). The generated class Company also provides the method marshal that is used to save the modified Company instance (you added a new employee) to a new XML file company2.xml.

Using Zeus to generate XML access code is certainly easier than writing your own SAX or DOM code. Once you install Zeus, you will probably prefer using it over writing your own SAX- or DOM-based XML access code for many applications.

Using Sun's JAXB Reference Implementation

To use the JAXB reference implementation, you must download and install Sun's Web Services Development Kit. Following the installation directions, you should set the environment variable JWSDP_HOME to the top-level directory for your Web Services Development Kit. You must also set the environment variable JAXB_HOME to the value $JWSDP_HOME/jaxb.

NOTE Sun's JAXB implementation is designed to work with XML Schemas in addition to DTDs. If you are unfamiliar with XML Schemas, please refer to the material at `www.w3.org/XML/Schema.html` or *XML Schemas* by Chelsea Valentine et al. (Sybex, 2002).

The directory `S12` contains, in addition to the Zeus Java XML bindings example, also the files required for the Sun JAXB reference implementation example: `company.xsd` (an XML Schema file) and the `TestJAXB.java` test program. Assuming that you have Sun's JAXB reference implementation installed (and temporarily, have the directory `$JAXB_HOME/bin` in your execution path), then you can use the JAXB tool xjc to generate Java code that accesses XML files that implement the schema in `company.xsd`:

```
xjc S12/company.xsd -p S12.jaxb_generated
```

This generates approximately 40 Java source files that require JAXB library JAR files at both compilation and runtime. Like the generated files produced by Zeus, you will probably never have look at this generated code, unless you are curious. In order to compile the `TestJAXB.java` example program, you will need to have the following JAR files in your CLASSPATH (these are all included with Sun's Java Web Services Development Kit): `xerces.jar`, `jaxb-api.jar`, `jaxb-libs.jar`, `jaxb-impl.jar`, `jaxp-api.jar`, `namespace.jar`, `relaxngDatatype.jar`.

The following code snippets are taken from the file `TestJAXB.java`. Here, I first created a JAXB context for a specific package (`S12.jaxb_generated`) and an unmarshaller:

```
JAXBContext jaxbContext = JAXBContext.newInstance("S12.jaxb_generated");
Unmarshaller unMarshaller = jaxbContext.createUnmarshaller();
unMarshaller.setValidating(false);
```

Note that the JAXB context is for the package of the automatically generated files (from running xjc). Now that you have created an unmarshaller, you can create an instance of the `CompanyImpl` class (referenced here by the `Company` interface):

```
Company company =
    (Company)unMarshaller.unmarshal(
            new FileInputStream("S12/company.xml"));
```

Using the `Company` interface, you can get the company name and a list of the employee elements (unmarshalled into Java objects):

```
String companyName = company.getName();
List employees = company.getEmployee();
System.out.println("Company name: " + companyName);
for (Iterator iter = employees.iterator();
     iter.hasNext();) {
    EmployeeType employee = (EmployeeType)iter.next();
    String last_name = employee.getLastName();
```

```
        String first_name = employee.getFirstName();
        System.out.println("  employee: " + first_name +
                           " " + last_name);
    }
```

As in the Zeus example, you can add a new employee to this company:

```
EmployeeTypeImpl employee3 = new EmployeeTypeImpl();
employee3.setFirstName("John Paul");
employee3.setLastName("Sartre");
employee3.setValue("");
employees.add(employee3);
```

Here, we save the modified company object to a new XML file:

```
Marshaller marshaller = jaxbContext.createMarshaller();
marshaller.setProperty(Marshaller.JAXB_FORMATTED_OUTPUT,
                       Boolean.TRUE);
marshaller.marshal(company,
                   new FileOutputStream(
                       new File("S12/company3.xml")));
```

As you have seen, once JAXB is installed, using JAXB is as simple as using Zeus. If you prefer to use XML Schema instead of DTDs, then you should use JAXB because the Schema support is incomplete in Zeus. If you want a lightweight Java XML binding mechanism and you don't mind using DTDs instead of XML Schemas to define your XML applications, then I recommend Zeus.

NOTE We have used several useful Java XML technologies in this chapter. Java and XML is a powerful combination. In the next chapter, you will see how the use of XML allows you to communicate with other programs written in different programming languages and running on different operating systems. The message here is clear: XML is a flexible and self-describing notation for storing and transmitting data. Some people argue, incorrectly I believe, that XML is too "heavyweight" or inefficient. Certainly, converting between XML and Java objects is not computationally free, but the flexibility of using XML seems like a fair tradeoff for a slight cost in computing resources.

Distributed Programming Using XML

SOLUTION 13

Using XML-RPC for Client/Server Programming

PROBLEM You want to be able to write both clients and servers that communicate with programs written in other programming languages.

SOLUTION You will use Apache XML-RPC (formerly known as Helma XML-RPC) to write both Java client and server processes that are compatible with other XML-RPC enabled applications that can be written in other programming languages.

Remote Procedure Calls (RPC) are procedure calls to processes running on different computers over a network. The website `www.xml-rpc.org` is a good general source of information on using XML-RPC with many different programming languages. XML-RPC supports scalar data types like integer and floating-point numbers and character strings. XML-RPC also supports the definition of structured data. The Apache XML-RPC toolkit makes handling many Java data types for remote method arguments and return types transparent.

The Apache XML-RPC toolkit is very lightweight, basically putting one JAR file in your CLASSPATH to support both client and server programs. You can download Apache XML-RPC at `ws.apache.org/xmlrpc/` (or search for "Apache XML-RPC").

Implementing a Server Side XML-RPC Process

The Apache XML-RPC library contains a built-in web server that can service remote requests. It is also possible to use the Apache XML-RPC library inside other web server containers like Apache Jakarta Tomcat; the interested reader can find documentation for doing this on the Apache XML-RPC website.

In order to implement an XML-RPC web service, you must implement a handler class that implements the `org.apache.xmlrpc.XmlRpcHandler` interface:

```
public interface XmlRpcHandler {
    Object execute(String methodName, Vector Arguments)
           throws Exception;
}
```

When using Apache XML-RPC, arguments for a remote procedure are always passed in a vector. In the example, we assume that the test remote procedure takes three arguments: a

String, a Double, and an Integer. The example file ExampleXmlRpcServer.java contains a nonpublic class ExampleXmlRpcHandler that implements the XmlRpcHandler interface:

```
class ExampleXmlRpcHandler implements XmlRpcHandler {
    public Object execute(String method, Vector v)
           throws Exception {
        if (method.equals("testMethod")) {
            return testMethod(v);
        }
        System.out.println(
          "ExampleXmlRpcServer error: unknown method name: " +
          method);
        return null;  // error: unknown method name
    }

    Vector testMethod(Vector v) {
        System.out.println("entered testMethod("+v+")");
        Vector ret = new Vector();
        // get the example arguments:
        String s = (String)v.get(0);
        Double f = (Double)v.get(1);
        Integer i = (Integer)v.get(2);
        ret.add(s + s);
        ret.add(new Float(2 * f.floatValue()));
        ret.add(new Integer(2 * i.intValue()));
        return ret;
    }
}
```

A single handler class can implement more than one method. Here, we compare the name of the execute method argument method with the string "testMethod" and if there is a match, call the local method testMethod to process the service request. The arguments for service requests are always passed in a Java vector. In the local method testMethod, we assume that the three methods are a String, a Double, and an Integer, and we cast them appropriately when accessing the elements of vector v.

Using the built-in web server class with this handler class is simple. In the following example, we set the built-in web server in "paranoid" mode: no service request is accepted from a client unless the client's IP address is registered using the acceptClient method. For a general web service that you want to publish to anyone on the Internet, omit both of the setParanoid and acceptClient calls.

```
WebServer ws = new WebServer(8100);
ws.addHandler("$default", new ExampleXmlRpcHandler());
ws.setParanoid(true);  // deny all clients
ws.acceptClient("127.0.0.1"); // allow local access
ws.start();
```

The first argument to the method `addHandler` is the name of the remote object for processing requests. For example, we could name the remote object `Test3` by using

```
ws.addHandler("Test3", new ExampleXmlRpcHandler());
```

In this case, we would access the web service using a URL like:

```
http://127.0.0.1:8100/Test3
```

In the original example, where the first argument to `addHandler` is `$default`, the URL we would use to access the web service would be:

```
http://127.0.0.1:8100
```

You will see in the next section how you can write a Java client application to use this example web service.

NOTE You will frequently see the absolute IP address 127.0.0.1 or the symbolic IP name localhost in examples in this book. This refers to the local computer. If for example, the web service was a server with the domain name aservername.com, you'd replace 127.0.0.1 with the server domain (in this example, aservername.com).

Implementing an XML-RPC Client

As you saw in the last section, the remote method `testMethod` expects three arguments: a `String`, a `Double`, and an `Integer`. You use the Apache XML-RPC utility class `XmlRpcClientLite` to make a connection to the server. You always need to define a vector to hold the arguments, fill the vector appropriately, and then use the `XmlRpcClientLite` method `execute` to call the remote web service. Here is an example of using the example web service from the last section:

```
String server_url = "http://localhost:8100";
// Create an object to represent the remote server:
XmlRpcClientLite server = new XmlRpcClientLite(server_url);
// Build a parameter list:
Vector params = new Vector();
params.addElement(new String("parrot"));
params.addElement(new Double(3.14159));
params.addElement(new Integer(1001));
// Call the server, and get the result as a Java Vector:
Vector v = (Vector)server.execute("testMethod", params);
// print out the retuned values:
for (int i=0, size=v.size(); i<size; i++) {
    System.out.println(" return value " + i +
                       " from remote 'testMethod':"+v.get(i));
}
```

XML-RPC is often used in applications like RSS news feed aggregation. I like XML-RPC in general, and the Apache XML-RPC library for Java in particular, because it is simple to use and lightweight.

In Solution 14, we will look at an even simpler way to publish and access web services (so simple, in fact, that you won't use any libraries except for standard `java.net` socket classes—server- and client-side code together is a few hundred lines of code).

In Solutions 15 and 16, we will look at SOAP, the "elephant" of XML-based messaging. SOAP is the most capable and flexible technique that you will use in this chapter, but it is also the most complex in terms of platform requirements (memory and CPU) and required support software.

SOLUTION 14

Using XML over HTTP for Web Services

PROBLEM You want to be able to publish and access web-based resources without the overhead of more complex schemes like SOAP and XML-RPC.

SOLUTION You will represent web-based resources and web services as URIs and access them using HTTP.

You will use a very simple technique in this solution. The ideas in this solution originated with the Representational State Transfer (REST) technology promoted principally by Roy Fielding and Mark Baker. REST uses standard HTTP GET/POST/PUT/DELETE operations to access URIs that identify resources and web services. In this solution, you will implement web services using HTTP GET requests to a server that parses a function name and optional named parameter values from the request and then returns an XML payload to the requestor. You will not use any libraries except the standard Java socket libraries to implement this: a server framework will be implemented in about 200 lines of Java code. Customizing this framework for a specific web services application requires only a few additional lines of code (plus the application that you want to publish as a web service).

In this solution, you will view published web services as being defined by a URI that encodes:

- Address and port number of server
- A "function" to execute
- Zero or more arguments to the "function"

For simplicity, you will only consider the model where HTTP GET operations are used to request an XML payload from a server. As a simple example, consider this URI that requests the stock price for the stock ticker from a service running on the local system (IP address 127.0.0.1) on port 9000:

```
http://127.0.0.1:9000/?getquote&ticker=AAPL
```

The function name is `getquote` and the single argument `ticker` has the value `AAPL` (the stock ticker for Apple Computer). The result is returned as an XML payload. One great advantage of this simple scheme is that it is trivial to write a client for a service in any programming language that either supports HTTP connection operations or, at a minimum, sockets. Because XML is self-describing, if you access this example URI and receive an XML payload, you can determine trivially what the format of the payload is and how to use it in your client-side programs; for example, you might receive this XML payload:

```
<stockquote ticker="AAPL" cost="19.25" />
```

For anyone who has built a large web services application using SOAP, the simplicity of this approach might be disturbing. However, the space of potential web applications is huge: while some applications call for the full complexity of SOAP, others are best implemented using the lighter weight XML-RPC, and still others are best implemented using something as simple as this solution of fetching XML payloads using HTTP GET requests. I prefer using XML-RPC if implementations are available for other platforms, but otherwise I use XML over HTTP, as discussed in this solution. Whatever your favorite, as a Java developer, you should have a full toolbox!

When writing XML over HTTP web services, the simplest test client is any utility that fetches the content of a web page, given a URL. I use the utilities `wget`, `fetch`, and `curl`, which are available under all common operating systems.

NOTE I use XML over HTTP when building web services using programming languages that do not have available existing SOAP or XML-RPC libraries. For example, all three implementations of Common LISP that I use lack robust SOAP and XML-RPC implementations, but XML over HTTP can be easily implemented in any programming language with good socket support and it's a good way to tie together Java and Common LISP processes in a distributed system.

Implementing a Java Web Server to Support XML over HTTP

The XML over HTTP enabled web server is implemented with two classes that you can find in the directory `src/S14`:

AbstractServer Accepts incoming socket connections, creates instances of the class `ServerConnection` to get the text for an HTTP GET request over an open socket connection, parses the GET HTML header to get the function name and arguments, and then calls the abstract method `getXmlPayload`.

ServerConnection Reads the contents of an HTTP GET request from an open socket and returns a payload to the requestor.

You can experiment with this example and read the source code; here, we will just look at a few implementation details. Together, these two classes are only about 200 lines of Java code. As promised, supporting XML over HTTP web services is simple! The constructor for the class `ServerConnection` takes two arguments:

```
public ServerConnection(AbstractServer server,
                        Socket client_socket)
```

The first argument is a reference to an instance of any class derived from `AbstractServer`. This reference will call the method `process` defined in the class `AbstractServer`. The method `process` is responsible for parsing an HTTP GET request and then calling the method `getXmlPayload` (that must be defined in any class derived from the `AbstractServer` class). The constructor for class `ServerConnection` creates a new thread and starts the thread after getting the input and output streams from the client socket input argument. The method `run` reads up to the first 1024 bytes from the input stream, calls the `AbstractServer` method process, and finally closes the input socket:

```
public void run() {
    String input_buf;
    byte[] buf = new byte[1024];
    try {
        int num = input_strm.read(buf);
        if (num >= 0) {
          input_buf = new String(buf, 0, num);
          if (input_buf.indexOf("GET") > -1) {
              myServer.process(input_buf, output_strm);
          }
        }
    } catch (Exception exception) {
    } finally {
      try {
         my_socket.close();
      } catch (Exception exception) {
    }
}
```

Here, the instance variable `myServer` is the reference to the instance of any class derived from `AbstractServer` that was passed as the first argument to the `ServerConnection` constructor.

In the next section, you will see how to customize this simple class framework by writing a subclass of `AbstractServer`.

NOTE I will cover Java socket programming in detail in Solutions 28 and 29.

Using the Java XML over HTTP-Enabled Web Server

We looked at the abstract class `AbstractServer` and some code from the `ServerConnection` class in the last section. This abstract class does all the work for implementing XML over HTTP services except for actually implementing the services. We will now look at the class `TestServer` that is derived from the abstract base class:

```
public class TestServer extends AbstractServer {

    public String getXmlPayload(String functionName,
                                String[] argumentNames,
                                String[] argumentValues) {
        System.out.println("getXmlPayload: functionName="+
                           functionName);
        for (int i=0, size=argumentNames.length; i<size; i++) {
           System.out.println("  "+argumentNames[i] + " : " +
                              argumentValues[i]);
        }
        return "<stockquote ticker=\"AAPL\" cost=\"19.25\" />";
    }

    public TestServer() {
        super();
    }
    static public void main(String[] args) {
        new TestServer();
    }
}
```

The method `getXmlPayload` is called with the name of a function and a set of argument name/value pairs by the abstract base class. Here, you simply print out the function name and the argument name/value pairs and return a legal XML element. There is very little memory footprint and processor overhead for building XML over HTTP-based web services.

As an example, if you used a client program or a utility like `wget` or `fetch` to retrieve the contents of the URL http://127.0.0.1:8080?foo&a=1&b=2, then the debug printout in this implementation of the method `getXmlPayload` would be:

```
getXmlPayload: functionName=foo
  a : 1
  b : 2
```

The class TestServer obviously does not do much except act as an example of receiving a function name and the function's arguments from the socket-handling code in the base class AbstractServer.

For your applications, you would write a subclass of AbstractServer that had a method getXmlPayload that actually performed a computation. Like the XML-RPC example in Solution 13, the getXmlPayload method could serve to process several different web services by checking the function name (first argument to getXmlPayload) and calling the appropriate local method based on this name.

SOLUTION 15

Using GLUE for SOAP-Based Web Services

PROBLEM You want to expose your Java code as SOAP-enabled web services.

SOLUTION You develop a sample SOAP service using the GLUE Standard Edition product and a client to access this service.

Simple Object Access Protocol (SOAP) is a standard protocol for remote web services and is considerably more complex than either XML-RPC or XML over HTTP. However, the GLUE product greatly simplifies the use of SOAP. After reviewing SOAP basics, you will implement both server and client side SOAP applications using GLUE (in this solution) and Apache Axis (in Solution 16).

Before starting this solution, it's a good idea to download and install GLUE standard (www.themindelectric.com). This installation includes very good documentation on web services in general and GLUE in particular. GLUE implements Sun's JAX-RPC API.

SOAP Basics

There are three technologies that can be used together: the Simple Object Access Protocol (SOAP), Web Services Description Language (WSDL), and Universal Description Discovery Integration (UDDI). In practice, SOAP and WSDL are almost always used together. UDDI is less frequently used and I will not cover it here.

NOTE You can get more information on UDDI at www.uddi.org.

SOAP is a protocol that allows two programs to communicate using messaging with XML message payloads. SOAP is usually used with HTTP but is sometimes used with e-mail servers or Java Messaging System (JMS) APIs. SOAP messages travel between end points that represent addresses of sender and receiver. With HTTP, SOAP is synchronous: a socket connection is opened to a SOAP-enabled server and an HTTP GET or POST request is used to send an XML payload (SOAP headers and message contents) to the server. With the original socket connection open, the server determines which local service to use to process the incoming message and calculate a response SOAP message, that is then returned to the requestor using the socket connection.

Two separate XML payloads are used in a synchronous SOAP-based RPC call: a SOAP request is sent to the remote service, and the remote service returns a SOAP response to the client application. You will see a SOAP response XML payload later when you look at an Apache Axis example in Solution 16. SOAP request and response payloads consist of three parts:

SOAP envelope Specifies what is in the message and what object on the server should handle the message.

SOAP encoding Specifies how simple and structured data types are serialized to XML. SOAP is extensible, so it must be possible to encode the data for arbitrary objects. (Solution 16 has a discussion of serializing Java objects to XML).

Message passing Specifies how the SOAP payload is to be delivered. At a minimum, specifies a URI for the target object, a method name, and parameters for the method.

NOTE You are limited to what Java data types you can use if you want to be interoperable with all SOAP platforms. Solution 16 has a section "Java Data Mapping to XML in Apache Axis." This discussion also applies to the use of GLUE. You can safely use most scalar Java types like Strings and numbers for method arguments and return values. The use of simple arrays is also very portable between implementations.

WSDL Basics

WDSL is an XML document that describes a web service. Later, you will be using GLUE and Apache Axis to implement web services. Both GLUE and Axis can automatically generate WSDL for deployed web services, and they also provide utilities to convert a WSDL document into Java stub code for accessing the web service. You will use this facility in an Axis-based example in Solution 16.

GLUE also provides the facility for dynamically generating bindings for a remote service by using the WSDL description for the service, and you will use this technique for this solution. Usually, a WSDL document is generated for a specific web service also contains information on the URI for the remote object implementing the service and port information. WSDL is not really intended for human readers—that said, when I do look at automatically generated WSDL documents, the most interesting information is in the port information that specifies the signatures of exposed methods.

The example ZIP file for Solution 16, `src/S16/axis.zip` contains the WSDL file `test.wsdl` for the example Axis web service. I use snippets from this file parts here as a quick introduction to WSDL; you can find WSDL tutorials on the Web that go into more detail for the WSDL specification. The top element in a WSDL document is `definitions` (in the `wsdl` XML namespace). Required attributes are the target name space for the remote service and the URI for the implementation remote object:

```
<wsdl:definitions
        targetNamespace="http://localhost:8080/axis/AxisTest.jws"
        xmlns:impl="http://localhost:8080/axis/AxisTest.jws"
```

The `portType` element specifies input and output message types for a service. In the following listing, you can see that the remote object `AxisTest` has a method `useLibToAdd` with method arguments `f1` and `f2`. Later, you will see how a `wsdl:message` element defines the types of these arguments.

```
<wsdl:portType name="AxisTest">
    <wsdl:operation name="useLibToAdd" parameterOrder="f1 f2">
      <wsdl:input message="intf:useLibToAddRequest"
                  name="useLibToAddRequest"/>
      <wsdl:output message="intf:useLibToAddResponse"
                   name="useLibToAddResponse" />
    </wsdl:operation>
</wsdl:portType>
```

Contained inside the `definitions` element are `wsdl:message` elements. These elements define argument types and the method return type. Here is the definition for the remote method `useLibToAdd` (you will also see this in the Axis example in Solution 16):

```
<wsdl:message name="useLibToAddRequest">
    <wsdl:part name="f1" type="xsd:float"/>
    <wsdl:part name="f2" type="xsd:float"/>
</wsdl:message>
<wsdl:message name="useLibToAddResponse">
    <wsdl:part name="useLibToAddReturn" type="xsd:float"/>
</wsdl:message>
```

The top-level `definitions` element also contains the `services` element that specifies the URI for accessing the web service `AxisTest`:

```
<wsdl:service name="AxisTestService">
    <wsdl:port binding="intf:AxisTestSoapBinding" name="AxisTest">
      <wsdlsoap:address
```

```
        location="http://localhost:8080/axis/AxisTest.jws"/>
    </wsdl:port>
</wsdl:service>
```

The binding specifies concrete formatting information and additional information for the protocols for portType elements. SOAP services are usually bound to a resource that is available via HTTP, as in this example. However, it is also possible to specify binding to other protocols, like SMTP.

NOTE When using tools like GLUE and Apache Axis, you really don't have to be too aware of the formats for SOAP messages and WSDL. I went into some detail for WSDL because you are more likely to inspect the contents of WSDL than SOAP messages. The power of WSDL and SOAP is that client programs written in most popular programming languages can use WSDL to access remote SOAP-enabled services written in other languages.

Example SOAP Applications Using GLUE

I assume that you have installed GLUE on your system in the standard GLUE installation directory /electric. To expose a Java program as a SOAP-enabled web service using GLUE, start by writing a Java interface for the methods that you want to expose. The example that you will work through is contained in the ZIP file S15/glue.zip. Here is a simple interface, IAdd, that specifies a single method add that adds to floating-point numbers and returns the sum of these numbers:

```
public interface IAdd {
    public float add(float f1, float f2);
}
```

You then need to implement this interface in a class that you can construct instances of:

```
public class Add implements IAdd {
    public float add(float f1, float f2) {
        return f1 + f2;
    }
}
```

This is just an example, of course; in general, you will have a Java application that you want to publish as a SOAP-enabled web service. I usually prefer to leave my standalone Java application as-is and write a new interface and wrapper class (that implements this interface) that calls the appropriate public methods in my application. This makes it easier to both maintain the code for a standalone Java application and separately maintain the code to expose it as a web service. In order to publish the IAdd interface, you need a short Java program that uses the GLUE libraries. The following short program uses the built-in GLUE web server to support remote access to the Add service:

```
import electric.server.http.HTTP;
import electric.registry.Registry;
```

```
public class PublishAddService {
    public static void main(String[] args) throws Exception {
        // start the internal GLUE web server specifying
        // port and domain:
        HTTP.startup("http://localhost:8004/glue");
        // publish the Add service:
        Registry.publish("add", new Add());
    }
}
```

Not bad! Less than ten lines of code and you have published the add method in the class Add in a standalone web server. You also need a test client to access this web service. There are two ways to write a client using the GLUE libraries but you will only use the simplest method here: get the WSDL for this web service and use GLUE libraries to dynamically make the connection to the remote server. Here is a sample client:

```
import electric.registry.Registry;

public class Client {
    public static void main(String[] args) {
        try  {
            // get the WSDL for the Add service and
            // build a local interface:
            String url = "http://localhost:8004/glue/add.wsdl";
            IAdd adder = (IAdd)Registry.bind(url, IAdd.class);

            // use the local interface to call the remote service
            float sum = adder.add(3.14159f, 10.0f);
            System.out.println("sum = " + sum);
        } catch (Exception ee) {
            ee.printStackTrace();
        }
    }
}
```

The built-in GLUE web server provides a dynamic WSDL generation service that we use here: note that instead of specifying just the service name add in the URL, we specify add.wsdl. If you fetch the contents of http://localhost:8004/glue/add.wsdl, you will see an XML WSDL document that describes the services for the object Add.

Using SOAP is complex, but the GLUE libraries hide this complexity. In order to compile these example files (assuming that GLUE is installed in /electric on Unix systems or \electric on Windows systems), specify the CLASSPATH as follows (for Windows, replace ":" with ";"):

```
javac -classpath .:/electric/lib/GLUE-STD.jar *.java
```

The following command will run the GLUE web server and the test service (the command should be all on one line):

```
java -classpath
      .:/electric/lib/GLUE-STD.jar:/electric/lib/servlet.jar
      PublishAddService
```

The following command will run the sample client (the command should be all on one line):

```
java -classpath
      .:/electric/lib/GLUE-STD.jar:/electric/lib/servlet.jar
      Client
```

NOTE GLUE is a good product. One thing that I appreciate about it is that it only takes a few minutes to install GLUE and to start hosting SOAP-based web services. In the next section, we will look at Apache Axis. It takes me about 15 minutes to install Axis and other required software—definitely more work than installing GLUE. The advantages of Axis is that it is open source software, has the liberal Apache license and, when combined with Apache Jakarta Tomcat, provides a very robust web services platform.

SOLUTION 16

Using Apache Axis for SOAP-Based Web Services

PROBLEM You want to implement SOAP-based web services using free open source software.

SOLUTION The combination of Apache Jakarta Tomcat and Apache Axis provides a robust and stable platform for hosting SOAP-based web services as well as Java servlet/JSP-based websites. Using Axis can be complex, but I will try to simplify it as much as possible to get you started quickly.

In Solution 15, we covered the basics of writing SOAP services and writing remote clients in Java to access these services with GLUE. If you have not already read Solution 15, you should go back and read the overview sections for SOAP and WSDL. In this solution, we will develop a similar example service and a client for that service using the Apache Axis package.

Before starting this solution, you need to download and install Apache Axis (`ws.apache.org/axis`). I assume that you already have the Apache Jakarta Tomcat servlet/JSP container installed on your system; you will need Tomcat for this solution (and also later in this book when we cover Java servlets and JSPs). Tomcat is available at the Apache website (`www.jakarta.apache.org/tomcat`); you need to install Axis in your Tomcat installation as per the directions in the Axis documentation. Apache AXIS implements Sun's JAX-RPC API.

NOTE The introduction to Solution 40 contains directions for starting Tomcat and administering Tomcat.

Java Data Mapping to XML in Apache Axis

A major goal of the SOAP specification and design is to support completely self-describing messages. If self-describing messages are not required, CORBA IIOP with IDL (see Solutions 32 and 33) is a more compact and efficient RPC mechanism.

For complete interoperability with other SOAP platforms (for example, Microsoft .NET, Perl SOAP::Lite, and so on), you are limited in the Java types that can be used for method arguments and return values. The following incomplete list shows the most frequently used Java data types to XML mappings supported by Axis (please see the Axis User Guide for a complete list):

- `java.lang.String (xsd:string)`
- `int xsd:int`
- `long (xsd:long)`
- `float (xsd:float)`
- `double (xsd:double)`
- `boolean (xsd:boolean)`
- `byte (xsd:byte)`
- `java.util.Calendar (xsd:dateTime)`
- `byte[] (xsd:hexBinary)`

The XML types are defined in the `xsd` namespace, which is used for XML Schemas. Interoperability with all SOAP-enabled platforms is more problematic when dealing with collection types. While the use of simple array types is "safe" for not breaking interoperability with other SOAP platforms, using Java collections in general is not.

NOTE The actual encoding for serializing Java objects to XML should not be a concern for programmers writing SOAP services and client applications because SOAP implementations take care of these details for you. However, you should be aware of the limitation on Java data types used for method arguments and return values.

Writing SOAP Services Using Axis

We will first look at deploying an existing Java program as a SOAP-enabled web service and later see how to write a standalone Java client for this web service.

NOTE If you install Tomcat and Axis to work through this solution, keep the installation on your system—you will need Tomcat again in the "Java Servlets" and "Java Server Pages (JSPs)" sections later in this book.

There are three ways to use Axis to provide SOAP-enabled web services:

- Copy the top level class for your web service to the `TOMCAT/webapps/axis` directory and change the file extension from `.java` to `.jws`. Add compiled classes required by this top-level class to the directory `TOMCAT/webapps/axis/WEB-INF/classes` (preserving the directory structure of your Java packaging scheme). Alternatively, you can place all required class files for your web service in a JAR file and place this JAR file in the directory `TOMCAT/webapps/axis/WEB-INF/lib`.
- Write an XML deployment descriptor (as per the documentation included with Axis). This option provides much more flexibility for only publishing some public methods, changing access names, etc.
- Embed Axis in an existing web application. If you have a large Java application, you might consider imbedding Axis in your application rather than running your application inside Axis.

The first option is very simple, the second is a bit more work, and the third is difficult. In this book we will only cover the first option; you can find details on the other two in the Axis Installation and User Guides.

The example directory `S16` contains a ZIP file named `axis.zip` that you should unzip into the directory `TOMCAT/webapps/axis`. This operation will create the Axis JWS file `AxisTest.jws` in the `TOMCAT/webapps/axis` directory and the source and compiled class files `TestLib.java` and `TestLib.class` in the directory `TOMCAT/webapps/axis/WEB-INF/classes`. The class `AxisTest` has two public methods that are both automatically exposed as SOAP-enabled web services:

```
public String getDate()
public float useLibToAdd(float f1, float f2)
```

The second method *useLibToAdd* uses the class `TestLib` and serves as an example of wrapping arbitrary Java programs as web services. You can wrap your Java programs as web serives by following these steps:

1. Copy the class files (preserving the package directory structure) for your application to the `TOMCAT/webapps/axis/WEB-INF/classes` directory.
2. Write a small Java wrapper class that provides a public method for calling any public methods in your program that you want to expose as web services. The file `AxisTest.jws` is an example of such a wrapper: it uses the library code in the class `S15.TestLib`.
3. Copy the Java wrapper file to the directory `TOMCAT/webapps/axis` and change the extension from `.java` to `.jws`.
4. Restart Tomcat.

For publishing public methods in an existing Java program, another alternative is to simply place a JAR file containing all compiled class files your application in the directory `TOMCAT/webapps/axis/WEB-INF/lib`. Then write a wrapper Java file (to be renamed with the `.jws` extension) that has public methods that use classes in this JAR file.

With Axis, you can test your deployed services without writing a test client because Axis supports a debug mode that uses HTTP GET requests to access SOAP services. Assuming that you unzipped the `axis.zip` file in the `TOMCAT/webapps/axis` directory and restarted Tomcat, try fetching the following URL in your web browser:

```
http://localhost:8080/axis/AxisTest.jws?method=getDate
```

This should return the following XML SOAP response payload:

```
<?xml version="1.0" encoding="UTF-8"?>
<soapenv:Envelope xmlns:soapenv="http://schemas.xmlsoap.org/soap/envelope/"
xmlns:xsd="http://www.w3.org/2001/XMLSchema" xmlns:xsi="http://www.w3.org/2001/
XMLSchema-instance">
 <soapenv:Body>
  <getDateResponse soapenv:encodingStyle="http://schemas.xmlsoap.org/soap/
encoding/">
   <getDateReturn xsi:type="xsd:string">Thu Jul 10 14:06:53 MST 2003</
getDateReturn>
  </getDateResponse>
 </soapenv:Body>
</soapenv:Envelope>
```

You can call the second public method in `AxisTest.jws` using the following URL, that encodes the object (`AxisTest`), the method name (`useLibToAdd`), and the method argument values (1 for the argument `f1` and 2 for the argument `f2`):

```
http://127.0.0.1:8080/axis/AxisTest.jws?method=useLibToAdd&f1=1&f2=2
```

You can fetch the SOAP response payload for this request using a utility like `wget`, `fetch`, or `curl`.

Writing SOAP Clients Using Axis

Axis provides a WSDL to the Java stub generator utility. To get WSDL for any SOAP-enabled web service deployed with Axis, append `?WSDL` to the URL for the web service; for example:

```
http://localhost:8080/axis/AxisTest.jws?WSDL
```

NOTE For later, get the result and save it in a file `test.wsdl`—you looked at parts of this file in Solution 15.

It is fine to be able to test Axis-deployed web services using HTTP GETs, but you should really , in general, access exposed web services with remote clients. To do this, you can either code clients manually or use the WSDL2Java Axis utility class, which requires you to set up a command file that specifies a CLASSPATH for the required Axis JAR files. The directory `S16` contains a file `wsdl2java` that I set up to work on my system; you can edit this file changing the location of the Tomcat installation to match your system. In a temporary directory, execute the following:

```
wsdl2java test.wsdl
```

The file `test.wsdl` contains the WSDL file generated by Axis for this example. This generates a Java package `localhost.axis.AxisTest_jws`.

NOTE The `client.zip` file already contains a directory `localhost` that contains the generated Java stub files. These stub files are compiled by the `run.sh` script for Mac OS X and Linux users included with this ZIP file and a `run.bat` script for Windows users.

The following test program uses this generated Java package to exercise both example web services (this is the example file `AxisTestClient.java` that is in the file `S16/client.zip`):

```
import localhost.axis.AxisTest_jws.*;

public class AxisTestClient {

    public static void main(String [] args) throws Exception {
        AxisTestService service = new AxisTestServiceLocator();
        AxisTest port = service.getAxisTest();
        String date = port.getDate();
        System.out.println("date="+date);
        float ff = port.useLibToAdd(10.0f, 33f);
        System.out.println("result="+ff);
    }
}
```

The `client.zip` file also contains a Unix-style script, `run.sh`, that compiles and runs this example client. You will have to edit this file by changing my TOMCAT path (`/Volumes/work/Tomcat-4.1.18`) to the TOMCAT path on your system.

NOTE Apache Axis is not as simple to use as GLUE because it takes a while to install Axis in Tomcat and set up your development environment. However, once you have Tomcat and Axis set up and you have the `wsdl2java` script set up for your system configuration, Axis is very easy to use. Web services using SOAP is now a standard technology. I recommend that you make the effort to try both GLUE and Axis and use them as appropriate in your projects. Another good alternative is to download Sun Microsystems Web Services Toolkit (you used this in Solution 12 on JAXB) that contains a complete software stack for developing and hosting web services. The Web Services Toolkit also includes support for JMS and JAXB, so you can try using SOAP with JMS.

Hypothetical Use of Web Services

We have covered a lot of material quickly in this chapter for developing and deploying web services. I will finish this chapter by discussing a scenario in which you might want to implement a system using web services.

The clients for other web services are likely to be web services themselves. For example, say your company wants to sell a web service for distributing news articles from multiple sources and that this web service then wants to use two additional web services:

- A spelling and grammar correction service—someone else at your company has developed and deployed a SOAP-enabled web service that tries to automatically correct spelling and grammar errors. This service is available on your corporate LAN and you can use it for free.
- A European company sells web services for automatically translating text between English, French, and German—you want to give your customers the option of having news stories delivered translated into French or German. You will pay the other company a fee per transaction for using their web services.

NOTE The advantage of using web services is that it allows you to use existing web services as components and to mix and match web services implemented using Microsoft's .NET platform, the Perl SOAP:Lite package, Python's ZSI or SOPE.py, VisualWorks Smalltalk, Web Services for Mac OS X, SOAP-Opera for Squeak Smalltalk, PHP-SOAP, etc.

A good alternative to using XML-based web services is Java RMI for systems written completely in Java. For interoperability between systems written in different programming languages, CORBA IIOP with IDL is a fine alternative. The main advantage of XML-based web services is the self-describing nature of XML messages. I will cover RMI in Solutions 30 and 31 and the use of CORBA technologies in Solutions 32 and 33.

Arrays, Vectors, and Hash Tables

SOLUTION 17

Efficient Conversion Between Arrays and Vectors

PROBLEM You need to frequently convert between simple Java arrays and Java collection types.

SOLUTION Simple arrays and Java collections each have their advantages. You will see how to efficiently convert between simple arrays, vectors, and `array lists`.

Java collection types are easier to use than simple array types. For most applications, the higher memory and computational overhead for using Java collection classes is a good tradeoff in return for ease of software development and software maintenance. However, it is important to understand that simple array types use memory and are more efficient in CPU use (see Solution 18), and it is important to use simple array types when efficiency is important.

NOTE Remember the main difference between `Vector` and `ArrayList` objects: vectors contain synchronization behavior to make them thread safe, which adds overhead when this protection is not required.

In this solution, we will look at a few examples for converting between simple array types and `Vector` and `ArrayList` objects.

The following example shows how to copy a vector containing string objects into a `String[]` array:

```
Vector v = new Vector();
v.add("the"); v.add("dog"); v.add("bit");
v.add("the"); v.add("cat");
String[] ss = (String[])v.toArray(new String[v.size()]);
```

The argument to the `Vector` method `toArray()` serves to specify the type of the array that is generated and provide storage. The following example shows the similar technique for converting an `ArrayList` containing instances of class `Float` into a `Float[]` array:

```
ArrayList al = new ArrayList();
al.add(new Float(3.14159f)); al.add(new Float(1));
Float[] ff = (Float[])al.toArray(new Float[al.size()]);
```

NOTE Java simple array types must contain objects of the same class or objects that can be cast to the class of the array type.

In the following example, we will convert the `String[]` array `ss` to both a `Vector` and an `ArrayList`:

```
Vector v2 = new Vector(Arrays.asList(ss));
ArrayList al2 = new ArrayList(Arrays.asList(ss));
```

It is common to see Java code that uses a `for` loop to copy elements or arrays to vectors and vice versa. This is a bad practice for two reasons: it makes your code longer (more prone to errors and increased maintenance costs), and it prevents your programs from taking advantage of optimizations in the standard class libraries.

SOLUTION 18

Save Memory in Java Applications

PROBLEM Your Java application stores many Java objects in memory. You want to reduce memory use even if it requires custom coding.

SOLUTION You will start by reviewing memory use of Java objects and then look at a few coding tricks to save memory.

Java is an efficient language for reducing programming time, but it is not always efficient in memory use. While the size of Java objects might change with different Java Virtual Machines (JVMs), the following list shows the approximate size of commonly used Java objects:

Object 8 bytes

Zero length string 40 bytes

char 2 bytes

int 4 bytes

Integer 16 bytes

The overhead for an array 16 bytes

Java primitive types like `byte`, `char`, `int`, and so on use less memory than Java types derived from the `Object` super class. In this solution, we will look at several coding tricks for saving memory: custom string handling, array use, object reuse, and a custom hash table.

NOTE Usually, you would not want to use the techniques I cover in this solution! It is generally more important to write clear, easy to read and maintain code than to save memory: memory is usually less expensive than software development effort spent on memory optimization. Sometimes, however, it is necessary to store a lot of data in memory, so it becomes important to use more compact data structures.

Measuring Memory Use

The JVM isolates the programmer from memory allocation concerns. This is usually a good thing, but it makes it tricky to accurately measure memory use. You can measure the amount of free, maximum, and total memory after forcing a garbage collection:

```
System.gc();
Runtime runtime = Runtime.getRuntime();
long freeMemory = runtime.freeMemory();
long maxMemory = runtime.maxMemory();
long totalMemory = runtime.totalMemory();
```

There are many problems with this, the worst being that calling `System.gc()` does not guarantee that the JVM will actually collect garbage (that is, unused memory). The best thing to do is to run memory-use tests several times and average the results. A simple but not too accurate way to estimate just the relative use of memory for different data structures is to serialize them into byte output streams and compare the final sizes of the streams for the objects that you are measuring. The following utility method can be used to measure the size in bytes of a serialized object:

```
public int estimateObjectSize(Object obj, String name)
       throws Exception {
   ByteArrayOutputStream byteOuputStream =
        new ByteArrayOutputStream();
   ObjectOutputStream objectStream =
        new ObjectOutputStream(byteOuputStream);
   objectStream.writeObject(obj);
   objectStream.flush();
   byte[] bytes = byteOuptutStream.toByteArray();
   int len = bytes.length;
   System.out.println(" Size of " + name + " is approximately " +
                      len + " bytes.");
   return len;
}
```

This method only works if the object tested implements the `java.io.Serializable` interface. It does not do a perfect job at comparing the relative size of different Java objects because it depends on how the JVM serializes different types. The relative size of serialized objects might not correspond exactly with the relative sizes of objects in memory.

TIP Use the debugger in your Java IDE to inspect data objects. This will allow you to estimate storage requirements and give you some appreciation for how the built-in collection classes work.

Custom String Handling

A common technique for reducing memory requirements for storing many strings when many of them might be duplicates is to intern the strings. Here is a simple example:

```
String the = "the";
the.intern();
String temp = "the";
if (the == temp) System.out.println("same string instance");
```

For applications where you are processing many strings in memory with many duplicates, this technique can make sense. An example application might be a program that is processing hundreds of megabytes of English text where each word is stored in a separate string and there will be many duplicate words in the input text.

WARNING JVMs can limit the total amount of interned string space. If you are interning a huge number of strings, you might encounter runtime errors.

A common problem with Java string memory use is caused by sharing characters between strings after performing common operations like substring. There is a trick to avoid sharing character memory (this can prevent garbage collection of the original string) and creating strings with no wasted space: use the `String(String)` constructor. For example:

```
String s1 = "The dog ran after the cat";
String s2 = s1.substring(4,7);
String s3 = new String(s1.substring(4,7));
```

Here, `s2` will share character memory with `s1`, while `s3` will not. As long as there are references to `s2`, the storage for `s1` cannot be garbage collected. As another advantage, `s3` will contain only data for three characters. Even though it may look odd and redundant, get used to using the `String(String)` constructor.

In general, using the `StringBuffer` class to manipulate strings will save the overhead of creating many new string objects. The Java compiler is usually smart enough to generate code that uses `StringBuffer` objects for simple string expressions. If you are incrementally adding text to an existing string, always use an instance of the `StringBuffer` class while adding text and then convert the string buffer to a final Java `String` object after the string data will no longer be modified.

TIP Avoid reading large amounts of text as Java strings. Because of character buffer sharing during substring operations, reading huge text files a line at a time into a Java string can waste memory. If you are reading hundreds of megabytes of text data, consider reading into `char[]` or `byte[]` arrays and extracting just the information that you will be using into Java strings.

Array Use

Because there is a 16-byte overhead for each array, you should take some care in declaring multidimensional arrays. Consider these two arrays:

```
int[][] ibuf1[1000][10]
int[][] ibuf2[10][1000]
```

The array `ibuf1` will take approximately 15840 more bytes to store than the array `ibuf2`. This is because multidimensional arrays in Java are really nested arrays, so there is a 16-byte overhead for each element in the first array dimension for two dimensional arrays.

At the cost of additional coding, you might consider allocating one-dimensional arrays and performing the indexing calculation yourself:

```
int[][] ibuf2[10][1000];
int[] ibuf3[10000];
// note:   ibuf3[i*1000 + j] == ibuf2[i][j];
```

Object Reuse

If your application creates and destroys many Java objects of a single type, try to prevent the large overhead of excessive object creation and destruction. As an example, if you are writing a graphics program with custom class for a `Line`, you can use a `Vector` to store instances of class `Line` that were created then no longer used. If you need a new instance of class `Line`, first check the `Vector` that you are using to store references to unused `Line` instances to see if any free instances are available.

NOTE This technique will actually increase memory use but it will often dramatically increase the runtime performance of your programs.

Custom Hash Table

The hash table classes supplied in the `java.util` package are highly optimized for both run–time performance and memory use. That said, for my own applications, I frequently use hash tables to maintain unique word use counts. By writing a custom hash table that supports only integer values and packs data in simple arrays, I can save over 50 percent of the memory that would be required to use a `java.util.Hashtable`. This memory savings comes with some costs:

- My custom hash table is approximately five times slower for `get()` method calls.
- My custom hash table is final—all entries have to be added and then the hash table is "finalized" and can accept no additional hash table entries.

For almost all applications, the standard Java class library hash tables and other maps (see Solution 19) are best because they are stable, easy to use, and efficient for most applications. However, it is important to be able to realize when standard libraries are not optimal for specific applications. For my applications (involving natural language processing—parsing English text and extracting semantic information), the memory use of huge hash tables is a problem. Reducing the size of hash tables that I use from over 200MB to less than 100MB is worth some programming effort and reduced runtime performance.

There are two classes in my custom hash table implementation:

StringIntHashtable This class functions as a regular hash table but saves little memory over a standard Java hash table. After it is populated with data, it contains a `toFinal()` method that creates a much more compact form of the hash table.

StringIntHashtableFinal A finalized version of a hash table that does not contain a `put()` method. Data is stored very compactly.

Both of these classes store key (string) and value (int) pairs in a set of bins. A hashing method converts a string into a bin index:

```
int hashFunction(String s)
Data in each hash bin is stored in sorted order. Because the final version of
the hash table uses arrays, we can use the standard static utility
Arrays.binarySearch(Object[], Object) to perform the binary search for a key
value:
public int get(String key) {
    int binIndex = hashFunction(key);
    // do a fast binary search:
    int index = Arrays.binarySearch(binKeys[binIndex], key);
    if (index == -1) return NO_VAL;
    return binValues[binIndex][index];
}
```

The time required to perform the binary search for data in any hash bin is responsible for the significantly slower performance over the standard Java hash tables—here we are using a hash function to quickly identify which bin the data is stored in (if it is in the hash table). This `searchIndex()` method is also implemented in the finalized class `StringIntHashtableFinal` but differs slightly because we use `ArrayList` objects for hash bin storage in the class

StringIntHashtable while we use a more compact String[] and int[] arrays to store bin data in the StringIntHashtableFinal class. The StringIntHashtable class contains an inner class HashEntry that is used to store a String key and int value data.

The code for the StringIntHashtable method put() is slightly complex because once it has calculated the hash bin index for the key string value, it must insert the new key/value pair in the correct location to maintain an alphabetically ordered key string list. This involves shifting data, so building large hash tables is slow:

```
public int put(String key, int value) {
    int binIndex = hashFunction(key);
    ArrayList al = entries[binIndex];
    // insert a new HashEntry into the array list in
    // sorted order:
    HashEntry he = new HashEntry(key, value);
    int size = al.size();
    int index = searchIndex(al, key);
    if (index != -1) return value; // already in hash table
    HashEntry h1;
    for (int i = 0; i < size; i++) {
        h1 = (HashEntry) al.get(i);
        if (h1.getKey().compareTo(key) == 0) return value;
        if (h1.getKey().compareTo(key) > 0) {
            // shift all values up in array list:
            al.add(null);
            for (int j = (size - 1); j >= i; j--) {
                al.set(j+1, al.get(j));
            }
            al.set(i, he);
            return value;
        }
    }
    // not inserted: add to end:
    al.add(he);
    return value;
}
```

For my application, the runtime costs for building huge hash tables is not a problem because I serialize the hash tables after creation and then reuse the serialized version.

The get() method is fairly simple: you must calculate the hash bin index for an input key string value and then do a binary search for the value using the method searchIndex() that you have already seen:

```
public int get(String key) {
    int binIndex = hashFunction(key);
    ArrayList al = entries[binIndex];
```

```
        // do a fast binary search:
        int index = searchIndex(al, key);
        if (index == -1)  return NO_VAL;
        HashEntry he = (HashEntry)al.get(index);
        return he.getValue();
    }
```

The simple class `StringIntHashtableFinal` contains package-visible data that the `StringIntHashtable` class can modify when creating a new instance of class `StringIntHashtableFinal`:

```
String[][] binKeys;
int[][] binValues;
int numBins;
```

You will now see how the class `StringIntHashtable` constructs a new instance of the class `StringIntHashtableFinal`:

```
public StringIntHashtableFinal toFinal() {
    StringIntHashtableFinal ret = new StringIntHashtableFinal();
    ret.binKeys = new String[numBins][];
    ret.binValues = new int[numBins][];
    ret.numBins = numBins;
    for (int i=0; i<numBins; i++) {
        ArrayList al = entries[i];
        int size = al.size();
        ret.binKeys[i] = new String[size];
        ret.binValues[i] = new int[size];
        for (int j=0; j<size; j++) {
            HashEntry he = (HashEntry)al.get(j);
            ret.binKeys[i][j] = he.getKey();
            ret.binValues[i][j] = he.getValue();
        }
    }
    return ret;
}
```

The constructor for the `StringIntHashtableFinal` class is not public, but it does have package visibility. The method `toFinal()` effectively copies `HashEntry` objects to `String[]` and `int[]` arrays. Note that I could not use the techniques in Solution 17 here because the `Arraylist` objects for each hash bin contain `HashEntry` objects that must be separated into key and value data.

NOTE The `StringIntHashtableFinal` class is serializable. For my applications, I construct instances of this class and serialize each one to a file. Applications that use these huge hash tables deserialize the data during program initialization.

SOLUTION 19

Implementing Sorted Key Hash Tables

PROBLEM You need to maintain a hash table of words used in a document. You would like the keys to be stored in alphabetical order.

SOLUTION You will use one of the new Java container classes, a `TreeMap`.

Several years ago, I needed to implement a custom Java hash table to store keys in alphabetical order; this custom class was several hundred lines of code. That effort is no longer required! The new Java collection classes solve the problem of sorting key maps. A map is a generalization of a hash table. In order to use a `TreeMap`, you start by defining a comparator class that implements the `Comparator` interface:

```
public int compare(Object o1, Object o2)
public boolean equals(Object o2)
```

I want to sort Java strings in ascending order, so this comparator class will serve (it inherits the `Object.equals()` method):

```
public class AlphaSortCompare implements Comparator {
    public int compare(Object o1, Object o2) {
        String s1 = (String)o1;
        String s2 = (String)o2;
        return s1.compareTo(s2);
    }
}
```

Here is an example of constructing a `TreeMap` with this custom comparator class and using it:

```
Map m = new TreeMap(new AlphaSortCompare());
m.put("the", new Integer(3));
m.put("dog", new Integer(1));
m.put("a", new Integer(4));
Set keySet = m.keySet();
Iterator iter = keySet.iterator();
while (iter.hasNext()) {
     Object obj = iter.next();
     System.out.println("next key: " + obj);
}
```

The output would be as follows:

```
next key: a
next key: dog
next key: the
```

This example used a nonsynchronized `TreeMap`. Using nonsynchronized collection classes saves significant runtime overhead in applications where multiple threads are not sharing data structures. In a multithreaded application, you should consider creating a synchronized `TreeMap`:

```
Map m = Collections.synchronizedMap(
            new TreeMap(new AlphaSortCompare()));
```

NOTE Java version 1.2 introduced the new collections framework. Joshua Bloch has written a good online tutorial for the new framework at `java.sun.com/docs/books/tutorial/collections/` that I recommend you read if you are not familiar with the new collection classes.

Searching and Sorting

SOLUTION 20

Using Depth First Search

PROBLEM You want to use a simple, low-memory-use search algorithm.

SOLUTION You will use depth first search.

The first three solutions in this chapter all cover search algorithms. I ordered Solutions 20, 21, and 22 in order of depth first, iterative deepening, and breadth first. The algorithm for Solutions 20 and 21 is similar because the class for Solution 21 is a subclass of the class for Solution 20.

In general, searching involves defining a search space, defining operators to move in this search space, and writing algorithms to move from a starting location in the search space to a goal location. In order to concentrate on the differences between search algorithms, I chose an easily specified but difficult to solve (in CPU time and memory requirements) problem: "nine-square" puzzles that have eight sliding tiles with one blank square. These puzzles are often also called "eight puzzles." The eight sliding tiles are labeled 1 though 8 as shown in the following illustration, which shows the starting (left) and goal (right) positions.

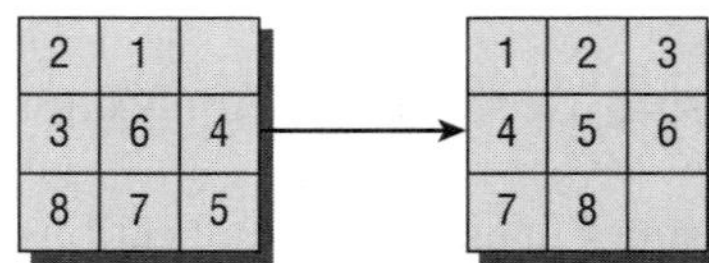

NOTE If you skip this solution and go straight to the more useful Solutions 21 and 22 material, at least read the following section about search space, as this material is required to understand Solutions 21 and 22 but is not repeated there. If you are interested in iterative deepening depth first search (Solution 21) then you should read this solution in its entirety.

The algorithm for depth first search is simple and consists of the following steps:

1. If the maximum search depth has not been reached, then from the current position in the search space, calculate all possible moves.
2. Select one of the possible moves and if this move does not equal the target goal state, go to step 1.
3. If the maximum search depth has been reached, back up one move, select the next possible move, and go to step 1.

The effect of this algorithm is to move in one long path in the search space until the maximum depth is reached, and then back up one move. Using this algorithm, preliminary search takes place "far away" from the starting location. This is in strong contrast to breadth-first search algorithms, which you will see in Solution 22.

Search Space for Nine-Square Puzzles

I will represent the nine-square boards seen in the previous illustration with the class `NineSquares`. This class provides the following utility methods:

NineSquares(String state) Converts a string in the form "1234 5678" to an internal representation.

String toString() Converts the internal representation to a string such as "38176 542".

boolean equals(NineSquares n) Checks to see if this `NineSquare` object is equal to another `NineSquare` object (this will be used to check to see if the goal state has been reached).

Vector possibleMoves() Returns a vector of possible square moves for a `NineSquare` object that will have one blank square. The position of the one blank square specifies which square indices could move into the blank area. A possible move is represented by an integer square index of the square to move into the empty board position.

In specifying search problems, in addition to a search space (or state) representation, you need operators that will generate possible moves from any point in the search space; here the method `possibleMoves()` implements the operator for calculating possible moves. In this context, a point in the search space is a given an instance of the class `NineSquares` with an internal position of the eight sliding squares. The possible move operator is implemented in the `possibleMoves()` method as a switch statement with a case statement for each of the nine possible locations of the blank square. The position of the blank square determines the indices of squares that can slide into the blank area.

NOTE I had a design decision to make when writing the search examples for this chapter: I would have liked to make the class `NineSquare` an abstract class (perhaps called `AbstractSearchSpace`) whose subclasses could represent any search space. However, I would then have needed an abstraction for specifying making moves. Because it is very easy to write search programs (with few lines of code), I decided that it was more important to make the search examples as simple as possible to illustrate the technique for implementing search. This simplicity comes at the cost of some nongenerality of the search examples.

Simplest Depth First Search

While I will start with a very simple search algorithm to cover the basic operations of graph search, in general, depth first search is not recommended because:

- It almost always fails to find optimum solutions. Depth first searches typically search in the wrong "direction" of the search space, search deeply, and eventually change directions and find a poor solution that contains far too many steps to reach the goal state.
- Depth first searches frequently take much longer to find solutions than more powerful techniques.

Depth first searches have two advantages:

- They are very simple to implement and serve as a good introduction to solving search problems.
- They use a relatively small amount of memory. You will see in Solution 22 that breadth first searches often require a lot of storage.

The example class `DepthFirst` uses a maximum search depth. When the search procedure gets to the maximum search depth without reaching the goal state, I back up and try other paths through the search space (or state space). The method `solve()` is responsible for move generation and depth first search through the search space (notice that this method calls itself recursively):

```
public void solve(int depth, int maxDepth,
                  NineSquares current, NineSquares goal) {
    if (depth > maxDepth) return;
    String s2 = current.toString();
    if (current.equals(goal)) {
        System.out.println("Found a solution at depth " +
                           depth + ":");
        for (int i = 0; i < depth; i++) {
            System.out.print("  " + moveList[i]);
        }
        System.out.println("

                           countExpanded);
        System.exit(0);
    }
    Vector possibleMoves = current.possibleMoves();
    for (int i = 0, size = possibleMoves.size(); i < size; i++) {
        int move =
            ((Integer) possibleMoves.elementAt(i)).intValue();
        NineSquares newBoard=NineSquares.makeMove(current,move);
        moveList[depth] = move;
        countExpanded++;
        solve(depth + 1, maxDepth, newBoard, goal);
    }
}
```

The first thing you do in this method is to test to see if you have searched deeper than your maximum search depth—if you have, you simply return from this method. The second thing you need to do is to see if the current position is equal to the goal position—if so, you print out the path to the current position and stop the program. If the current position is not equal to the goal position, then you call the class `NineSquares` method `getPossibleMoves()` to get the possible square movements from the current position. For each of these possible moves, you create a new instance of class `NineSquares` and recursively call the method `solve()` with this new "current" position and add one to the value of the current search depth.

To set up a problem, you create a starting position as an instance of the class `NineSquares` and a goal position as another instance of the class `NineSquares`:

```
NineSquares start = new NineSquares("6173 4582");
NineSquares goal = new NineSquares("1238 4765");
DepthFirst searcher = new DepthFirst();
searcher.solve(start, goal);
```

There are two methods named `solve()`, but they have different method signatures. You then call one of the `solve()` methods to start the search (this method calls the other `solve()` method that we have already looked at):

```
public void solve(NineSquares start, NineSquares goal) {
    solve(0, 20, start, goal);
}
```

As is, this depth first search program is not very useful because it is inefficient. There are a few simple things that you can do to improve it:

Keep a list of already "visited" points in the search space When you generate possible moves, discard any new position that has already been "visited" or searched. The class `DepthFirstNoDuplicates` is identical to the `DepthFirst` class except for the trivial changes required to avoid visiting a point in the search space more than one time. It is worth taking the time to look at the source code to the class `DepthFirstNoDuplicates` because the search programs in Solutions 21 and 22 will have similar code. In the class `DepthFirstNoDuplicates`, you use a hash table to remember board positions (as represented by a string produced by the method `toString()` in the class `NineSquares`). Remembering already visited board positions greatly reduces the running time for any search algorithm if the test for being visited is fast. In this case, this test is a simple hash table lookup.

Perform an "iterative deepening" depth first search. This is Solution 21. Iterative deepening search is like depth first search except you start by searching only to a depth of one, then to a depth of two, and so on, until either a solution is found or the maximum search depth is reached (in which case the search ends in failure).

SOLUTION 21

Making Searches More Space Efficient: Iterative Deepening Search

PROBLEM You want your search programs to run faster than simple depth first search and to find better solutions, but you also want smaller data storage requirements than breadth first algorithms has.

SOLUTION You will use iterative deepening depth first search for CPU efficiency and data storage efficiency and to find good solutions to search problems.

You saw in Solution 20 that depth first search has the advantage of small memory requirements but poor runtime performance and the tendency to find bad solutions that contain many more search steps than optimal solutions. These problems will be solved in Solution 22 at the cost of extra required memory. In this solution, you will use a powerful technique that uses little memory, is reasonably fast, and finds good solutions: iterative deepening search.

The idea behind iterative deepening search is simple: the flaw in depth first search is that it usually finds a solution by searching wildly in the wrong direction—to make it eventually turn around and find a solution takes many more steps than a breadth first search requires. The solution used in iterative deepening search is to perform a depth first search limited to a maximum depth of 1, 2, 3, … N until a solution is found. If a good solution exists for a number of steps equal to N, then an iterative deepening search will find either this solution, or another solution that only takes N steps.

It might seem like you are doing a lot of extra work repeating search operations (that is, setting a maximum search depth to 1, failing to find a solution, setting the maximum search depth to 2, repeating the work done with the maximum depth set to 1, and so on), but in practice this is not such a bad thing to do. The reason is simple: the number of possible moves that are explored as a function of search depth is exponential as a function of search depth. For the eight square puzzles, there are either 2, 3, or 4 possible moves from any position—this is determined by the index of the blank square. Setting the maximum search depth to 1 means that you must search a maximum 4 raised to the first power, or 4 possible positions. For a maximum search depth of 2, you search a maximum of 4 raised to the second power, or 16 possible positions. For a search depth of 3, you search a maximum or 4 to the third power or 64 positions. So, you can see that repeating search operations is not such a bad thing if you can minimize the maximum search depth that you must use to find a solution to a given problem.

I hope you read Solution 20 on depth first search, because the following discussion assumes that you understand the method `solve()` that is identical in both `DepthFirstNoDuplicates.java` and the example for this solution, `IterativeDeepening.java`. The class `IterativeDeepening` is a subclass of the class `DepthFirstNoDuplicates` and uses the base class method `solve()`. The method signature for method `solve()` is

```
void solve(int depth, int maxDepth, NineSquares start,
           NineSquares goal)
```

The only real difference between the example code for this solution and for that for Solution 20 is how the method `solve()` is called. In Solution 20, you called method `solve()` specifying the current search depth as zero and the maximum search depth as 20:

```
solve(0, 20, start, goal);
```

In this solution, you call method `solve()` in a loop:

```
for (int maxDepth = 0; maxDepth < 20; maxDepth++) {
    avoidDuplicates = new Hashtable();
    solve(0, maxDepth, start, goal);
}
```

Here you set the hash table `avoidDuplicates` to a new empty hash table each time you increase the maximum search depth. You can experiment with both the classes `DepthFirstNoDuplicates` and `IterativeDeepening` with different initial and goal board positions to see how much more efficient iterative deepening search is.

SOLUTION 22

Making Searches More CPU Efficient: A* Search

PROBLEM You want your search programs to run faster.

SOLUTION You will look at breadth first search algorithms that run much faster than depth first search algorithms but use much more temporary data storage.

You saw in Solution 20 that while depth first search has the advantage of using relatively little memory for search operations, usually they find poor search solutions and have poor runtime performance. A solution to these limitations of depth first search is to perform one of the varieties of breadth first search.

The algorithm for breadth first search uses a queue (implemented with the collection class `LinkedList`) of possible moves to make in the search space. As new possible moves are calculated, they are added to the back of the search queue. To explore new moves in the search space, a possible move is removed from the front of the search queue. Extra memory is required to hold the possible move search queue, and for some search problems the amount of memory for the queue can get very large. A breadth first search "fans out" from the starting position: think of a wave slowly moving away from the starting location. When the wave intersects the goal position in the search space, the search process is complete (although you have to do some additional work to get the search path through the search space).

The class `BreadthFirst` in package `S22` implements three varieties of breadth first search:

Simple Newly calculated possible moves are added as they are calculated to the end of the possible move queue.

A* For a given position in search space, newly calculated possible moves are sorted based on a calculated Euclidean distance to the goal state (this calculation is not required to be accurate, but it should tend to identify moves in the "best" direction of search space). Moves are added to the back of the move queue in sorted order, "best" moves that bring you closer to the goal location are added first to the queue.

Manhattan For a given position in search space, newly calculated possible moves are sorted based on a calculation of the Manhattan distance to the goal state. The Manhattan distance assumes movement only along dimensional axis of the search space.

Three constant values are specified at the top of the file `BreadthFirst.java` to specify these three varieties of breadth first search:

```
static final public int BREADTH_FIRST = 1;
static final public int A_STAR_MANHATTAN = 2;
static final public int A_STAR_COUNT = 3;
```

Setting up an eight square puzzle is similar to using the depth first search class:

```
BreadthFirst p = new BreadthFirst();
boolean success =
    p.solve(new NineSquares("21 364875"),
            new NineSquares("12345678 "),
            A_STAR_MANHATTAN);
System.out.println("Success of search: " + success);
```

Here I specified that the Manhattan version of the A* search be used. As seen in the last code snippet, the method `solve()` takes three arguments: starting and goal board positions and an integer constant specifying the variety of breadth first search to use. The method signature for the method `solve()` is

```
public boolean solve(NineSquares start, NineSquares goal,
                     int strategy)
```

Method `solve()` does not use recursion. We will look at the method `solve()` in some detail later, but first we will look at the utility classes and methods that method `solve()` uses. An instance of the class `LinkedList` is used to implement the queue used to store possible moves; method `solve()` uses a loop that takes a possible move off of the front of the queue, tests to see if it is the goal state and if the goal has not been reached, then generates more possible moves from the new state that are added to the back of the queue. The objects stored in the move queue are instances of the nonpublic class `State`. The nonpublic class `State` defines the following public instance data:

```
public NineSquares currentPosition = null;
public Vector moveList = null;
public Vector moveHistory = new Vector();
```

An instance of class `State` maintains a complete list of moves that were used to reach this state from the starting state. This information will be used to print a solution when the goal state is reached. You can read the code of the inner utility class `State` in the file `BreadthFirst.java`.

NOTE You use the collection class `LinkedList` to implement a queue by using the method `addLast()` to add any object to the end of the queue and the method `removeFirst()` to pull an object off of the front of the queue.

The top-level method `solve()` uses several utility methods to find a path to the goal node:

void printMoveHistory(State s) Prints the move history from an instance of the `State` class after the goal state has been reached.

State expand(int strategy, NineSquares board, Vector possibleMoves, Vector oldMoveHistory) Calculates a new instance of the `State` class using a specified breadth first search strategy, a current board position, a list of possible moves from the current board position, and the old move history that was used to reach the current board position.

int count(NineSquares b1, NineSquares b2) In an A* search, calculates the Euclidean distance between two board positions. The distance is simply a count of how many squares are already in their proper positions.

int manhattan(NineSquares b1, NineSquares b2) In an A* search with Manhattan distance, calculates the Manhattan distance between two board positions. The distance is a fairly complex calculation of the number of squares each board piece needs to be moved to transform one board position into another board position.

These utility methods are fairly straightforward, and I will leave it to you to read the code in the file `DepthFirst.java`. We will now look at the method `solve()` in detail. You start by allocating a new (empty) instance of the nonpublic class Queue and adding the starting board position to the queue:

```
public boolean solve(NineSquares start, NineSquares goal,
                     int strategy) {
    currentGoal = goal;  // for use in method expand
    LinkedList queue = new LinkedList();
    int countDuplicates = 0;
    int countExpanded = 0;
    // add initial nodes:
    queue.addLast(expand(strategy, start, start.possibleMoves(),
                     new Vector()));
```

You then enter a while loop that exits only if the goal position is reached or the queue every contains no more possible moves (as represented by instances of the class State):

```
while (true) {
    if (queue.isEmpty()) break;  // failure to find a solution
    State nextState = (State) queue.remove();
    // breadth first, so first check to see if goal is reached:
    if (nextState.currentPosition.equals(goal)) {
        System.out.println("Goal met for board: " +
                           nextState.currentPosition);
        System.out.println("Number of duplicate board " +
                           "positions  avoided = " +
                           countDuplicates);
        System.out.println("Number of expanded nodes " +
                           "(not including duplicates)="
                           + countExpanded);
        printMoveHistory(nextState);
        return true;
    }
```

So far, the logic is simple: if the move queue is empty, then break out of the while loop (failing to find the goal position). If the move queue is not empty, remove the instance of class State at the front of the queue and check to see if it matches the goal position. If the next state is not the goal state, then you should generate possible moves and add them to the back of the possible move queue:

```
for (int i=0, size=nextState.moveList.size(); i<size; i++) {
    int move =
((Integer)nextState.moveList.elementAt(i)).intValue();
    NineSquares b =
       NineSquares.makeMove(nextState.currentPosition, move);
    String s2 = b.toString();
    if (avoidDuplicates.get(s2) != null) {
        countDuplicates++;
```

```
            continue; // already looked at this position, so skip it
        }
        countExpanded++;
        avoidDuplicates.put(s2, new Boolean(true));
        Vector possibleMoves = b.possibleMoves();
        Vector v2 = new Vector(nextState.moveHistory);
        v2.add(new Integer(move));
        State state = expand(strategy, b, possibleMoves, v2);
        queue.addLast(state);
    }  // end of for loop
```

The rest of method `solve()` is the end of the `while` loop and a return value of false for failing to find a path to the goal position:

```
        } // end of while loop
        return false;
    }
```

As with the depth first search, keeping track of already visited board positions and avoiding revisiting these positions makes the search much faster. I avoided searching duplicate board positions by storing the string representation of visited board in the hash table `avoidDuplicates`.

NOTE As with the depth first search, most of the work in writing a search program is setting up a representation for the search space and defining operators to calculate possible moves from any location in this search space. For all search examples in this chapter, this domain-specific code is isolated in the class `NineSquares`.

SOLUTION 23

Using Merge Sort in Applications

PROBLEM You need to sort large amount of data quickly.

SOLUTION You will use the recursive merge sort.

We will look closely at two efficient recursive sort algorithms in this solution and in Solution 24 (where we look at the quicksort algorithm). I usually use quicksort in my own applications rather than merge sort. However, merge sort can have runtime advantages (that is, better worst case performance), and I believe that the recursive algorithm for merge sort is simpler to understand than the recursive algorithm for quicksort. I recommend that you take the time to work through the algorithms used for both merge sort and quicksort. Both sort algorithms can be implemented in few lines of code, but really understanding the algorithms is not easy and reading the code will not easily teach you how these algorithms really work, so I will go into more detail than usual. There are advantages to both quicksort and merge sort. The advantages of quicksort are

- In-place sorting (merge sort uses auxiliary storage)
- Usual runtime on the order or N * log(N) with small constant multiplier

The advantage of merge sort is

- Worst case runtime is on the order of N * log(N) (note that quicksort worst case runtime is N * N)

NOTE You will sort arrays of floating-point numbers in both the merge sort and quicksort examples. These examples can be easily modified to use other Java data types. The purpose of the sort example programs is to teach you how the algorithms work.

The merge sort algorithm is recursive but still fairly easy to understand:

- Divide a sequence of data in two
- Recursively call merge sort on both halves of the original data to sort the data
- Combine the sorted data into longer sorted sequences

The following illustration shows the merge sort algorithm operating on a four number sequence: 7, 3, 2, and 1. The one-element sequences [7] and [3] are merged into the two-element sequence [3, 7], and the one-element sequences [2] and [1] are merged into the two-element sequence [1, 2]. Then the two-element sequences [3, 7] and [1, 2] are merged into the final four-element sequence [1, 2, 3, 7], as shown in the following illustration.

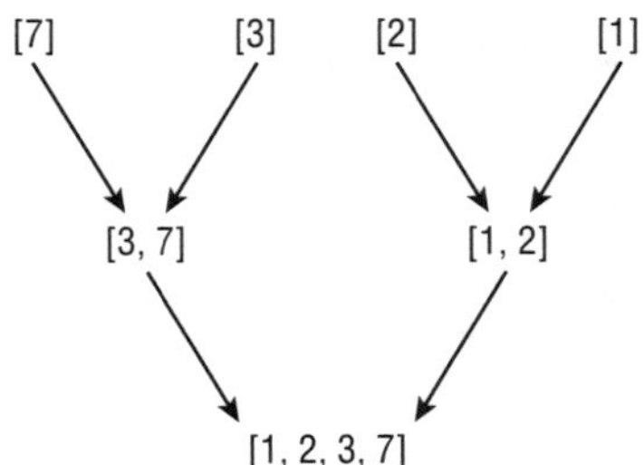

This illustration shows the steps taken at the bottom of the recursion: the merging process is performed as the recursive calls return. In order to make it more understandable, we will look at the calling sequence for the methods to split the sequence into two pieces (method doMergeSort()) and to merge subsequences together (method doMerge()) for sorting the sequence [7, 3, 2, 1] seen in the illustration:

```
doMergeSort(0, 3)
doMergeSort(0, 1)
doMergeSort(0, 0)
doMergeSort(1, 1)
  doMerge(0, 0, 1) [ 7.0 3.0 ] --> [ 3.0 7.0 ]
doMergeSort(2, 3)
doMergeSort(2, 2)
doMergeSort(3, 3)
  doMerge(2, 2, 3) [ 2.0 1.0 ] --> [ 1.0 2.0 ]
  doMerge(0, 1, 3) [ 3.0 7.0 1.0 2.0 ] --> [ 1.0 2.0 3.0 7.0 ]
```

In this output, the arguments to the method doMergeSort() are the starting index and the ending index in the array to be sorted. The arguments for the method doMerge() are the starting index, the middle index, and the ending index that specify two subsequences to be merged together. The output after doMerge() shows the array slice before and after merging.

The constructor for class MergeSort takes an array of floating point numbers to sort, creates a working storage array of the same size named results, and calls the recursive doMergeSort() method:

```
public MergeSort(float[] array) {
    results = new float[array.length];
    this.array = array;
    doMergeSort(0, array.length - 1);
}
private float[] results;
private float[] array;
```

The recursive method doMergeSort() takes a starting and ending index in the original data array, calls itself recursively on the two halves of this array, and then calls the utility method doMerge() to merge the results into the array results:

```
private void doMergeSort(float[] arr, int start, int end) {
    if (start < end) {
        int mid = (start + end) / 2;
        doMergeSort(arr, start, mid);
        doMergeSort(arr, mid + 1, end);
        doMerge(arr, start, mid, end);
    }
}
```

Although the result of the sort is also left in the original data array, the following public method is used to get the sorted results from the newly allocated working storage:

```
public float[] getResults() {
    return  results;
}
```

All of the real work in the merge sort algorithm is performed in the method `doMerge()` that is called with a starting index into the data to be sorted, the middle index for the data to be sorted, and the ending index of the data to be sorted:

```
private void doMerge(int start, int mid, int end) {
    int i1 = start;
    int j1 = mid;
    int i2 = mid+1;
    int j2 = end;
    int i = start;
    while (i1 <= j1 && i2 <= j2) {
        if (array[i1] < array[i2]) {
            results[i] = array[i1];
            i1++;
        }else {
            results[i] = array[i2];
            i2++;
        }
        i++;
    }
    while (i1 <= j1) {
        results[i] = array[i1];
        i++;
        i1++;
    }
    while (i2 <= j2) {
        results[i] = array[i2];
        i++;
        i2++;
    }
    for (int k=start; k<=end; k++)  array[k] = results[k];
}
```

The code in the method `doMerge()` might look a little complex, but keep in mind what the responsibility of this method is: given a "slice" of the data array between starting and ending indices, merge the two halves of this data into the results array. The variables `i1` and `i2` are used as the starting indices for the two halves of the input array slice. The variables `j1` and `j2` are the ending indices for the two halves of the input array slice. The first `while` loop merges most of the data, and the second two `while` loops copy any remaining data if the two halves of the input slice are not the same size.

NOTE You might find it useful to uncomment the print statements in the `MergeSort` example program and re-run the example. This will help you understand how the bottom-up recursive merge sort algorithm works. You can do this by changing the value of the variable `DEBUG` at the top of the class definition.

SOLUTION 24

Using Quicksort in Applications

PROBLEM The merge sort algorithm is efficient, but you want to avoid allocating extra working memory for the sort operation.

SOLUTION You will use the quicksort algorithm that does not use extra memory for the sort operation.

Although the theoretical worst case performance of quicksort is on the order of N * N (where N is the number of elements being sorted), in practice, the runtime performance of quicksort is N * log(N) with a small constant multiplier. Quicksort has the further advantage of sorting in place with no extra storage required.

Quicksort Algorithm

There are two parts to the quicksort algorithm: a recursive driver and a utility to partition an arbitrary array into two parts where all elements of the lower part are less than all elements of the upper part. Here, "lower" and "upper" refer to relative index values in the array. The code for the recursive driver is trivial, so we will first look into detail at the partition operation. Because quicksort works with data in place, you will implement a `QuickSort` class that maintains the data to be sorted in instance data so the method `partition()`needs to be passed only starting and ending indices of this instance data. The array that holds the data being sorted is `result`. The method signature is

```
private int partition(int firstIndex, int lastIndex) {
```

I will refer to the elements of the array `results` between `firstIndex` and `lastIndex` as an array "slice." I will choose one data element in the array `result` between the index values `firstIndex` to `lastIndex` inclusive and call this the pivot point or pivot element. You can choose this pivot element to be the first value in the array slice:

```
float partitionElement = result[firstIndex];
```

The method `partition()` will return the final index of the pivot element, so allocate a local variable for this position in the array:

```
int partitionElementFinalIndex = firstIndex;
```

While you are swapping elements on either side of the pivot element, use the following two index values:

```
int swapLowIndex = firstIndex;
int swapHighIndex = lastIndex;
```

The method `partition()` contains a `do` loop that is used to process all elements in the array slice. The first thing that you do inside this loop is to find an element of the array slice above the pivot element that is less than the value of the pivot element:

```
while (swapHighIndex > swapLowIndex &&
       result[swapHighIndex] >= partitionElement)
  swapHighIndex--;
```

If you find a high index element to swap with the pivot element, then you do the following:

```
result[swapLowIndex] = result[swapHighIndex];
while (swapHighIndex > swapLowIndex &&
       result[swapLowIndex] <= partitionElement)
    swapLowIndex++;
partitionElementFinalIndex = swapLowIndex;
if (swapHighIndex != swapLowIndex)
    result[swapHighIndex] = result[swapLowIndex];
```

This is not much code, and if you keep in mind what the responsibilities of the method `partition()` are, it should now be fairly easy to read and understand the code for this method in the file `QuickSort.java`. The top-level recursive driver method `doQuickSort()` is simple:

```
private void doQuickSort(int first, int last) {
    if (first < last) {
        int partitionElementIndex = partition(first, last);
        doQuickSort(first, partitionElementIndex - 1);
        doQuickSort(partitionElementIndex + 1, last);
    }
}
```

The method `doQuickSort()` is also passed first and last indices that define an array slice. If the first index is less than the last index, then you call partition with the entire array slice, then recursively call `doQuickSort` with the sub array slice up to, but not including, the pivot element and recursively call `doQuickSort` with the sub array slice after the pivot element index (labeled *`pi`* in the printout below).

The following program output shows the call sequence for methods `doQuickSort()` and `partition()` when sorting the sequence [7, 3, 2, 1]:

```
doQuickSort(0, 3)
  partition(0, 3) [7.0 3.0 2.0 1.0] --> [1.0 3.0 2.0 7.0] pi=3
doQuickSort(0, 2)
  partition(0, 2) [1.0 3.0 2.0] --> [1.0 3.0 2.0] pi=0
doQuickSort(0, -1)
doQuickSort(1, 2)
  partition(1, 2) [3.0 2.0] --> [2.0 3.0] pi=2
doQuickSort(1, 1)
doQuickSort(3, 2)
doQuickSort(4, 3)
```

The output after `partition` is the array slice specified by the input arguments when entering and leaving the method `partition()`. The value `pi` is the pivot element index retuned by the method `partition()`.

The class constructor takes an input array and performs the sort:

```
QuickSort(float[] data) {
    // the original data will be over written:
    this.results = data;
    doQuickSort(0, data.length - 1);
}
private float[] results;
```

Although the original array passed into the class constructor is modified so you can use the original array for the sorted results, you also define a method to get a reference to the sorted results array:

```
public float[] getResults() {
    return results;
}
```

Note that the array `results` is a reference to the same array passed to the class constructor.

NOTE You might find it useful to uncomment the print statements in the QuickSort example program and re-run the example. This will help you understand how the top-down recursive quicksort algorithm works. You can do this by changing the value of the variable `DEBUG` at the top of the class definition.

Threads

SOLUTION 25

Using Work Threads for Background Processing

PROBLEM You want to perform several computational tasks in a single Java program.

SOLUTION You will look at two techniques for writing multithreaded Java applications.

One of the advantages of the Java language is that it provides direct support for multiple thread programming. The Java Virtual Machine (JVM) provides runtime support for multiple threads running inside a single Java application. There are two basic techniques for writing multithreaded applications in Java and we will look at both of them:

- Writing a subclass of class `Thread` and overriding the public method `run`
- Implementing a `Runnable` interface, which requires implementing a public method `run`

We will look at thread efficiency considerations in Solution 26 and thread management issues in Solution 27. Later in this solution, we will also look at an example of using a timer thread that runs a task at a specified time interval.

How do you decide which of the two thread-writing techniques to use? In general, if your class needs to be derived from another class (not the `Thread` class), then derive from the other class and implement the `Runnable` interface. If an instance of a class needs to manage more than one thread, then implement an inner class that extends the class `Thread` and create as many instances of this inner class as required. (See Solution 27 for information on managing multiple threads).

Writing a Subclass of Thread

In this section, you will write a subclass of the Java `Thread` class. You can customize subclasses of `Thread` by overriding the public `run` method. The `run` method is executed in the new thread. The example class `CountThread` in package `S25` is so short that I will list it here and then discuss the code:

```
public class CountThread extends Thread {
    private int count = 5; // number of times to print message
    public void run() {
        while (true) {
            if (count-- > 0) {
                System.out.println("thread " + this +
                                   " count=" + count);
                try {
```

```
                    Thread.sleep(1000L);
                } catch (Exception e) {
                } // sleep 1 second
            } else {
                break; // out of the 'while' loop
            }
        }
    }
    public static void main(String[] args) throws Exception {
        new CountThread().start();
        Thread.sleep(2000); // sleep 2 seconds
        new CountThread().start();
    }
}
```

NOTE If you want control over stopping a thread, you can add a *stop()* method to your thread class that sets a flag that is tested in the *run()* method. Later, you will also see how to stop threads using the thread APIs.

There are two things to learn from this example: the first is how to write a custom run method, and the second is how to create an instance of the Thread class and start the thread executing. Typically, work threads in applications "run forever" until the application is terminated. The standard pattern for implementing a custom public run() method is to first perform any thread-specific initialization and then to enter a while loop. Initialization can also be done in the class constructor. In this example, the public run() method simply loops five times, printing a message each time through the loop. When the instance variable count's value is decremented to zero, then the break statement exits the while loop. When a thread's public run() method returns, the thread stops execution. This public run() method sleeps for one second after printing each message so the thread will run for approximately five seconds.

NOTE There is a deprecated method stop() in the Thread class for stopping a thread's execution. Because this method is deprecated, you should not use it. If you need to stop a thread, add appropriate logic to your run() method to return if specific events occur that would indicate that the thread should stop. One possibility is adding a method exit() to your thread subclass that sets an instance variable that is checked in the run() method.

The public static main() method creates two instances of the class CountThread and starts each thread. In this example, a thread is created and started in one line of code:

```
new CountThread().start();
```

This single line of code has the same functionality as the following two lines:

```
CountThread ct = new CountThread();
ct.start();
```

There is a two-second delay between creating and starting the first thread and the second thread. This makes the program debug output more interesting; the following 10 lines are the output from this example program:

```
thread Thread[Thread-1,5,main] count=4
thread Thread[Thread-1,5,main] count=3
thread Thread[Thread-2,5,main] count=4
thread Thread[Thread-1,5,main] count=2
thread Thread[Thread-2,5,main] count=3
thread Thread[Thread-1,5,main] count=1
thread Thread[Thread-2,5,main] count=2
thread Thread[Thread-1,5,main] count=0
thread Thread[Thread-2,5,main] count=1
thread Thread[Thread-2,5,main] count=0
```

The method `toString()` in the class `Thread` prints out the thread name, the number of threads active in the current thread group (5 in this case, including the 2 that I started in this example), and the name of the current thread group. Here, the names of the two threads are `Thread-1` and `Thread-2`, and the name of the thread group is `main`.

NOTE I will cover thread groups in some detail in Solution 27.

Implementing a Runnable Interface

In the last section, you saw how to derive a subclass from the class `Thread` and give the thread subclass specific behavior by overriding the public `run()` method. The approach used in this section is very similar: I will write a class `CountRunnable` that implements the `Runnable` interface and then create a instance of the class `Thread` by passing a new instance of the class `CountRunnable` to the class `Thread` constructor. In the demo class `CountRunnable` (in package `S25`), you see an example of implementing the `Runnable` interface by implementing a public method `run()`:

```
public class CountRunnable implements Runnable {
    public void run() {
        for (int i=0; i<5; i++) {
            System.out.println("thread " + this + "  i = " + i);
            try { Thread.sleep(200L); } catch (Exception e) { }
        }
    }
    public static void main(String[] args) {
        new Thread(new CountRunnable()).start();
        for (int k=0; k<5; k++) {
            System.out.println("thread main k="+k);
            try { Thread.sleep(100L); } catch (Exception e) { }
        }
    }
}
```

The public run() method is functionally similar to the public run() method that we implemented in the last section (although I use a for loop here instead of a while loop). The public run() method loops five times, printing a message and then sleeping for 0.2 seconds each time through the loop.

The public static method main() creates a new instance of the class Thread and passes a reference to a new instance of the class CountRunnable to the Thread class constructor. Notice that as soon as a new instance of the class Thread is created, you immediately call its method start to start the thread. After the thread is created and started, the public static method run() also enters a loop where a message is printed, and the main thread sleeps for 0.1 seconds each time through the loop. Here is the output from running this demo program:

```
thread S25.CountRunnable@ca318a  i = 0
thread main k=0
thread main k=1
thread S25.CountRunnable@ca318a  i = 1
thread main k=2
thread main k=3
thread S25.CountRunnable@ca318a  i = 2
thread main k=4
thread S25.CountRunnable@ca318a  i = 3
thread S25.CountRunnable@ca318a  i = 4
```

Notice that the time delay in the thread is 0.2 seconds, while the time delay in the method main() is 0.1 seconds, so on average you see two printouts from the method main for every printout from the thread. Thread scheduling is not exact, and there is no guarantee of real-time performance, especially when the JVM needs to perform garbage collection.

NOTE If you do need to use Java in a "real time" application, it is important to initialize all of the objects required for program execution and then avoid creating or destroying any new objects while real-time performance is required. Avoiding garbage collection will minimize the chance that the threads in your Java application will not frequently get run by the thread scheduler in the JVM.

Using a Timer Thread

The timer classes were added to the standard Java class libraries with the introduction of the JDK 1.3. You will use two new classes in the java.util package:

TimerTask You will write subclasses of this abstract class overriding the public abstract method run() to perform any work to be done at specific time intervals.

Timer This is a utility class for running an instance of TimerTask in a new thread to either run one time at a specific time or run repetitively at a specified time interval. You can optionally specify that the spawned thread run as a daemon thread.

NOTE By default, any thread that is started in a Java application that is still running when the application exits will keep the application active until the thread itself terminates. If you specify that a thread is a daemon thread, then the thread will automatically quit when the application exits. The class Thread constructor takes an optional boolean argument; if this argument is `true`, then the thread starts as a daemon thread.

The example class `TimerDemo` in package `S25` creates two instances of the class `Timer`: one that waits two seconds and then runs the work task (as implemented in a `TimerTask` subclass run method) one time; the other `Timer` object runs the work task every one second. The class `TimerDemo` contains an inner class that is a subclass of `TimerTask`. Here is the implementation of the inner class `MessageTask` that extends `TimerTask`:

```
class MessageTask extends TimerTask {
    private int max_prints = 3;
    private int count = 0;
    public void run() {
        System.out.println("TimerTask " + this +
                           ", count="+count);
        if (count++ > max_prints)  timer.cancel();
    }
}
```

An instance of the class `Timer` will manage an instance of this inner class. Depending on how the instance of the `Timer` class is created, the `run()` method in this inner class will be either called one time or called repetitively at a specified time interval. If the `Timer` instance is set up to call this `run()` method repetitively, the value of the `count` variable determines when to stop the thread that this timer is running in. The `TimerDemo` class has two class constructors: the first constructor runs the task implemented in the method `run()` just one time after a specified time period (the first argument `seconds`) and then the thread stops:

```
public TimerDemo(int seconds) {
    timer = new Timer(true);
    // run task hust one time:
    timer.schedule(new MessageTask(), seconds*1000);
}
```

The second constructor waits a specified number of seconds and then runs the specified task repetitively at a specified time interval (the second argument `seconds`):

```
public TimerDemo(int wait_seconds, int seconds) {
    timer = new Timer();
    // run the task repetitively:
    timer.schedule(new MessageTask(), wait_seconds * 1000,
                   seconds*1000);
}
```

The key difference in these two constructors is the extra argument to the `Timer` class method `schedule`. The public static method `main` uses both of these constructors:

```
public static void main(String args[]) {
    System.out.println("Create two instances of TimerDemo...");
    // run task 1 time after waiting 2 seconds:
    new TimerDemo(2);
    // wait 5 seconds, then run task once every 1 second:
    new TimerDemo(5, 1);
    System.out.println("Threads started: wait for completion");
}
```

Here is the output from this example program:

```
Create two instances of TimerDemo...
Threads started: wait for completion
TimerTask S25.TimerDemo$MessageTask@7a8913, count=0
TimerTask S25.TimerDemo$MessageTask@bd747e, count=0
TimerTask S25.TimerDemo$MessageTask@bd747e, count=1
TimerTask S25.TimerDemo$MessageTask@bd747e, count=2
TimerTask S25.TimerDemo$MessageTask@bd747e, count=3
TimerTask S25.TimerDemo$MessageTask@bd747e, count=4
```

The third line of output is from the "run once" timer. The "run repetitively" timer prints lines 4 through 8.

NOTE For tasks that should run periodically, using the `Timer` and `TimerTask` classes is much preferable to creating a standard thread with timed delays in the thread's `run()` method. Using these newer classes simplifies application code.

SOLUTION 26

Efficient Thread Synchronization

PROBLEM You want to make data synchronization between threads more efficient and prevent program errors due to concurrent write access to data shared between threads.

SOLUTION You will look at programming techniques for efficient thread synchronization.

The Java language provides direct support for multiple thread programming, and the Java Virtual Machine (JVM) provides runtime support for multiple threads running inside a single

Java application. The only real difficulties that you may encounter when writing multiple threaded Java applications are in three areas:

- Failing to synchronize data access for multiple threads. This can lead to execution errors if more than one thread has concurrent write access to data or if one thread is writing to data while another thread is reading shared data. This problem is most severe for complex data structures such as linked lists.
- Performance problems due to unnecessary data synchronization or inefficient synchronization.
- Deadlock problems due to waiting forever for a resource that another thread has locked; the other thread is similarly waiting forever for a locked resource.

In this solution, you should concentrate on understanding data synchronization issues—once these issues are understood, the Java code for proper data synchronization is simple to implement. Java programs use two distinct types of data memory: the heap and a stack. All threads in an application share the same heap. Each thread has its own stack. Local method variables and method argument values are stored in a thread's stack. There is little danger of two threads accessing each other's stacks—it will never happen unless a local object (declared in a method) is passed as an argument. There is one possible problem when passing references to arrays to methods in separate threads: arrays are passed by reference, so although each thread has its own reference, if the referenced array data is stored on the heap or on the stack, data access collision is possible.

So, what is the problem if two threads access the same data at the same time? If two threads are reading the same data there is no problem. It can be a problem if one thread is writing heap data while another thread is reading the same data. It is also a problem when two threads write to the same heap data. These problems are made worse when the common data is a complex data structure like a linked list; for example: one thread is traversing a linked list while another thread is changing list pointers.

NOTE You cannot adequately test multiple threaded applications on a computer that only has a single CPU. This is because two threads cannot truly access data "at the same time" on a single CPU system. I have found thread related coding errors that only manifest themselves on multiple CPU systems.

Heap storage is a different matter from thread-specific stack space. Different threads will, in general, need to access common heap data. Only Java objects reside on the heap. The JVM maintains a lock for each object on the heap. This lock is often called a monitor lock and is an integer count for the number of times the object has been locked; when this count is zero, then the object is free to be locked by another thread. The lock for each object does not necessarily have to be used; however, a thread can request ownership of a lock on any object. If no other thread already has the lock, then the JVM assigns the lock to the requesting thread immediately. If another thread owns the lock, the requesting thread has to wait until the thread that currently owns the lock releases it. A condition where two or more threads are stuck waiting for locks that other threads own is called deadlock.

NOTE It is important to understand that there is nothing to prevent code in a thread from accessing (reading or writing) a Java object that is locked by another thread. Owning a lock does not prevent access by incorrectly written code in other threads to the locked object. Objects that can be accessed by multiple threads should be accessed in synchronized code blocks.

Thread Safe Data Types

The original collection classes in the `java.util` package are inherently threadsafe. Some of the newer collection classes added to the `java.util` package are not threadsafe and are inherently much more efficient to use when it's known that multiple threads will not need concurrent access. I touched on this briefly in Solution 17. For example, the class `Vector` is guaranteed to be threadsafe: two threads can access the same `Vector` object without any special code to synchronize access. The class `ArrayList` has a very similar API to the older class `Vector`, but access to instances of the class `ArrayList` is not automatically synchronized.

NOTE I am very conservative in most of the example code in this book: I usually favor the use of slower classes such as `Vector` that provide automatic synchronization. This design decision is on purpose: always favor safety over efficiency unless proper analysis shows that the less safe solution is adequate. In this case, I prefer the automatically synchronized collection classes in case readers use the example code as-is in a multithreaded application.

It is worthwhile to list the common collection class and indicate which are automatically synchronized:

Array Not synchronized (simple arrays are not instances of collection classes; I list Array here just for reference)

ArrayList Not synchronized

HashMap Not synchronized

HashSet Not synchronized

Hashtable Synchronized

LinkedList Not synchronized

TreeMap Not synchronized

TreeSet Not synchronized

Vector Synchronized

Iterators for synchronized collection classes throw a `ConcurrentModificationException` if the synchronized collection is modified while the iterator is being used. Iterators are preferred to enumerations because enumerations are not threadsafe.

If you are writing a single threaded application, always prefer the use of nonsynchronized collection classes or simple arrays: why slow down your programs unnecessarily? If you are writing multithreaded applications and performance is a priority, then do some analysis and only use synchronized collection classes when more than one thread requires access to the data (with at least one thread writing to the data—concurrent read-only access is never a problem, with or without synchronization). In the next section, we will look at explicitly synchronizing data access.

Explicitly Synchronizing Data Access

It is simple to explicitly synchronize access to data in Java programs. There are two strategies:

- Synchronize an entire method: all instance data for an object is locked while the method is executed.
- Synchronize a single object: only a single Java object is locked.

The example class `SynchronizationDemo` in the package `S25` declares two instance variables that are declared public for discussion purposes:

```
public Integer value = new Integer(0);
public ArrayList unusedData = new ArrayList();
```

This class contains a method that uses the `synchronized` keyword in the method signature to synchronize both of the instance objects `value` and `unusedData`:

```
public synchronized void SynchedMethod(int new_value) {
    value = new Integer(new_value);
}
```

Here, all instance data is locked while this method executes. If another thread has locked the instance of class `SynchronizationDemo` or either of its two public instance variables, then the JVM will not execute this method until the other thread releases its lock. The next method only synchronizes access to the instance variable `value`:

```
public void SynchObject(int new_value) {
    synchronized (value) {
        value = new Integer(new_value);
    }
}
```

For possible efficiency reasons, I always use the second method: I only synchronize specific objects as I need them.

SOLUTION 27

Controlling Your Applications Using Thread Groups and Custom Security Managers

PROBLEM Your Java application uses many threads and you want better control of thread priorities and the ability to monitor the threads.

SOLUTION You will use thread groups to manage multiple threads and look at the use of a custom security manager for a thread group.

All threads belong to a thread group. In the examples in Solutions 25 and 26, we did not specify a thread group when creating threads, so the threads that we created belong to the thread group that the creating thread belonged to. This default thread group is called `main`. I use threads in most applications that I write, but I frequently do not bother explicitly using thread groups. However, using thread groups is useful when you want to manage groups of threads or you want to write a custom security manager for a group of threads.

There are three public constructors that allow the thread group to be explicitly set:

```
public Thread(ThreadGroup group, String name)
public Thread(ThreadGroup group, Runnable runnable)
public Thread(ThreadGroup group, Runnable runnable, String name)
```

Before I cover the use of these three constructors, we will first look at the class `ThreadGroup` in some detail.

ThreadGroup Class

Instances of the class `ThreadGroup` can contain both threads and other thread groups. You will be using the example class `ThreadGroupPriorityTest` in the package `S27` to look at thread group creation and the most useful operations on thread groups. This class implements the `Runnable` interface so it can conveniently be used to create test threads (see Solution 25):

```
public class ThreadGroupPriorityTest implements Runnable
```

The public method `run()` implemented in this class has no practical use except for demonstrating thread group operations:

```
public void run() {
    // wait 1 second so the main method can print 'main' thread
```

```
        // group information:
        try { Thread.sleep(1000L); } catch (Exception ee) { }
        ThreadGroup tg = Thread.currentThread().getThreadGroup();
        String tgName = tg.getName();
        String tgParent = tg.getParent().getName();
        for (int i=0; i<100; i++) {
            System.out.println(name + ": i = " + i +
                               " thread group name="+tgName+
                               ", parent thread group name="+
                               tgParent);
        }
        // before exiting thread, print out all threads in
        // the current thread group:
        int num = tg.activeCount();
        Thread[] threads = new Thread[num];
        tg.enumerate(threads);
        System.out.print("Threads in thread group "+tgName+":");
        for (int i=0; i<num; i++) {
            System.out.print(" " + threads[i].getName());
        }
        System.out.println();
    }
```

When a thread is created using an instance of the class `ThreadGroupPriorityTest` and is started using the method `start()`, this method `run()` is executed in the new thread. In the main test program, you will want to print out the top-level (`main`) thread group information, so the first thing that this method `run()` does is sleep for one second (this will give the `main()` method time to print out information). The class `Thread` has a static method, `currentThread`, that returns the thread that is currently running. The class `Thread` method `getThreadGroup()` returns the thread group for a thread instance. These methods are used to get the thread group name and the parent thread group name for debug printout.

This thread's `run()` method loops 100 times, printing a message each time through the loop. As you will see shortly, the test `main()` method creates three thread groups (with low, medium, and high thread priority), with one thread in each group. When all three threads are running at once, you might see these lines of output:

```
high: i = 60 thread group=high, parent thread group name=main
medium: i = 34 thread group=medium, parent thread group name=main
low: i = 7 thread group=low, parent thread group name=main
```

The first item printed is a print name that is set by a string argument to the `ThreadGroupPriorityTest` class constructor, then you print the loop index, thread group name, and the parent thread group name.

As you have probably guessed from the demo class name, you will modify the thread priority for each thread group that you create. The following code is from the static method `main()` in the class `ThreadGroupPriorityTest`:

```
ThreadGroup low = new ThreadGroup("low");
ThreadGroup medium = new ThreadGroup("medium");
ThreadGroup high = new ThreadGroup("high");
low.setMaxPriority(Thread.MIN_PRIORITY);
medium.setMaxPriority(Thread.NORM_PRIORITY);
high.setMaxPriority(Thread.MAX_PRIORITY);
```

Here I created three thread groups and explicitly set the priority of any threads that are later added to each thread group. Calling the method `setMaxPriority()` has no effect on threads that are already added to a thread group, so you will usually create a thread group, set the priority, and then add threads to the group. After I set the thread group priorities, I will add one thread to each thread group:

```
Thread lowThread =
  new Thread(low, new ThreadGroupPriorityTest("low"));
Thread mediumThread =
  new Thread(medium, new ThreadGroupPriorityTest("medium"));
Thread highThread =
  new Thread(high, new ThreadGroupPriorityTest("high"),
             "highPThread"); // here, we name the thread
```

Here we create threads by specifying an owning thread group and a new instance of a class that implements the `Runnable` interface. The last thread created (`highThread`) uses a constructor that also takes a string name to explicitly name a thread. By default, threads are named `Thread-1`, `Thread-2`, etc. Next, in the public static `main()` method, I start these threads and then print out information from the top-level default thread group `main`:

```
// start the test threads:
lowThread.start();
mediumThread.start();
highThread.start();
// show threads in "main" thread group:
ThreadGroup main = Thread.currentThread().getThreadGroup();
int num = main.activeCount();
System.out.println("Number of thread in group 'main'="+num);
Thread[] threads = new Thread[num];
main.enumerate(threads);
System.out.print("Threads in thread group 'main':");
for (int i=0; i<num; i++) {
    // note: do not use thread.getName() because some threads
    // may be null; use thread.toString() so a null thread
    // will print as "null":
    System.out.print(" "+threads[i]); // use implicit toString()
}
System.out.println();
```

The static method `Thread.currentThread` will return the top-level `main` thread group. The method `getThreadGroup()` returns the thread group that a thread belongs to. I use the `activeCount()` method to get the number of threads in the top-level thread group and print out this information:

```
Number of thread in group 'main'=5
Threads in thread group 'main': Thread[main,5,main] Thread[Thread-1,1,low]
Thread[Thread-2,5,medium] Thread[highPThread,5,high] null
```

Notice in this printout that threads in thread groups contained in the main thread group are included in the enumeration of the top-level thread groups' active threads.

This example created three thread groups with different runtime priorities. Be aware, however, that a thread's runtime priority is just a request to the JVM's scheduler: higher priority threads will on the average be run more often in a specific time interval than lower priority threads. If you run the example program several times, you will see this effect: usually the high-priority thread's `run()` method is called more frequently than the medium-priority thread, and the medium-priority thread's `run()` method is usually called more often than the low-priority thread's `run()` method. Note that after looping 100 times and printing out the thread group information, the method `run()` returns to the caller, and at that point the thread is no longer active.

Custom Thread Security Manager

The Java language and JVM provide default security: checking for runtime exceptions, verifying class files at load time, etc. It is also possible to customize the security restrictions on Java applications and threads. You are probably aware of security restrictions on Java applets that execute in the context of a web browser. I do not cover Java applets in this book.

By default, Java applications do not have a default security manager, as can be seen by running this code:

```
SecurityManager securityManager = System.getSecurityManager();
if (securityManager != null) {
    Object securityContext=securityManager.getSecurityContext();
    System.out.println("securityContext=" + securityContext);
} else {
    System.out.println("No security manager set");
}
```

The message "No security manager set" will be printed unless you install your own security manager or if this code is running, for example, as a web application in a servlet container such as Tomcat (see Solutions 40 through 49) or an EJB container (see Solutions 50 through 53). You will first write an example security manager class and then see how to install it. The following inner class is defined in the class `SecurityManagerDemo` in package `S27`:

```
class DemoSecurityManager extends SecurityManager {
    public void checkDelete(String fileName)
```

```
            throws SecurityException {
        // never allow file deletes:
        throw new SecurityException("Not allowed to delete file "
                                    + fileName);
    }
    public void checkConnect(String host, int port)
            throws SecurityException {
        // never allow remote socket connections:
        throw new SecurityException(
            "Not allowed to connect to host" +
            host + " port: " + port);
    }
    public void checkAccess(ThreadGroup tg)
            throws SecurityException {
        // never allow changing thread group parameters:
        throw new SecurityException(
            "Not allowed modify thread group " + tg);
    }
    public void checkExit(int status) throws SecurityException {
        // never allow exiting the JVM:
        throw new SecurityException(
            "Not to exit JVM with status=" + status);
    }
}
```

The class `SecurityManager` has many methods that you can override in subclasses—here we just overrode four methods to serve as an example. You should consult the complete API for the `SecurityManager` class. After you install this custom security manager class, any thread in the application (including the main default thread) is subject to the restrictions of this custom security manager class. Here is the code for installing a security manager:

```
System.setSecurityManager(new DemoSecurityManager());
```

Once a custom security manager has been set in a JVM, it cannot be modified or replaced. In the public static method `main()` in class `SecurityManagerDemo`, I purposefully violate two restrictions set by the custom security manager:

```
try {
    System.exit(1);
} catch (Exception e) {
    System.out.println("exit error: " + e);
}
try {
    ThreadGroup high = new ThreadGroup("high");
    high.setMaxPriority(Thread.MAX_PRIORITY);
} catch (Exception e) {
    System.out.println("thread group modification error: " + e);
}
```

The program output shows two security exceptions thrown:

```
exit error: java.lang.SecurityException: Not to exit JVM with
status=1

thread group modification error: java.lang.SecurityException: Not
allowed modify thread group
java.lang.ThreadGroup[name=main,maxpri=10]
```

NOTE If you are using compiled code libraries written by people you do not know, then using a custom security manager in your application makes a lot of sense to avoid any possibly malicious code in third-party libraries.

Network Programming

SOLUTION 28

Programming with Server Sockets

PROBLEM You want to write a server application that uses low-level sockets to service client programs written in any programming language that supports sockets.

SOLUTION You will look at two techniques implementing server-side TCP sockets and briefly cover UDP sockets in the last section of this solution.

One of the advantages of the Java language is that it provides direct and high level support for socket-based network programming. Because socket-based programs often wait for remote resources, it is common to write multithreaded programs to handle socket connections. You will write two functionally similar Transmission Control Protocol (TCP) server socket example programs: one does not use separate threads and one is multithreaded.

There are two common protocols used for socket programming: TCP and User Data Protocol (UDP). TCP provides guaranteed delivery or failure behavior: if an error does not occur, then you can be sure that the process on the other side of the socket connection received data transferred over the socket connection. UDP does not provide guaranteed delivery but is more efficient, especially when transferring data packets small enough to fit inside one physical packet. I will cover UDP in the last section of this solution; keep in mind that for network broadcast applications you will probably want to use UDP. I have used UDP for programming network games where network efficiency and low latency were more important than guaranteed data delivery.

TCP sockets are referred to as connection-oriented sockets because once a connection is made, programs at both ends of the connection can read and write from the socket as long as the connection is open (that is, not explicitly closed or closed due to a network error). Data that one end of the connection writes to the socket is available for reading at the other end of the socket connection.

UDP sockets are referred to as connectionless sockets because a physical datagram of data is sent to a remote receiver defined by a host name (or IP address) and a port number. There is no real coordination between sender and receiver; for example, the sender does not know for sure that the recipient program actually received the data.

NOTE I will use two example TCP socket programs and one example UDP socket program both in this solution and Solution 29.

In order to keep the TCP example programs in this solution and in Solution 29 short and simple to understand, we will make one assumption: client and server processes will send a single Java string and then close the socket connection. TCP sockets provide a persistent data communications channel: for many applications, you will want to open a socket connection between two processes and keep the connection open. As you will see, an open socket connection can provide a buffered reader and a print writer to read and write from/to the socket connection. So, the two TCP example server programs in this solution each accept incoming socket connections, read a single Java string from the buffered reader for the connection, convert this string to all uppercase characters, send the new string to the remote client, and then terminate the connection. The example client developed in Solution 29 will send a test string to either of the example programs in this solution, print the response string, and terminate. If you look in the directory `src/S28` you will see three Java source files:

ServerSocketDemo.java This program processes only one incoming socket connection at a time. You configure the server socket to store up to 20 (although this can be changed easily) incoming connection requests—more than 20 pending requests causes new requests to generate a socket error on the remote client. This technique works well (and is very simple to implement) when handling service requests is fast (that is, do not block).

ServerSocketThreadedDemo.java This program uses an inner class derived from the `Thread` class to process incoming connections in parallel. This technique works best when processing service requests might take a while (that is, block for a while).

UDPSocketReceiver.java This program demonstrates receiving and printing the contents of incoming datagram packets. No response is returned to the sender.

Nonthreaded Server Example

The file `ServerSocketDemo.java` contains the code snippets that I use in this section. I define a few constants to define host name, port number, and the maximum number of queued connections for the server socket:

```
final static public String host = "127.0.0.1"; // local host
final static public int port = 8000;
final static public int maxConnectionQueueLength = 20;
```

When you open a server socket, you must specify a port number and can optionally specify a maximum connection queue length. In this example, you are configuring the server socket to maintain a queue of up to 20 pending client connection requests. This connection request wait queue serves a very useful purpose: if the server is busy processing a client connection, other clients can still attempt to make a socket connection—although they will have to wait their turn for a connection. In the next section, you will use multiple threads to avoid causing clients to wait for a connection.

The following code snippet (from the file `ServerSocketDemo.java`) shows how to create a server socket and then use a `while` loop to accept incoming client socket connection requests, one at a time:

```
ServerSocket serverSocket = null;
try {
    serverSocket=new ServerSocket(port,maxConnectionQueueLength);
} catch (IOException e) {
    e.printStackTrace();
    return; // error - server not started
}
Socket clientSocket = null;
```

You will now loop (forever, or until this program is externally terminated) accepting incoming connection requests from clients. Once a client socket is opened from calling the server socket `accept()` method, you can get both a `PrintWriter` output stream for writing back to the client and a `BufferedReader` input stream for reading from the client. Because you opened the input stream for reading output from the client as a buffered reader object, you are limited to reading Unicode characters (either Java `char[]` arrays or Java strings). If you were writing Java servers that interact with clients that use simple 8-bit characters, then you would not create a buffered reader. Instead, you'd directly use the input stream and use the `read()` method of the input stream class. In the following example, I read Unicode characters into a Java string, copy the string converting all characters to uppercase, and return the new modified string to the client by writing it to the print writer object:

```
while (true) {
    try {
        try {
            clientSocket = serverSocket.accept();
        } catch (IOException e) {
            e.printStackTrace();
            continue;    // wait for another client connection
        }

        PrintWriter out =
           new PrintWriter(clientSocket.getOutputStream(),true);
        BufferedReader in =
           new BufferedReader(
               new InputStreamReader(
                   clientSocket.getInputStream()));
        String input_buf = in.readLine();
        System.out.println("received on socket: " + input_buf);
        // return modified string to the client:
        out.println(input_buf.toUpperCase());
        out.close();
        in.close();
```

```
            clientSocket.close();
        } catch (Exception e) {
            e.printStackTrace();
        } finally {
            try {
                clientSocket.close();
            } catch (Exception e2) {
                e2.printStackTrace();
            }
        }
    }
```

For your applications, you will certainly want to do more processing than simply echoing a string (converted to uppercase) back to the client. Still, this code snippet shows how simple it is to handle server sockets.

NOTE The last code snippet contains an infinite loop for waiting for and servicing client connections. Usually you should avoid infinite loops in your programs, but an infinite loop makes sense here because you want the service to run until either the program is terminated or the computer is rebooted.

In order to run this example, change to the `src` directory and enter the following commands:

```
javac -d . S28/*.java
java S28.ServerSocketDemo
```

You will want to run the Solution 29 demo program `ClientSocketDemo` while running this program.

Threaded Server Example

The example code in the last section showed how to open and use TCP server sockets. In this section, you will extend the previous code to use TCP separate sockets to handle incoming client connection requests. This technique is especially useful if the server-side code for processing client requests takes a while to run because other clients will not have to wait for a connection.

The example code for this solution is in the file `ServerSocketThreadedDemo.java` in the directory `src/S28`. I define a few constants to define host name, port number, and the maximum number of queued connections for the server socket:

```
final static public String host = "127.0.0.1"; // local host
final static public int port = 8000;
final static public int maxConnectionQueueLength = 20;
```

In the last section, you saw how a socket connection from a client could be directly handled in the same thread that accepted the client connection. In this section, I use nonpublic class

HandleConnectionThread (defined at the bottom of the file ServerSocketThreadedDemo.java) that manages a separate thread to process each client connection. The constructor for this non-public class takes one argument: a socket that I will get by calling the accept() method on the server socket. Refer to Solution 25 for more information on Java thread programming.

```
class HandleConnectionThread extends Thread {
    protected transient Socket client_socket;
    protected transient BufferedReader input_strm;
    protected transient PrintStream output_strm;

    public HandleConnectionThread(Socket client_socket) {
        this.client_socket = client_socket;
        try {
            input_strm =
                new BufferedReader(
                    new InputStreamReader(
                        client_socket.getInputStream()));
            output_strm =
                new PrintStream(client_socket.getOutputStream());
        } catch (IOException io_exception) {
            try {
                client_socket.close();
            } catch (IOException e) {
                e.printStackTrace();
            }
            io_exception.printStackTrace();
            return;
        }
        this.start(); // start the thread
    }

    public void run() {
        String input_buf;
        try {
            input_buf = input_strm.readLine();
            System.out.println("received on socket: " +
                               input_buf);
            // modify string and return to client:
            output_strm.println(input_buf.toUpperCase());
            output_strm.flush();
            output_strm.close();
        } catch (Exception e) {
            e.printStackTrace();
        } finally {
            try {
```

```
                    client_socket.close();
                } catch (Exception e) {
                    //e.printStackTrace();
                }
            }
        }
    }
```

The class constructor in this nonpublic class gets a buffered reader and a print writer from the client socket, as you saw in the last section. The `run()` method in this nonpublic class uses the same code that you saw in the last section for reading from a buffered reader and writing to a print writer.

The code for initializing the TCP server socket and accepting connections from clients is similar to the example server in the last section. The constructor for the class `ServerSocketThreadedDemo` contains the following code for creating a server socket and for using a `while` loop to wait for incoming client connection requests:

```
ServerSocket serverSocket;
try {
    serverSocket =
       new ServerSocket(port, maxConnectionQueueLength);
} catch (IOException e) {
    System.out.println("Error in setting up server socket: " + e);
    return;
}

try {
    while (true) {
        Socket socket = serverSocket.accept();
        new HandleConnectionThread(socket);
    }
} catch (IOException e) {
    System.out.println("Error in getting connection: " + e);
} finally {
    try {
        serverSocket.close();
    } catch (IOException e) {
        System.out.println("Error closing connection: " + e);
    }
}
```

Using multiple threads to handle client connections is slightly more complex than the non-threaded example in the last section, but it does provide the advantage of allowing multiple client connections at the same time.

NOTE This example is not as efficient as it could be: new instances of the nonpublic class `HandleConnectionThread` are created for each incoming connection request. You could prevent excess object creation and destruction overhead by modifying this class slightly to allow resetting the client socket—then a pool of these objects could be reused for handling connection requests. As is, this example is easier to understand but is slightly less efficient than it could be.

In order to run this example, change to the `src` directory and enter the following commands:

```
javac -d . S28/*.java
java S28.ServerSocketThreadedDemo
```

You should run the Solution 29 demo program `ClientSocketDemo` while running this program.

Implementing a UDP Socket Receiver

UDP sockets are used for connectionless communication. In order to write Java programs that use UDP sockets, you need to use two classes:

DatagramPacket This class contains raw data, the address information for the recipient, and the sender's address information.

DatagramSocket This class represents a datagram socket that is used for sending and receiving datagram packets.

While it is possible for the recipient of a datagram packet to determine the address (that is, the host name and port number) of the sender in order to send replies back to the sender, I do not usually use UDP sockets in a send-and-receive-a-response mode (that is, a client/server programming model). Instead, I use UDP sockets in applications where one application needs to broadcast data to one or more recipients. The file `UDPSocketReceiver.java` contains the demonstration program for this section. This program opens a datagram socket on port 8000 and loops forever receiving datagram packets. For each packet received, you print out the data in the packet and address information. This program requires the `java.net` package libraries:

```
package S28;

import java.net.*;
import java.io.IOException;

public class UDPSocketReceiver {
    final static public int port = 8000;
```

The public static main method throws an `IOException` on any errors so I do not have to explicitly handle `IOException` errors in the demo code:

```
    public static void main(String[] args) throws IOException {
```

I open a datagram socket on port 8000, allocate a reference to a byte array, and enter an infinite loop waiting for incoming packets:

```
        DatagramSocket socket = new DatagramSocket(port);
        byte[] buffer = new byte[256];
        while (true) {
```

I create a datagram packet and then use the datagram socket method receive to block (that is, to wait) until an incoming datagram is available:

```
            DatagramPacket packet =
                new DatagramPacket(buffer, buffer.length);
            socket.receive(packet);
```

After receiving a datagram, I get information from the datagram and print it out:

```
            InetAddress address = packet.getAddress();
            int p = packet.getPort();
            byte[] data = packet.getData();
            String dataAsString = new String(data);
            System.out.println("Received data packet:");
            System.out.println("   address : " + address) ;
            System.out.println("   port    : " + p) ;
            System.out.println("   data    : " + dataAsString) ;
        }
    }
}
```

Running this UDP demo receiver program and the UDP demo sender program from Solution 29 produces the following output on the receiver side:

```
Received data packet:
   address : /127.0.0.1
   port    : 49640
   data    : hello from a UDP socket sender
```

The last section of Solution 29 contains a demo program for sending a datagram over a datagram socket.

NOTE Sending and receiving many small packets of information with UDP is much more efficient than using TCP. Keep in mind, however, that UDP does not guarantee delivery of packets.

SOLUTION 29

Writing Client Socket Applications

PROBLEM You want to write a Java socket-based client program.

SOLUTION You will write a Java example TCP socket client that can connect with socket-based servers written in any programming language that supports sockets. You will also see how to send datagram packets over a UDP socket connection.

The TCP and UDP socket client example programs in this solution work with the example programs in Solution 28.

Implementing a TCP Socket Client

The Java language provides high-level support for socket programming. You will see that it takes only a few lines of code to write a socket-based Java client program. The file `ClientSocketDemo.java` contains the code snippets seen in this section.

The following code snippet shows how to open a TCP socket connection to a remote server, send one Java string to the server, and wait for and receive one string back from the server. After the string is received back from the server, this client code closes the socket connection that also serves to notify the remote server code to close the socket connection at the server end of the connection. Note that the following code needs to process both `UnknownHostException` and `IOException` errors. Error handling code is not shown here for brevity:

```
String host = "127.0.0.1"; // local host
int port = 8000;
Socket socket = new Socket(host, port);
BufferedReader in =
  new BufferedReader(
    new InputStreamReader(socket.getInputStream()));
PrintWriter out=new PrintWriter(socket.getOutputStream(),true);
out.println("Sending test message");
String str = in.readLine();
System.out.println(" response from server=" + str);
socket.close();
```

The constructor for the class `Socket` takes two arguments: a host name and a port number. A socket can be read and written to. As you saw in Solution 28, you can get both a buffered reader to read from a socket and a print writer to write to a socket.

NOTE This example uses Unicode characters. If you want to read and write plain 8-bit characters or binary data, then you simply get the input stream from the socket without creating a buffered reader and get the output stream from the socket without creating a print writer.

In this example, I use the `println()` method to write a string through the print writer and socket to the remote server. Similarly I use the `readLine()` method to read a string containing one line of output that the server wrote to this client back over the open socket connection.

Implementing a UDP Socket Sender

You saw how to implement a receiver of datagram packets in the last section of Solution 28. In this section, you will learn how to write a complementary demo program that sends a datagram to a receiver. You should read the last section of Solution 28 if you have not already done so.

The file `UDPSocketSender.java` contains the example code for this section. This code requires the libraries in the package `java.net`:

```
package S29;

import java.net.*;

public class UDPSocketSender {
    final static public int port = 8000;
```

The `public static main()` method throws a general exception to handle array bounds errors if the `args` argument is of zero length and to handle any other errors caused by network-related errors:

```
    public static void main(String[] args) throws Exception {
```

You need the host name of the receiver—this is a mandatory command-line argument when running this demo program:

```
        String host = args[0]; // mandatory argument!
```

You need to create a byte array containing data to send; here I simply create a Java string and then get the byte array from the string:

```
        String testMessage = "hello from a UDP socket sender";
        byte[] buffer = testMessage.getBytes();
```

You need to get the address of the host. This can throw an `UnknownHostException` error:

```
        InetAddress address = InetAddress.getByName(host);
```

You need to create a datagram socket; this can throw a `java.net.SocketException`:

```
        DatagramSocket udpSocket = new DatagramSocket();
```

You need to create a datagram packet using the byte array from the test string and address information for the remote receiver:

```
        DatagramPacket packet =
            new DatagramPacket(buffer, buffer.length,
                               address, port);
```

You are now ready to send the packet to the remote receiver; this can throw an `IOException`:

```
        udpSocket.send(packet);
        udpSocket.close();
    }
}
```

Run this example program with the UDP socket receiver demo program from the last section of Solution 28.

NOTE This example is not a client application because it does not receive a response back from the remote receiver. This UDP socket example and the example in the last section of Solution 28 were added to introduce readers to a network programming technique that is too often overlooked in favor of using less efficient TCP sockets.

SOLUTION 30

Using Server-Side RMI

PROBLEM You want to write a server application for use by other Java applications for performing specific tasks provided by the server application.

SOLUTION You will use Java Remote Method Invocation (RMI) to expose specific methods of a server class to remote clients.

RMI is a simple and efficient method for calling methods on objects running in remote Java Virtual Machines (JVMs). In order to locate named objects to use, you will use an `rmiregistry` naming service. When you write objects that will act as servers, you will register these objects with an `rmiregistry` naming service. (You will see later how to run the `rmiregistry` program.)

The example server program written in this solution works with the example RMI client application written in Solution 31.

The example programs in this solution and in Solution 31 demonstrate a very useful feature of RMI: dynamic remote class loading. With RMI, not only data but objects with behavior are available (that is, code for the methods is remotely byte code loaded).

NOTE The information on RMI in this solution and Solution 31 is brief. If you want more detail, Ann Wollrath and Jim Waldo wrote a good RMI tutorial that you can find at `java.sun.com/docs/books/tutorial/rmi/`.

Implementing the RMI Server

The first step in implementing an RMI-based service is to write a Java interface that defines the API for the service. The file `S30/FortuneCookie.java` implements the interface for our example service:

```
public interface FortuneCookie extends java.rmi.Remote {
    public String getFortune(String firstName)
           throws RemoteException;
    public SimpleClass getAnObject() throws RemoteException;
}
```

The class `SimpleClass` (see the source file `SimpleClass.java`) is serializable (a requirement) and defines a `toString()` method that the test RMI client in Solution 31 will use after fetching an instance of this class. All the Java classes for all arguments and returned values used to define an RMI-based service API must be serializable. Here I use the Java String class and the example `SimpleClass` class, which both implement the `java.io.Serializable` interface.

The next step in implementing the example service is to write a Java class that implements the `FortuneCookie` interface:

```
public class FortuneCookieImpl extends UnicastRemoteObject implements
FortuneCookie {

  public FortuneCookieImpl(String name) throws RemoteException {
    super(); // UnicastRemoteObject constructor
    try {
        Naming.rebind(name, this);
    } catch (Exception e) {
        System.out.println(e);
    }
  }

  public String getFortune(String firstName) {
    return "You will be happy";
  }
```

```
    public SimpleClass getAnObject() throws RemoteException {
      return new SimpleClass();
    }
  }
```

There are three RMI-specific implementation details in this class:

Class is derived from the `UnicastRemoteObject` class: If this is not done, you must additionally override a few `java.lang.Object` methods.

The class constructor throws a `RemoteException`: The super class constructor can throw this exception.

The constructor binds the service to a specific name: This is optional. If not specified, remote clients use the interface name (in this case, `FortuneCookie`) to request this service.

I could have included a `main()` method to launch the fortune cookie service in the `FortuneCookieImpl` class, but I preferred to write a separate main application class:

```
import java.rmi.*;
public class FortuneCookieServer {
    public static void main(String[] args) throws Exception {
        if (System.getSecurityManager() == null) {
            System.setSecurityManager(new RMISecurityManager());
        }
        new FortuneCookieImpl("Wise-one");
        System.out.println("FortuneCookieServer started OK.");
    }

}
```

I will cover setting up a security policy file in the next section. The `RMISecurityManager` will use the Java properties `java.security.policy` to find the security file to use for this service.

Building and Running the RMI Server

To run the example server application, open two shell windows (called command windows on Windows systems). You will start the Java RMI naming registry and leave this program running while running the examples in both this solution and Solution 31:

```
rmiregistry
```

It is important that the `rmiregistry` program not have your application classes in its CLASSPATH—this is necessary to properly handle remote loading of classes by client applications—later, when you run the server example, you will define the Java property `java.rmi.server.codebase` to point to the file path for the example `src` directory. This information will allow the `rmiregistry` program to pass remote clients the appropriate stub code to use the service. Remember not to run the `rmiregistry` program in the example `src` directory.

In the other command window, change to the top-level source directory `src`. After compiling the Java source files, you will use the `rmic` utility to generate Java skeleton code to handle the low level details of providing RMI-based services and for generating stub code that is transferred to the remote client. By default, the `rmic` tool does not keep generated Java source files; it produces only compiled class files for the required stubs. You can use the `rmic` command-line option `keepgenerated` if you want to see the generated code. In the other shell window, type the following commands:

```
javac -d . S30/*.java
rmic -d . S30.FortuneCookieImpl
java -classpath . -Djava.security.policy=security_policy.txt  -
Djava.rmi.server.codebase=file:/Users/markw/Content/Java_10_minute_solutions/src
S30.FortuneCookieServer
```

The last three lines should be typed on one command line—the text wraps here because the line is not long enough for the entire command. In this example, I set the codebase to the location of my client stub class files for the server. You will have to change the file path to match where the `src` directory is on your computer.

The security management policy file that is in the source directory allows all permissions:

```
grant {
   permission java.security.AllPermission;
};
```

In general, you will want to restrict IP addresses of clients that can access remote services, etc.

SOLUTION 31

Writing RMI Clients

PROBLEM You want to remotely access services on an RMI-enabled server.

SOLUTION You will write a Java client that uses the RMI APIs.

RMI-based clients can both load the data for objects and use a remote class loader to load compiled code for a remote object. The compiled code that is remotely loaded is the stub code generated by the `rmic` utility and remotely defined classes.

Implementing the RMI Client

Writing RMI-based clients is simple: only a few lines of code are required to set up a security manager to allow loading remote code and to get a local stub object that represents a remote object and allows calling methods on the remote object.

You need to import both the RMI classes and the Java interface `S30.FortuneCookie` that you defined in Solution 30:

```
import S30.FortuneCookie;
import java.rmi.*;


public class FortuneCookieClient {
    public static void main(String[] args) {
        try {
            if (System.getSecurityManager() == null) {
                System.setSecurityManager(
                       new RMISecurityManager());
            }
            FortuneCookie cookie =
       (FortuneCookie) Naming.lookup("rmi://localhost/Wise-one");
            // get 2 fortunes:
            for (int i=0; i<2; i++) {
                String fortune = cookie.getFortune("Mark");
                System.out.println(fortune);
            }
            // now try to gt a remote object:
            Object obj = cookie.getAnObject();
            System.out.println("fetched a remote object: " +
                                   obj.toString());
        } catch (Exception e) {
            System.out.println(e);
        }
    }
}
```

The first thing that this client does is create a custom security manager. In the next section, you will see how to specify an initialization file for security management as a command-line argument. The client program then performs a name service lookup on the `rmiregistry` program running on the local computer (that is, `localhost`). For most applications, you would access the `rmiregistry` server on a remote server; for example:

```
(FortuneCookie) Naming.lookup("rmi://a-server-123.com/Wise-one");
```

This lookup call will return a stub object instance that must be cast to the interface for the remote service. You get a fortune as a Java string using:

```
String fortune = cookie.getFortune("Mark");
```

The cookie object is a stub created by the `rmic` tool (see Solution 30) and remotely loaded from the remote server. This stub contains the code to access the remote object registered with the remote `rmiregistry` name server.

When you remotely load an instance of `SimpleClass`, you are (if necessary) loading compiled code and data from the remote server:

```
Object obj = cookie.getAnObject();
```

Here I could have cast this object to the class `SimpleClass`, but I choose to leave the reference as a Java object. In the print statement, I call the *`toString()`* method on this object, which is the *`toString()`* method defined for class *`SimpleClass`*. You will see sample output in the next section.

Building and Running the RMI Client

To compile and run the client (run the `rmiregistry` program and the Solution 30 server program as per the directions in Solution 30), change directory to the `src` directory and run the following commands:

```
javac -d . S31/*.java
java -Djava.security.policy=security_policy.txt S31.FortuneCookieClient
```

The last two lines should be entered on the same line in a shell window (or command window if you are running Windows). You will see output like the following if you also run the `rmiregistry` name server and RMI server as per the instructions in Solution 30:

```
Mark, you will be happy
Mark, you will be happy
fetched a remote object: You will win 4 dollars!
```

SOLUTION 32

Using Server-Side CORBA

PROBLEM You want to be able to interoperate with CORBA-based clients written in other programming languages besides Java.

SOLUTION You will write a CORBA-based server that interoperates with all CORBA clients.

CORBA (Common Object Request Broker Architecture) is a programming language–neutral way to build robust and efficient distributed services using Internet Inter-ORB Protocol

(IIOP). If you want to only use Java client and server programs it is much simpler to use RMI (see Solutions 30 and 31). RMI-based programs can optionally use IIOP for compatibility with CORBA services.

CORBA Object Request Brokers (ORBs) allow a program to invoke methods on remote objects without knowledge of the remote object's location, what programming language the object is written in, or the operating system that hosts the remote object. To be brief, CORBA is a very good technology for building distributed systems and well worth the effort to learn how to effectively use it.

NOTE Why is CORBA not more widely used? Many companies use CORBA for large-scale distributed systems, but CORBA is not used as much as you would think based on the high quality and efficiency of the CORBA architecture and implementations. The reason is fairly simple: at least initially, CORBA implementations for different programming languages and operating systems were expensive. For Java programmers, this situation has changed because CORBA is now built into Java.

I will briefly cover the definitions of terms used in the CORBA architecture before implementing a CORBA service in this solution and a CORBA client in Solution 33:

IDL Interface Definition Language: this defines the APIs for CORBA services.

Object Implements an interface defined in IDL.

Servant Implements the functionality defined in IDL. Remote client code uses this implementation via an object.

Client Requests references to remote objects and then uses these references as if they were local objects for calling methods on remote objects.

ORB Object Request Broker: responsible for delivering a request from a client to a remote object and returning the result to the client.

Object adapter Maps an interface (object) to a servant.

Implementing the Advice CORBA Service

Writing CORBA server and client applications in Java is not as simple as using RMI (see Solutions 30 and 31). However, the examples in this solution and Solution 33 will get you started using CORBA quickly and can serve as development templates for your own CORBA-based applications. Code in the examples that you can change for your own applications is clearly marked with comments.

You start by writing an IDL file that specifies the API for the services. Sun's Java IDL is based on the Common Object Request Brokerage Architecture (CORBA). You will use the tool `idlj` (which used to be called idltojava) to process an IDL file and automatically generate most of the code that you will need for a CORBA-based service written in Java. You will go through the same process in Solution 33 for Java CORBA-based clients.

NOTE The default CORBA server model generated by the `idlj` tool has changed with JDK1.4. The examples in this solution and in Solution 33 require JDK1.4 or later—they will not work unmodified with JDK1.3 because they use the newer server Portable Object Adapter (POA) model.

As an example for this solution and Solution 33, you will define a service to give random advice. The files for both server and client examples are in the directory `src/S32S33`. Only three files in this directory are hand edited:

Advice.idl Defines the API for the CORBA-based service.

AdviceServer.java Defines the main method to initialize an ORB and a nonpublic class that implements the actual service APIs.

AdviceClient.java This file is the subject of Solution 33.

The other Java source files are automatically generated and, except for briefly describing their purpose, will not be discussed. The contents of the IDL file `Advice.idl` is as follows:

```
// idl interface
module S32S33 {
    interface Advice {
        string getAdvice();
    };
};
```

NOTE You will notice that I use the same Java package `S32S33` in this solution and Solution 33. It is simpler to have both the client and main server class in the same package when using CORBA. An alternative is to not use the module statement in your IDL source file and put the generated top-level interface in the default (unnamed) package.

It is beyond the scope of this brief tutorial to go into many details for the IDL language. Simple Java types have corresponding IDL types; for example a Java `String` is an IDL `string`, a Java `int` is an IDL `long`, a Java `float` is an IDL `float`, etc. Handling simple types in IDL is simple; handling collection types is complex and beyond the scope of this discussion. The file `Advice.idl` defines a method `getAdvice` that will have this Java method signature:

```
String getAdvice();
```

The file `AdviceServer.java` contains both the public class `AdviceServer` and the nonpublic utility class `AdviceImpl`. Lines in this file that are specific to this example (and that you will want to change if you use this file as a template for your own projects) are marked with the comment "`!!`" to indicate that you should modify these lines if you reuse this code. Implementing CORBA-based services is complex, so I will break the `AdviceServer.java` code into small pieces intermixed with discussion of it. To make this example and the example in Solution 33 easier to write, all the code will reside in the package S3233:

```
package S32S33;
```

You need to import CORBA classes from for Java packages:

```
import org.omg.CosNaming.*;
import org.omg.CORBA.*;
import org.omg.PortableServer.*;
```

The public class AdviceServer consists of a public main class that uses the AdviceImpl non-public class defined at the bottom of the file AdviceServer.java, the automatically generated Java classes produced by idlj, and the CORBA library implementation for Java:

```
public class AdviceServer {
    public static void main(String args[]) {
        try{
```

You need access to a local Object Request Broker (ORB), so the first thing that you need to do is to create an instance of the class org.omg.CORBA.ORB that takes two arguments: the command-line arguments from running the service and an instance of the class java.util.Properties (here you pass null instead of an instance of the Properties class):

```
            ORB orb = ORB.init(args, null);
```

The command-line arguments will include the definition of a parameter ORBInitialPort that defines the port number that the CORBA ORB is using. The second argument can be used to override default Java properties. Next, you need to get a Portable Object Adapter (POA), which helps transfer client requests to a local ORB by generating object references and activating and deactivating servants for the remote service:

```
            POA rootpoa =
              POAHelper.narrow(
                 orb.resolve_initial_references("RootPOA"));
            rootpoa.the_POAManager().activate();
```

You now create an instance of the servant helper class AdviceImpl that is defined at the bottom of this file:

```
            AdviceImpl helloImpl = new AdviceImpl(); // !!
            org.omg.CORBA.Object ref =
                rootpoa.servant_to_reference(helloImpl); // !!
```

You have now registered an instance of the implementation class with the ORB; now you need to register the local Advice interface implementation object with the ORB's name server using the name Advice:

```
            Advice href = AdviceHelper.narrow(ref);
            org.omg.CORBA.Object objRef =
                orb.resolve_initial_references("NameService");
```

```
            NamingContextExt ncRef =
                NamingContextExtHelper.narrow(objRef);
            String name = "Advice";   // !!
            NameComponent path[] = ncRef.to_name(name);
            ncRef.rebind(path, href);
```

Finally, you start the ORB:

```
            orb.run();
```

The following error handling code prints an error message if an exception is thrown:

```
        } catch (Exception e) {
            System.err.println("AdviceServer error: " + e);
            e.printStackTrace(System.out);
        }
    }
}
```

The nonpublic class `AdviceImpl` is derived from the class `AdvicePOA` that is a portable object adapter derived from the base class `org.omg.PortableServer.Servant`. This class is required to define the public method `getAdvice`:

```
class AdviceImpl extends AdvicePOA {
    public String getAdvice() {
        return "Relax - you have been too tense lately.";
    }
}
```

You will find this class defined at the bottom of the file `AdviceServer.java`.

Using the *idlj* Utility to Generate Client/Server Utility Classes

You use the `idlj` program to automatically generate several Java source files—these are CORBA "boilerplate" files that you will not be editing. You need to run the following command from the top-level `src` directory:

```
idlj -fall S32S33/Advice.idl
```

The option `-fall` specifies that server and client side Java files will be created that are required for both the server (this solution) and the client (Solution 33). After running this `idlj` command, the following files will be automatically generated:

AdviceOperations.java Defines the Java interface `AdviceOperations` that both server and clients will use to pick up the method signature for the method `getAdvice`. The IDL file `Advice.idl` defines this interface using the CORBA IDL to Java type mappings.

AdvicePOA.java Implements the `InvokeHandler` interface and the interface methods defined in the `Advice.idl` file.

AdviceHelper.java Provides the method `narrow` that you will use later to cast a local (to a client) object to the correct Java type. This is used in Solution 33 when you write a CORBA-based client.

AdviceStub.java Gets loaded on the remote client to access the CORBA-based service.

These generated files might look like a hassle, but you don't need to do anything with them except to compile them. For this tutorial, you do have to write one Java file that you looked at in detail in the last section: `AdviceServer.java`. It contains the class `AdviceServer` boilerplate code that you will want to copy for your own server classes (changing "Advice" to the root name of your IDL file)—only four lines of code need to be changed when reusing this code in your projects and these four lines of code are marked with "`!!`" in end-of-line comments. This file also contains a nonpublic class `AdviceImpl`, where you have to define the method `getAdvice`.

Running the CORBA Server Example

To compile the Java source files, run this command in the `src` directory:

```
javac -d . S32S33/*.java
```

To run the server-side code, open up two shell windows and run these two commands in the `src` directory:

```
tnameserv -ORBInitialPort 7000
java S32S33.AdviceServer -ORBInitialPort 7000
```

You will use the command-line argument `-ORBInitialPort` when running both the `tnameserv` program and the server application to define which port the ORB will use for socket connections. You will use the same port number and command-line argument in Solution 33 when you run the CORBA-based client.

SOLUTION 33

Writing CORBA Clients

PROBLEM You want to interoperate with CORBA-based services.

SOLUTION You will use Java CORBA support to write Java CORBA clients.

The directory `src/S32S33` contains three files that are hand edited: `Advice.idl`, `AdviceServer.java`, and `AdviceClient.java`. You looked at the first two of these files in Solution 32 for implementing a CORBA-based service. In this solution, you will look at the file `AdviceClient.java`, which implements my example CORBA client.

Implementing the CORBA Client

You will list the CORBA client defined in the file `AdviceClient.java`, adding comments as required. You place the client in the same package as the server in order to have access to the Advice interface and import the required CORBA Java classes and declare the class:

```
package S32S33;
import org.omg.CORBA.*;
import org.omg.CosNaming.*;

public class AdviceClient {
```

The `public static main()` method initializes the ORB from command-line arguments (in this case picking up the `-ORBInitialPort` argument and value) and an instance of the class `Property` (here you pass null for the `Property` instance):

```
    public static void main(String args[])throws Exception  {
        ORB orb = ORB.init(args, null);
```

Next, you need to get the a context for the CORBA name service:

```
        org.omg.CORBA.Object objRef =
            orb.resolve_initial_references("NameService");
        NamingContextExt ncRef =
            NamingContextExtHelper.narrow(objRef);
```

Now you define the name of the remote service (`"Advice"`) and get an interface for this service:

```
        String name = "Advice";   // !!
        Advice helloImpl =
            AdviceHelper.narrow(ncRef.resolve_str(name));//!!
```

Finally, you are ready to use the local object (that is, stub for the remote object) to call the method `getAdvice()`:

```
        System.out.println(helloImpl.getAdvice());  // !!
    }
}
```

I have marked lines of code that are specific to this example with the comment "`!!`". You can reuse this code to write your own CORBA clients by copying this file and changing the lines marked with "`!!`" as appropriate for your application.

Building and Running the CORBA Client

I assume that you have followed the directions in Solution 32 for running `tnameserv` and the example CORBA-based server, and that they are still running on your computer—if not, please refer back to the last section of Solution 32 now and follow the directions there for starting these two programs.

In order to generate the required CORBA Java client support files and compile the client, type the following commands in the top-level `src` directory:

```
idlj -fall S32S33/Advice.idl
javac -d . S32S33/*.java
```

These steps are unnecessary if you performed them while you were reading Solution 32. To run the client, run the service as per Solution 32, then run the following:

```
java S32S33.AdviceClient -ORBInitialPort 7000
```

You should see the output provided by the remote server object:

```
Relax - you have been too tense lately.
```

JDBC Database Access

SOLUTION **34** Configuring JDBC

SOLUTION **35** Performing Database Updates

SOLUTION **36** Performing Database Queries

SOLUTION **37** Performing Batch Updates

SOLUTION **38** Using Transactions to Insure Data Integrity

SOLUTION **39** Dynamic Database Exploration Using the Metadata API

SOLUTION 34

Configuring JDBC

PROBLEM You need to configure JDBC access to a database.

SOLUTION You will look at configuring JDBC for several popular databases and cover some potential problems.

The Java Database Connectivity (JDBC) specification allows Java programmers to write database applications that are portable to different database products and operating systems without modifying Java source code. Unless specified otherwise, this section assumes that you are using JDBC version 2.

NOTE I will cover persistent Enterprise Java Beans (EJBs) in Solution 51. At that time we will discuss some issues of using databases with Java Enterprise (J2EE) applications. This section (Solutions 34 through 39) will cover only the use of JDBC with the standard edition of Java.

You will see how simple it is in general to configure JDBC for any specific database implemented on a database server. However, setting up a database server, creating new databases, administering the database server, backing up databases, and so on are all nontrivial tasks and are topics that are outside the scope of this book. In this solution, we will discuss configuring JDBC to work with a database that is already set up and ready to use. Solutions 35 through 39 will cover Java JDBC programming techniques.

NOTE I will cover the important aspects of using JDBC in Solutions 34 through 39 using short code examples. If you want a complete JDBC tutorial, please refer to the tutorial at `java.sun.com/docs/books/tutorial/jdbc/` written by Maydene Fisher.

Using JDBC Drivers

JDBC drivers for popular database systems are available as JAR files. For example, I usually use the popular and free database PostgreSQL for my development and for most deployments to customer sites. PostgreSQL is only available for Linux, Unix, and Mac OS X, however, so I usually use the free database MySQL under Windows. Depending on customer requests, I also use DB2 and Oracle for some projects. Regardless of which database product I use, I always stick with the standard JDBC APIs and avoid database-specific extensions—this ensures Java code portability.

The first step that you need to perform is to find an up-to-date JDBC driver for your particular database. For example, to support PostgreSQL, I use the driver in the file `pg73jdbc3.jar` that supports the JDBC 1, 2, and 3 APIs. You will need to have your JDBC driver JAR file in your Java CLASSPATH both during development and on deployed systems.

You must specify some information to configure JDBC:

- The name of the JDBC driver class
- The database URL that can optionally contain username and password database login information
- Optional username login name
- Optional user password

For both development and deployment, I usually specify these values in a Java class as static data by following static initialization code that allows me to override the default settings using Java properties (see Solution 8).

NOTE You will see in "Enterprise JavaBeans (EJBs)" how JDBC configuration data such as the driver name, username, etc. can be obtained via JNDI.

Java Code for Reconfigurable JDBC and Database Setup

There are many ways to implement reconfigurable JDBC programs. In this section, I will discuss how I set up my JDBC initialization code so that it is possible to set default values in the code (usually set up for my development environment) and allow users of my code to simply override the default setup information at runtime. I find the following hierarchy of settings works best for me:

- Setting default JDBC and database setup statically in the code: these values are set for my development environment.
- Reading a program-wide XML configuration file at class load time that sets all program parameters, including JDBC and database configuration information: these values override what is statically defined in the Java source code.
- Checking Java property values at class load time: these values override both XML input file values and values set statically in the Java source code.

This hierarchy of settings works well for me: during development, I simply use the default settings in the source code. During deployment, I use values in an XML configuration file.

Occasionally, I will set Java properties to temporarily override what is in the XML configuration file.

NOTE Because we covered the use of XML configuration files in Solution 10, the example code in this section will only demonstrate setting default development values in the source code and overriding these values from Java properties.

The following code snippet is typical initialization code that I use (taken from the example file `JdbcInitialization.java` in the `S34` directory):

```
public static String DBurl = "jdbc:postgresql://localhost:5432/
db123?user=postgres";
public static String DBdriver = "org.postgresql.Driver";

static {
    /**
     * Check to see if parameters are set to override defaults:
     */
    try {
        DBurl = System.getProperty("DBurl", DBurl);
        DBdriver = System.getProperty("DBdriver", DBdriver);
    } catch (Exception e) {
        e.printStackTrace();
    }
    try {
        Class.forName(DBdriver).newInstance();
    } catch (Exception e) {
        System.err.println("Could not open JDBC driver " +
                           DBdriver);
        e.printStackTrace();
    }
}
```

Notice that while default JDBC configuration data is specified, these values can be easily overridden by using Java properties for property names `DBurl` and `DBdriver`.

NOTE We will redefine this class in Solution 35 (placing the new version in the Java package `S35S36`) to add initialization code to insure that the database tables required for an example application are created if they do not already exist.

Separating JDBC Code from the Rest of Your Application

Even though JDBC code is portable to different database products (once the setup and configuration has been done), I recommend that you encapsulate your JDBC code in separate classes that provide an API for your application to use for all database access. For small projects,

I usually have a single JDBC utility class. I extend the database access API in this class (that is, add new methods) on an as-needed basis. Using the "Extreme Programming" paradigm, I prefer to not write utility code until I need it. For larger projects, I write multiple JDBC utility classes, one for each major component of the system that requires database access.

There are other good alternatives for handling data persistence:

- Free and commercial Java object-oriented databases
- The Java Data Objects (JDO) specification at `www.jcp.org/en/jsr/detail?id=12` (I cover JDO in Solutions 59 and 60)
- Using EJB container managed persistence (see Solution 51)

However, for my JDBC-based applications, I usually prefer a simple approach: write simple (no behavior except for `get/set` methods) data-centric, application-specific classes and separate JDBC-based utility classes to save and load these Java data-centric classes to a database. This simple approach does require extra coding, but I find the resulting implementation to be easy to understand and to maintain. We will use this approach in Solutions 35 and 36 with example data-centric classes `Customer`, `Product`, and `Inventory`.

Use a Database Client While Developing JDBC Applications

While you are developing JDBC-based applications, you should get in the habit of keeping a database client application open on the database that you are using. I provide short SQL tutorials in Solutions 35 and 36 that you should work through using a client application for the database you use for development. You can use a database client to immediately inspect the state of a database before and after running new code.

Unit Testing JDBC Code

I will cover the use of the ant build tool and the JUnit unit testing tool later in this book (Ant, JUnit, and XDoclet). Ant and JUnit should be used by Java developers on all but the smallest projects. Some Java IDEs support ant build files directly.

Assuming that you already use JUnit, I encourage you to write unit tests that use separate test databases, create test tables, and test all aspects of application-specific JDBC utility classes that you use to separate JDBC code from the rest of your application. Automating the testing of your application-specific JDBC code will save you time and effort.

NOTE You can download ant from `ant.apache.org` and download junit from `www.junit.org`. We will look at ant and JUnit in detail later in this book.

SOLUTION 35

Performing Database Updates

PROBLEM You have set up JDBC and created a test database. Now you want to add data to a relational database and modify it.

SOLUTION You will use the standard JDBC APIs to perform database updates, keeping your Java code portable between database products.

I will cover the simpler techniques for creating and modifying data in a database. Later, in Solutions 37 and 38, we will look at advanced techniques for database modifications (batch updates and transactions). I will begin this solution with a brief overview of SQL required for database updates. Then you will extend the database setup code that you used in the last section by insuring that database tables required by your example application are created. Finally, you will define three data-centric example application classes `Customer`, `Product`, and `Inventory` and write a JDBC utility class for saving and loading these objects to a database.

Sample Database

You will use a simple database in Solutions 35 through 39. This database contains three tables: customer, product, and inventory. The customer table uses five columns:

`CustomerID: int`

`Name: varchar`

`Address: varchar`

`Email: varchar`

`Phone: varchar`

The `varchar` data type supports variable length text strings. The product table uses three columns:

- `productID int`
- `name varchar`
- `cost float`

The inventory table uses two columns:

- `productID int`
- `count int`

WARNING This database is inadequate to use to run a business; it is intended only for learning JDBC. In a production system, the inventory count would simply be stored in the product table. (This sample database is not normalized.)

Short SQL Tutorial for Database Updates

I will cover SQL basics here: creating tables in a database, adding rows, modifying rows, and deleting rows. SQL is an expressive language, and I will barely scratch the surface here. I will not cover interactive database creation operations that are database specific. After reading this short SQL tutorial you might also want to read the user manual for the database that you are using.

The following three SQL statements create the three sample database tables that we will be using:

```
CREATE TABLE customer (customerID int PRIMARY KEY, name varchar, address
varchar, email varchar, phone varchar);
CREATE TABLE product (productID int PRIMARY KEY, name varchar, cost float);
CREATE TABLE inventory (productID int PRIMARY KEY, count int);
```

The semicolon is used to end an SQL statement when using a database client application. Note that when you later imbed SQL statements in JDBC calls you will not need the semicolon. SQL is case insensitive, but I sometimes use capital letters to make SQL statements more readable.

All three tables use a unique integer identifier to act as a primary key. A database system will maintain indices on columns that are specified as primary keys. While you can search for information by matching on any column in a database table, this search will be much faster on a column that is a primary key.

In this example, one column in each table is specified to be the primary key. A primary key that contains multiple columns is called a composite primary key. If you want to maintain indices for fast search on other columns, you can explicitly create an index for other columns in a database table.

After creating the three example database tables, you can add data. One way to use SQL for adding a new row of data is to use an expression of the form:

```
insert into <table name> values(…);
```

where integer and floating point values are entered as numbers and any character data is enclosed in single quote marks; for example:

```
insert into customer values(12345, 'Mary Smith',
    '1 Main Street', 'mary@smithcompany.com', '(415)312-0123');
insert into product values(9912, 'widget21', 10.00);
insert into inventory values(9912, 20);
```

Individual fields (or columns) in a row can be modified using the `set` and `where` keywords. The `where` option will select a subset of rows in the database and the `set` option changes the name of a column for the selected rows; for example:

```
update inventory set count=19 where productID=9912;
```

You can delete a row by using the `delete` SQL command with the `where` option to select a subset of rows to delete:

```
delete from customer where customerID=12345;
```

If you leave off the `where` option, all rows in the table will be deleted:

```
delete from customer;
```

Preventing JDBC-Related Memory Leaks

You will be using three JDBC-related classes that you need to free resources for after instances are no longer used:

Connection Opens a client socket interface with a database using a JDBC driver. If your programs create many connections and never close them, it is likely that your database server will eventually run out of available client connections.

Statement A data structure used for both querying and updating a table in a database. Not closing statements will cause memory leaks inside your JVM.

Result Set A data structure used to hold return values from database queries. A result set shares memory with the statement that it is created from, so closing a statement will invalidate a result set. Not closing result sets will probably cause memory leaks inside your JVM.

Creating a database connection has computational overhead and some applications keep database connections open for long periods of time. I prefer the slight loss of efficiency in opening and closing connections as needed to make it less likely to leave unclosed database connections open.

NOTE In "Enterprise JavaBeans (EJBs)," you will see that EJB containers can maintain a pool of available connections and thus eliminate this overhead. Many applications also pool connections—if you do decide to reuse connections in your JDBC-based programs, be sure to close all of them before the program terminates.

I enclose all JDBC calls for querying a database table inside a `try/catch` block using `finally` statements to close connections, statements, and result sets used inside the `try/catch` block. A negative side effect to this careful management of JDBC-related objects is that it is difficult to factor out common code in JDBC application-specific utility classes that perform database queries: you will see later that the utility database query methods in the class `JdbcUtilApis` look "baroque," that is, they tend to have repeated `try/catch/finally` blocks containing similar-looking code. This is because there is no straightforward way to return a valid result set after closing a database statement.

You will see that because database updates return only an integer number of rows changed in the database you can write a single update utility method and reuse it.

Extending the JDBC Initialization Class

I covered JDBC initialization in Solution 34 using the class `JdbcInitialization` in the package `S34`. I will reimplement this class in package `S35S36`, which is used in this solution and Solutions 36 through 39 to also insure that the three example database tables that we need are created. The new code for insuring that these tables are created uses the following pattern: try to do a query on a table (covered in Solution 36 in some detail); if an exception is thrown, assume that the table does not exist and create it. Note that in general, trying to re-create a database table that already exists does no harm, but this test saves the effort if the table can be shown to exist. We will look at the creation code for table customer (the code for the other two tables is similar):

```
Connection conn = null;
Statement stmt = null;
try {
    conn = DriverManager.getConnection(DBurl);
    stmt = conn.createStatement();
    stmt.executeQuery(
          "select * from customer where customerID=-1");
} catch (Exception any) {
    /**
     * The query failed on error, so try to create the table:
     */
    try {
        System.out.println("We probably need to create the"+
           " table 'customer'. Error thrown was: " + any);
        stmt.executeUpdate("create table customer (customerID int PRIMARY KEY,
name varchar, address varchar, email varchar, phone varchar)");
    } catch (Exception e2) {
    }
} finally {
    try {
        stmt.close();
    } catch (Exception ee) {
    }
    try {
        conn.close();
    } catch (Exception ee) {
    }
}
```

If you also create indices for any nonprimary key columns, use a separate call to `stmt.executeUpdate()` for creating indices after the table is created. I will not cover separate indices in this book.

NOTE Why create database tables in application-specific code? I have found that I can save myself a lot of development and deployment time by adding code to create tables if necessary when I perform JDBC setup. Moving to a new platform is as simple as creating a database, changing the database URL (and optionally the username and password information), and then running my application code that will then create required database tables the first time the code is run.

Implementing the *JdbcUtilApis* Application-Specific Utility Class for Database Updates

For the example database containing the customer, product, and inventory database tables, you also implement two data-centric Java classes:

Customer Contains the data represented in a row of the customer table.

Product Contains the data represented in both a row of the product table and an associated row (indexed by a unique product ID) in the inventory table.

These data-centric classes have no behavior except for `get/set` methods. The private data for the `Customer` class is

```
private int customerID;
private String name;
private String address;
private String email;
private String phone;
```

These class variables correspond to the five columns in the customer table. The `Product` class private data is

```
private int productID;
private String name;
private int numberInInventory;
```

These variables correspond to the shared primary index `productID` in the tables product and inventory, the name stored in the product table, and the number of items in inventory stored in the column count in the inventory table.

The classes `Customer` and `Product` will be primarily used in discussing database queries in Solution 36—they are introduced here because this solution and Solution 36 use the same package, `S35S36`.

NOTE The three sample database tables are trivial and serve only demo purposes. The inventory count could have been more properly contained in the product table, but I wanted to give some sense of linked tables. A better but more complicated example might use another table "order" that would be linked to a customer table row and a product table row.

The class `JdbcUtilApis` contains several similar methods for creating and modifying rows in the three sample tables. This class has additional query specific methods that we will look at in Solution 36.

Because database updates return only the number of rows affected in the database, you can define a single update utility method that takes an SQL update statement as an argument:

```
private int doUpdate(String updateSQL) {
    int count = 0;
```

You define references for a connection and a statement outside of the `try` code block so that they can be closed (if they do not have null values) in the `finally` code block:

```
    Connection conn = null;
    Statement stmt = null;
    try {
```

The `Dburl` string (as seen in Solution 34) contains the database name and optionally the database account name and password. This information is used by the driver (loaded during class loading of class `JdbcInitialization`) to create a connection to the database:

```
        conn =
          DriverManager.getConnection(JdbcInitialization.DBurl);
```

A statement is created from the connection. Here I use the statement only once before closing it, but in general, a connection and a statement can be used repetitively for multiple database updates and queries before they are closed:

```
        stmt = conn.createStatement();
```

The method `executeUpdate()` is passed a string that is a valid SQL update command:

```
        count = stmt.executeUpdate(updateSQL);
    } catch (Exception ee) {
        ee.printStackTrace(System.err);
```

The `finally` code block guarantees that I close the statement and connection:

```
    } finally {
        if (stmt != null) {
            try {
                stmt.close();
            } catch (Exception e2) {
            }
        }
```

```
            if (conn != null) {
                try {
                    conn.close();
                } catch (Exception e2) {
                }
            }
        }
        return count;
    }
```

This simple method is used in other update methods in the class `JdbcUtilApis` in order to factor out common JDBC update-specific code. For example, this method is used to add a new row to the product database:

```
    public int addProduct(String name, float cost) {
```

The method `generateRandomKey` creates random keys until a key is found that is not already in use in the database (we will look at the implementation details of this method in Solution 36):

```
        int key = generateRandomKey("product");
```

You call the `doUpdate()` method with a valid SQL update command and the return value is the number of rows affected in the database. You should note that since the column "name" is of type `varchar` (that is, a string type), you need to surround the name value in single quotes:

```
        int rowCount = doUpdate(
             "insert into product VALUES(" + key + ", '" +
             name + "', " + cost + ")");
```

The returned number of rows affected in the database should be 1:

```
        if (rowCount == 1) return key;
        return -1; // error code
    }
```

You can also use the utility method `doUpdate` to delete rows in a database; here I delete a row in the customer database with a specific unique customer ID:

```
    public int deleteCustomer(int customerID) {
        int rowsDeletedCount =
            doUpdate("delete from customer where customerID=" +
                     customerID);
        return rowsDeletedCount;
    }
```

You can also use the SQL `UPDATE/SET` commands to modify the column of a specific row in the inventory database (remember that SQL statements are case insensitive except for string literals, so the capitalization of `UPDATE` and `SET` is just for readability):

```
    public int updateInventory(int productID, int newCount) {
        int rowsModifiedCount =
```

```
        doUpdate("UPDATE inventory SET count=" +
                 newCount + " where productID=" + productID);
    return rowsModifiedCount;
}
```

SOLUTION 36

Performing Database Queries

PROBLEM You need to query a database from your Java application.

SOLUTION You will use the JDBC APIs to query a database.

This solution uses the three example database tables that I used in Solution 35: customer, product, and inventory. This solution also uses the utility class `JdbcUtilApis` (in package `S35S36`) that you saw in Solution 35; here I will cover the utility methods in this class used for database queries.

Short SQL Tutorial for Database Queries

You saw the SQL syntax and examples for database updates in Solution 35. Here I will briefly cover SQL used for querying a database. In general, you will use the `select` command with the `where` option (that you saw in Solution 35) to select a subset of the rows in a database table:

```
select <column name list> from <table name>
       where <match expression>;
```

For example, if you knew that a product-unique key in the database was 99822, you could find the rows in the product and inventory tables using these SQL statements:

```
select * from product where productID=99822;
select name, cost from product where productID=99822;
select count from inventory where productID=99822;
```

The first `select` command used an asterisk for the column name list so all columns of matching rows are returned by the query. The second `select` command only fetches the "name" and "cost" columns from matching rows. The third select command selects a single column "count" from the inventory table.

In these three examples, the `where` clause matched a numeric value (in this case 99822). If the `where` clause tested the value of a column with character data (for example, `varchar`), then the test string would be enclosed in single quotes.

NOTE I am only covering sufficient SQL for using to learn JDBC. You can find many tutorials on the Web by searching for "SQL tutorial."

Implementing the *JdbcUtilApis* Application-Specific Utility Class for Database Queries

You looked at the class `JdbcUtilApis` in Solution 35 when I covered JDBC programming techniques for adding rows, deleting rows, and updating column values in a database. I will use the same class here to cover the JDBC programming techniques for querying database tables.

Because database queries using JDBC return instances of the class `ResultSet` that share data with JDBC `Statement` objects, you cannot simply write a query utility method and reuse it. As a result, the query utility methods in the class `JdbcUtilApis` must all contain connection setup, statement creation, query code, and JDBC object cleanup code. You will look at one example for populating the data of an instance of the class `Customer`. The utility methods for querying the sample database are similar. You first create an "empty" customer object and define references for JDBC as result set, connection, and statement:

```
public Customer getCustomerData(int customerID) {
    Customer customer = new Customer();
    ResultSet rs = null;
    Connection conn = null;
    Statement stmt = null;
```

You then wrap all JDBC-related calls inside a `try/catch/finally` block so that you can guarantee that the JDBC result set, connection, and statement objects get closed properly:

```
    try {
        conn =
          DriverManager.getConnection(JdbcInitialization.DBurl);
        stmt = conn.createStatement();
```

When you perform the SQL query, you do not use "*" for the column selection list because you do not need all columns in the table:

```
        rs = stmt.executeQuery("select name, address, email, phone from customer
where customerID=" + customerID);
```

The result set method `next()` makes the next selected row available and returns Boolean true if another row is available. Here, because you are querying using a primary key, you know that you will get either zero or one row back, so a simple `if` test checking the value of the method `next()` is okay. In the general case where many rows might be returned, you would use a `while` loop instead:

```
        if (rs.next()) {
            customer.setCustomerID(customerID);
```

The `ResultSet` class provides methods for retrieving column values in a row supporting many Java types like `String`, `int`, `float`, and so on. These "`get`" methods take either an integer column index (based on the returned result set, not the original columns in the database), or a string column name. It is much more efficient to use integer indices because the use of string column names requires additional metadata access (see Solution 39). The column indices start with the value 1, not 0:

```
customer.setName(rs.getString(1));
            customer.setAddress(rs.getString(2));
            customer.setEmail(rs.getString(3));
            customer.setPhone(rs.getString(4));
        }
    } catch (Exception ee) {
        ee.printStackTrace(System.err);
```

The `finally` block must close the result set, statement, and database connection to avoid both crashing the database server (if it runs out of pooled connections) and creating allocated memory in the JVM that cannot be garbage collected:

```
    } finally {
        if (rs != null) {
            try {
                rs.close();
            } catch (Exception e2) {
            }
        }
        if (stmt != null) {
            try {
                stmt.close();
            } catch (Exception e2) {
            }
        }
        if (conn != null) {
            try {
                conn.close();
            } catch (Exception e2) {
            }
        }
    }
    return customer;
}
```

The other query methods in the class `JdbcUtilApis` are very similar to this method—I will not cover the other code except for showing the JDBC query code in the method `getProduct`; this code is interesting in that it uses data from two tables to fill in the data for an instance of class `Product`:

```
rs = stmt.executeQuery(
  "select name from product where productID=" + productID);
if (rs.next()) {
     product.setProductID(productID);
     product.setName(rs.getString(1));
}
rs.close();
rs = stmt.executeQuery(
  "select count from inventory where productID=" + productID);
if (rs.next()) {
     product.setNumberInInventory(rs.getInt(1));
}
```

Here, I closed the first result set; the second result set will be closed in the `finally` code block.

NOTE While you can refer to column names by name, it is much more efficient to reference them by integer index. This avoids a metadata access for the database. I will cover the metadata APIs in Solution 39.

SOLUTION 37

Performing Batch Updates

PROBLEM You want to efficiently make batch updates to a database.

SOLUTION You will use JDBC version 2 features for prepared statements and batch updates.

Performing batch updates in this solution and using transactions (in Solution 38) is similar to the JDBC update examples seen in Solution 35. Here, you will look at the differences required for batch updates—you can read the source code to the full example in the class `BatchUpdateExample` in the package `S37`. Performing batch updates is often done using transactions, so the material in this solution is complementary to Solution 38. The JDBC 2 specification added an API method `addBatch()` to maintain a list of operations for JDBC classes `Statement`, `PreparedStatement`, and `CallableStatement`.

Here, you will use this new API only with the `Statement` class. There are two modes for using batch updates: turning auto commit off, or leaving auto commit on (the default for JDBC). In the following code snippet, the calls to `setAutoCommit(false)` and `commit()` are commented out so any batch updates that occur before an error will affect the database:

```
Connection conn = null;
Statement stmt = null;
try {
```

Initialize JDBC, clear all data from test database tables, and create a connection and statement:

```
    new S35S36.JdbcInitialization();
    (new S35S36.JdbcUtilApis()).removeAllData();
    conn = DriverManager.getConnection(
                 S35S36.JdbcInitialization.DBurl);
    stmt = conn.createStatement();
```

If you wanted to use transactions in this example, you would uncomment the following line of code:

```
    //conn.setAutoCommit(false);
```

The argument for `addBatch()` is a valid SQL update statement (like you use when calling `executeUpdate`). This SQL update is stored and not yet performed:

```
    stmt.addBatch("insert into product values (10001, 'Anti-virus program',
29.95)");
    stmt.addBatch("insert into product values (10002, 'Disk-Defrag program',
39.95)");
```

You may want to experiment with the example program by uncommenting out the following statement that causes the execute batch command (seen later in this code snippet) to throw an exception while processing this illegal SQL update request (the table `UNKNOWN_TABLE` is not in the example database):

```
    // test: throw an exception on purpose:
    //stmt.addBatch("insert into UNKNOWN_TABLE values (1,2,3)");
    stmt.addBatch("insert into product values (10003, 'Undelete-File program',
19.95)");
```

The method `executeBatch()` executes in order all stored SQL update requests and returns an `int[]` array indicating how many rows in the database were affected by each individual SQL update request:

```
    int[] rowsChanged = stmt.executeBatch();
    for (int i = 0; i < rowsChanged.length; i++) {
        System.out.println(" rows changed: " + rowsChanged[i]);
    }
```

```
        //conn.commit();
    } catch (Exception batchOrSqlException) {
        System.out.println("Error during batch update: " +
                           batchOrSqlException);
```

As always, you should use code to close open JDBC objects:

```
    } finally {
        if (stmt != null) {
            try {
                stmt.close();
            } catch (Exception e) {
            }
        }
        if (conn != null) {
            try {
                conn.close();
            } catch (Exception e) {
            }
        }
    }
```

This example is contrived in the sense that batch updates are usually used with transactions. However, it is useful for you to experiment with this example program to see the effect of errors during batch updates.

SOLUTION 38

Using Transactions to Insure Data Integrity

PROBLEM You need to need to make a series of associated updates to a database. If any update fails, you do not want any of the updates to affect the database.

SOLUTION You will use the JDBC transaction APIs.

Frequently you need to make a series of associated updates to a database. To maintain the integrity of the database, it is often mandatory to make a set of updates do all or nothing, that is, all of the updates must work or none should affect the state of the database. The example for this solution is very similar to the batch update example seen in Solution 37. The difference is that if any failures occurred during the batch updates, the updates that were already performed are kept in the database. In the example for this solution in the class `TransactionExample`, if any errors occur, the database will roll back to its initial state.

Using JDBC Transactions

The example program for this solution is `TransactionExample.java` in the `S38` directory. This program is nearly identical to the example program in Solution 37, except that the two statements to enable transaction support are not commented out and I use the `rollback()` method. The following code snippet shows transaction support enabled (I will discuss the error handling code later—the `finally` code block will use the `rollback()` method):

```
conn = DriverManager.getConnection(JdbcInitialization.DBurl);
stmt = conn.createStatement();
```

You enable transaction support by turning off `AutoCommit`:

```
conn.setAutoCommit(false);
stmt.addBatch("insert into product values (10001, 'Anti-virus program',
29.95)");
stmt.addBatch("insert into product values (10002, 'Disk-Defrag program',
39.95)");
// test: throw an exception on purpose:
stmt.addBatch("insert into UNKNOWN_TABLE values (1, 2, 3)");
stmt.addBatch("insert into product values (10003, 'Undelete-File program',
19.95)");
```

Execute the batched updates:

```
int[] rowsChanged = stmt.executeBatch();
```

If there have been no errors, then you can commit transactions:

```
conn.commit();
```

If any errors occur, the example program closes the JDBC objects as usual but first uses the `rollback()` method:

```
} catch (Exception batchOrSqlException) {
    System.out.println("Error during batch update: " +
                       batchOrSqlException);
    try {
        conn.rollback();
    } catch (Exception sqle) {
        System.out.println("Error during update rollback: "
                           + sqle);
    }
} finally {
    if (stmt != null) {
        try {
```

```
                stmt.close();
            } catch (Exception e) {
            }
        }
        if (conn != null) {
            try {
                conn.close();
            } catch (Exception e) {
            }
        }
    }
```

Using transactions greatly simplifies the logic in database applications. If a database did not support transactions, you would have to make updates one at a time and record the updates yourself. If any errors occurred, you would have to "undo" the database updates that occurred before the error. Worse, if your application program crashed, updates that occurred before the error would permanently affect the state of the database.

NOTE You will see a powerful combination in Solution 53: combining transaction support for both JDBC and Java Messaging System (JMS) guaranteed delivery messages. You can combine in one transaction database updates with guaranteed message delivery notification to other processes.

SOLUTION **39**

Dynamic Database Exploration Using the Metadata API

PROBLEM You want to be able to explore available tables and schema for the tables in a relational database.

SOLUTION You will use the JDBC metadata APIs.

As a developer, you usually either design a database with your application or you build your applications using an existing database. In either of these two development scenarios, you know the tables in a database and the formats of the tables.

For some applications, however, it can be useful to be able to write JDBC-based applications that can explore available databases; for example, to try to find all tables with a column named "customer" or "email".

The example Java program for this solution is the file `MetadataExmaple.java` in the `S39` package. You will get two types of metadata: from an open connection and from a result set after initializing a database connection. Start by opening a database connection:

```
new S35S36.JdbcInitialization();
Connection conn =
  DriverManager.getConnection(S35S36.JdbcInitialization.DBurl);
Statement stmt = conn.createStatement();
```

I assume that the `DBurl` is still set for the database `"test"`. Then you can get the database-specific metadata from the open connection:

```
DatabaseMetaData metaData = conn.getMetaData();
```

`DatabaseMetaData` is an interface. According to the JDBC specification, the `Connection` class must provide a method `getMetaData()` for returning a nonabstract class instance that implements the `DatabaseMetaData` interface. For your specific database and JDBC implementation, try printing the return value of the `getMetaData()` method; for example, this statement:

```
System.out.println("Concrete DatabaseMetaData class: " + conn.getMetaData());
```

prints out:

```
Concrete DatabaseMetaData class: org.postgresql.jdbc2.DatabaseMetaData@bb7465
```

You can see that I am using the `PostgreSQL` database with a version 2 JDBC driver. The following method call will return a result set containing all of the table names and data associated with the `"test"` database:

```
metaData.getTables("test", null, null, null)
```

The four arguments for the *`getTables()`* method are as follows:

String catalogName The catalog name is the name of a database. In this book, we are using a local database named `"test"`.

String schemaMatchPattern This is a matching pattern for database schema. A null value indicates not to use this pattern in finding tables in the database. An empty string (`""`) indicates to match all tables with no schema defined.

String tableNamePattern If null, all tables (including index tables) are matched. If I know the name of a table (for example, "customer"), I sometimes specify a table name pattern to get just the information for the table that I am interested in.

String tableTypePattern If null, this matches on all table types. Typical types are "INDEX" and "TABLE".

The example program contains a utility method for printing out the column names and column data type for a specific database metadata, database, and table combination:

```
public static void printTableColumns(DatabaseMetaData metaData,
                                     String database,
                                     String table)
        throws Exception {
    ResultSet rs = metaData.getColumns(database, null,
                                       table, null);
    ResultSetMetaData rsMetaData = rs.getMetaData();
    int num = rsMetaData.getColumnCount();
    System.out.println("\nDatabase: " + database + "\ttable: " +
                       table + "\nColumn names and types:");
    while (rs.next()) {
        String columnName = rs.getString(4); // name in column 4
        String typeName = rs.getString(6);   // type in column 6
        System.out.println("\t" + columnName + "\t" + typeName);
    }
}
```

You may be wondering how I knew that the fourth column of the result set metadata was the column name, and the sixth column was the type name. This information is in the JDBC specification, but I found it by printing out the column names and row values for the result set metadata for all three example tables that we have been using. I used the method `printResultSet()` in the example class `MetadataExample` to print out all available metadata information for the example table:

```
public static void printResultSet(String title, ResultSet rs) {
System.out.println("\nResult Set: " + title + "\n");
    try {
        ResultSetMetaData rsMetaData = rs.getMetaData();
        int num = rsMetaData.getColumnCount();
        // print column names:
        for (int i = 0; i < num; i++) {
            String columnName = rsMetaData.getColumnName(i + 1);
            System.out.print("\t" + columnName);
        }
        System.out.println();
        while (rs.next()) {
            System.out.print("new row : ");
            for (int i = 0; i < num; i++) {
                String s = rs.getString(i + 1);
                System.out.print(s + "\t");
            }
```

```
                System.out.println();
            }
        } catch (Exception e) {
            e.printStackTrace();
        }
    }
```

This method is called several times in the public static method `main` in the example program; you are invited to run the example program, look at the output, and experiment with the metadata APIs that I have discussed here. If you look at the full API available in the interface `ResultSetMetaData`, you will see that I have just scratched the surface. However, I have covered the subset of the metadata APIs that I have found useful in my own programs.

NOTE Suggested project: write a database browser client that uses the metadata APIs. Your browser could prompt for a database name and then display all tables and table schema information for the specified database.

Java Servlets

SOLUTION 40

Handling Browser Requests

PROBLEM You want to get started using Java Servlets, starting with handling simple requests.

SOLUTION I will give you quick instructions for setting up the Tomcat servlet/JSP container and web server and cover the basics of writing servlets.

Servlets are web application–specific Java classes that rely on a servlet container to perform the work of handling network connections, preparing request data for a servlet, and returning an output data stream written by a servlet to a remote client (typically a web browser). I will begin this solution with a short section of advice on setting up the Tomcat servlet/JSP container and web server. You will be using Tomcat (or another server of your choice) in Solutions 40 through 49. I will then cover the basics of handling browser requests in servlets.

NOTE The source code for the examples for Solutions 40 through 44 can be found in the `src` directory in the ZIP file `part10.zip`. In order to install these servlet examples, copy this ZIP file to your Tomcat `webapps` directory and unzip the file there. This will create subdirectories in the `webapps` directory named `S40`, `S41`, `S42`, `S43`, and `S44`.

Setting Up Tomcat

The servlet examples in this book were written and tested using Tomcat version 4.1.x. You should get the latest stable release of Tomcat and install Tomcat following the directions provided on the Tomcat website: `jakarta.apache.org/tomcat`. In the following discussion, I will use TOMCAT (spelled in all capital letters) to indicate the directory path where Tomcat is installed; for example, I will refer to `TOMCAT/bin` as the full file directory path to the Tomcat bin subdirectory.

NOTE The servlet/JSP container in the latest version of Tomcat is called Catalina, so some people refer to the installation directory as CATALINA.

After you have installed Tomcat, you will see nine directories:

bin Contains the scripts to start Tomcat under Windows, Linux, and Unix.

common Contains shared code as Java JAR files.

conf Contains configuration files for Tomcat.

logs Contains runtime output logs. Files starting with "Catalina" will contain error messages and any debug printout in your servlets.

server Contains compiled JAR files to implement Tomcat and contains a `webapps` directory for the manager and admin webapps.

shared Contains (initially empty) subdirectories code shared among different web applications.

temp Contains temporary files.

webapps The directory where you install new directories for your own web applications.

work A working directory for Tomcat. For example, when the Tomcat JSP container compiles your JSP files into Java source files, it will place compiled versions in this directory.

For the purposes of this discussion, we are only concerned with the `bin`, `logs`, and `webapps` directories.

NOTE Tomcat's default installation provides servlet and JSP examples in the `webapps` directory. By copying the `config/server-noexamples.xml.config` over the file `src/server.xml`, you can disable the examples. By editing the `tomcat-users.xml` file, you can enable a management user to allow dynamic deployment of web applications; this is very useful for using special ant tasks for auto-deploying web applications as part of the ant build process. You can read the detailed Tomcat documentation for these options—we will use Tomcat "as is" after the normal installation.

To start Tomcat, change directory to `TOMCAT/bin` and use one of two startup scripts:

startup Starts Tomcat as a background process; it will run until you run the shutdown script.

catalina Starts Tomcat in the foreground. One advantage of running Tomcat in the foreground is that printout appears in the same command window where you run Tomcat. You stop Tomcat by typing Control-C in this window.

A Demo Servlet That Handles Browser Request from Parameters

I will show you a complete servlet example that is configured to run with Tomcat. You will look at both the Java code for the servlet and the required `web.xml` deployment file. There are two types of HTTP request types that we will handle in our demo servlet: GET and POST. GET requests are simpler; all data is encoded in a URL, for example:

http://localhost:8080/S40

http://localhost:8080/S40?x=2&y=1122

http://localhost:8080/S40?printdate

All three of these URLs refer to the demo servlet for this solution deployed on Tomcat running on localhost (that is, your development computer). POST requests use an open socket connection to pass both header and data to a web server. The Tomcat web server and servlet container handles the details of both GET and POST requests.

You will see later how to specify the context name for a servlet when you look at the `web.xml` file for this servlet. The first example URL encoded GET request just listed runs the servlet with no parameters. The second URL passes two parameters to the servlet: parameter *x* has the value 2 and parameter *y* has the value 1122. The third URL has the parameter ***`printdate`*** that has no value. I will show you how to access these parameters in a servlet.

NOTE I assume that you have unzipped the file `part10.zip` in your `TOMCAT/webappsdirectory`, creating subdirectories `TOMCAT/webapps/S40`, etc. The source for the demo applet is in the file `TOMCAT/webapps/S40/WEB-INF/classes`. I use the ant build tool for my development and keep my web application source code separate from the deployed files. However, the simplest possible setup for development is to simply place the Java source code for servlets in the deployment directory and edit and compile the servlet there. Every time you recompile the servlet, restart Tomcat.

I list most of the file `DemoServlet.java` here with explanations of the code as required. Start by including both the servlet specific classes, the `PrintWriter` class, and the `Enumeration` class:

```
import javax.servlet.http.HttpServlet;
import javax.servlet.http.HttpServletRequest;
import javax.servlet.http.HttpServletResponse;
import javax.servlet.ServletException;
import java.io.PrintWriter;
import java.util.Enumeration;
import java.util.Date;
public class DemoServlet extends HttpServlet {
```

The Tomcat servlet container does the work for you of handling both GET and POST requests. Tomcat will call `doGet()` for GET HTTP requests and `doPost()` for POST requests. Here you can handle both types of requests with the same method, `doPost()`. Method `doGet()` simply calls `doPost()` with the servlet request and response arguments passed to it by the Tomcat servlet container:

```
    public void doGet(HttpServletRequest req,
                      HttpServletResponse res)
          throws ServletException {
        doPost(req, res);
    }
```

In the demo servlet, the following listed method handles all requests. The first argument is a request object that contains session data, parameters and values, etc. In this example, you will only use parameters stored in the request object. The second argument is a response object.

Response objects contain the output stream for writing back to the clients' remote browser and have methods for setting content type, redirecting to a different URL, etc.

```
public void doPost(HttpServletRequest req,
                   HttpServletResponse res)
    throws ServletException {
```

You use the `getWriter()` method on the response object to get a print stream for writing data back to the remote web browser client:

```
PrintWriter out = null;
try {
    out = res.getWriter();
} catch (Exception e2) {
    e2.printStackTrace();
}
```

You set the content type for the response object to HTML text. Other possibilities are XML and plain text. For example, I sometimes set the response type to XML when the client is a PDA device and expects XML data for a client side application. In this book, we will only use HTML output.

```
res.setContentType("text/html");
```

You can now use the output stream (that is the object out) to write HTML:

```
out.println(
  "<html><head><title>Demo Applet</title></head><body>");
out.println("<h2>Demo Applet</h2>");
```

In Solution 41, you will use parameters to get data that users have entered in web forms. Here you will simply print out all parameter names and values and also look for two special cases: if a parameter is *printdate*, then you will write out HTML to show the current date, and if there are parameters *x* and *y* with numeric values, you will print out the sum to the HTML output stream:

```
Enumeration enum = req.getParameterNames();
while (enum.hasMoreElements()) {
     String name = (String) enum.nextElement();
     String value = (String) req.getParameter(name);
```

You can use the `println()` method on the output stream object to write data back to the client web browser:

```
     out.println("<h4>Parameter=" + name + " value=" +
                 value + "</h4>");
}
if (req.getParameter("x") != null &&
    req.getParameter("y") != null) {
     try {
         float x=Float.parseFloat(req.getParameter("x"));
```

```
                float y=Float.parseFloat(req.getParameter("y"));
                float sum = x + y;
                out.println("<p>" + x + " + " + y + " = " +
                            sum + "</p>");
            } catch (Exception ee) {
                ee.printStackTrace();
            }
}
```

You can print the current date to the output stream if the parameter *printdate* is defined:

```
        if (req.getParameter("printdate") != null) {
            out.println("<p>Current date is " + new Date() +
                        "</p>");
        }

        return;
    }
}
```

For example, typing this URL in my web browser:

`http://localhost:8080/S40?x=2&y=1122&printdate=yes`

produced the following output seen in my web browser:

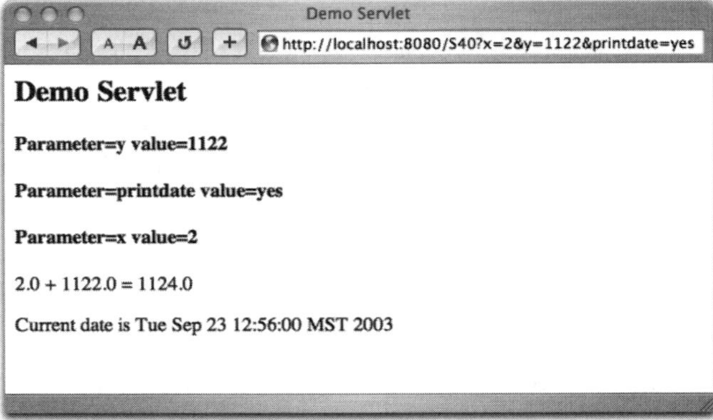

Deploying the Demo Servlet to Tomcat

I assume that you have unzipped the file `part10.zip` in your TOMCAT/webapps directory. This deploys the demo servlet (after restarting Tomcat), so I will explain the purpose of the files in `TOMCAT/webapps/S40` directory and its subdirectories:

S40/ Top-level directory for the Solution 40 demo servlet. If any plain HTML files were used with this servlet, they would be placed in this directory.

S40/WEB-INF/ Contains compiled servlet class file, library JAR files, and the `web.xml` configuration file.

S40/WEB-INF/classes/ Contains both the source code and compiled class file for the servlet.

S40/WEB-INF/lib/ This directory is empty in this example, but if your servlet required library JAR files, you would place the JAR files here.

S40/WEB-INF/web.xml Servlet configuration file.

The following code snippet shows the contents of the `web.xml` configuration file:

```
<?xml version="1.0" encoding="ISO-8859-1"?>

<!DOCTYPE web-app
    PUBLIC "-//Sun Microsystems, Inc.//DTD Web Application 2.3//EN"
    "http://java.sun.com/dtd/web-app_2_3.dtd">

<web-app>
 <servlet>
  <servlet-name>DemoServlet</servlet-name>
   <servlet-class>DemoServlet</servlet-class>
  </servlet>

  <servlet-mapping>
      <servlet-name>DemoServlet</servlet-name>
      <url-pattern>/</url-pattern>
  </servlet-mapping>
</web-app>
```

The `web.xml` configuration files uses a DTD and must have elements in the correct order. All `<servlet>` elements appear first in the configuration file followed by the `<servlet-mapping>` elements. The `<servlet>` elements are used, one per servlet (in this example, I have only defined one servlet—many web applications use multiple servlets) to set a symbolic name for the servlet and the name of the Java class that implements the servlet. The `<servlet-mapping>` element is optional and is used to assign a URL pattern relative to the top-level base URL for the web application. Because this demo servlet is in the `webapps` subdirectory `S40`, the base URL (that is, the context) for this web application will have the form:

```
http://<server>:<port>/S40
```

The servlet mapping specifies that the URL pattern for this servlet is `/`, so assuming that you are accessing Tomcat running on your local development computer, the URL for accessing the demo servlet would be

```
http://localhost:8080/S40
```

If, for example, the URL pattern was */demo* instead of */*, then you would use the following URL to access the servlet:

```
http://localhost:8080/S40/demo
```

NOTE Why study servlets at all when most developers prefer Java Server Pages (JSPs)? Because JSPs are based on servlet technology and an understanding of servlets is important to effectively using JSPs. There are also some applications where servlets make more sense than JSPs; for example, when you want to use work threads in web services. Later, in Solution 49, you will use the struts web application framework, which uses a controller servlet to implement a Model View Controller architecture.

Lifecycle of Servlets

The servlet container is responsible for loading the compiled code for a servlet as required. If there is a request for a servlet that is not already loaded, the servlet container uses a custom class loader to load the compiled code before calling either the `doGet()` or `doPost()` methods. This is shown in the following illustration:

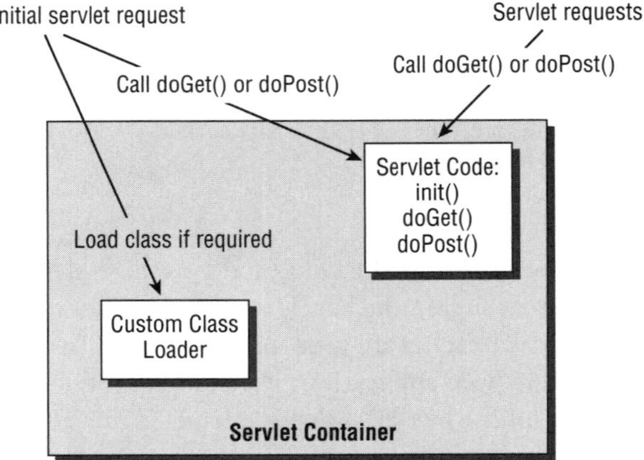

After a servlet is loaded, the servlet container creates request and response objects and calls `doGet()` or `doPost()`. An output stream for writing data back to the client browser is contained in the response object. Although I did not include this in the example servlet, you can add a custom `destroy()` method to your servlet classes that can perform any "tear down" activities when the servlet container frees a servlet object.

SOLUTION 41

Handling Form Data

PROBLEM You want to allow a user to enter data on a web form that your web application will process and then return information to the user.

SOLUTION You will implement a servlet that presents a text input field. When the user enters text, your servlet processes the text and refreshes the client web browser display showing both the original entry form followed by the output from your web application.

You learned how to use parameters passed to a servlet in Solution 40. You will build on this knowledge to learn how to handle web forms in this solution. Solution 46 will show an alternative or handling web forms using Java Server Pages (JSPs).

In the demo servlet `FormServlet` that I present in this solution, you will place code for displaying an HTML form in the servlet. Another good alternative is to write a static HTML page that contains a HTML form that has a target URL that is a form-handling servlet. Although I assume that you know HTML, I will review how to set up HTML forms. The directory `S41` contains the file `form.html` that shows an example form:

```
<html>
<HEAD>
        <TITLE>Demo HTML Form Page</TITLE>
</HEAD>
<body>

<h2>Enter test data and select 'submit data'</h2>

<FORM action="/S40" method="get">
  <INPUT TYPE="text" NAME="query" size="60" />
  <BR />
  <INPUT TYPE="submit" NAME="doit" VALUE="submit data" />
  <INPUT TYPE="HIDDEN" NAME="product" VALUE="0" />
</FORM>

</body>
</html>
```

The form action is the target URL that handles the form data. Here, you have three input form items: an input text field named `query`, a submit button named `doit`, and a hidden input item. Hidden inputs are sometimes used to pass data to another web page when you do not want the user to see the data. Note, however, that a user can always "view source" on a web page and see any hidden input elements.

If this form action specified the demo servlet in Solution 40 that echoes all parameters, you would see, assuming that the user typed "test 1 2 3" in the text field:

```
Parameter=product value=0
Parameter=query value=test 1 2 3
Parameter=doit value=submit data
```

The HTML form had a hidden input product with a value of 0. When your web applications dynamically generate HTML forms for users, using hidden input tags is a useful way to pass state information to a servlet (you will also look at using session data in Solution 43). The value of the input text field shows as "test 1 2 3" because that is what I typed into my web browser when running this test.

The `FormServlet` example displays a form (like the one you just saw in the static `form.html` example) and if the text input field contains text, processes this text using an example library.

NOTE The processing performed by `FormServlet` is trivial—I use a library in `S41/WEB-INF/lib/str.jar` to show you how to use external Java utility classes in your servlets.

The example servlet in this solution is identical to the one in Solution 40 except for the class name and the definition of the `doPost()` method, so I will only list the `doPost()` method here:

```
public void doPost(HttpServletRequest req,
                   HttpServletResponse res)
       throws ServletException {
    PrintWriter out = null;
    try {
        out = res.getWriter();
    } catch (Exception e2) {
    }
    res.setContentType("text/html");
    out.println(
      "<html><head><title>Form Applet</title></head><body>");
    out.println(
      "<h2>Enter test data and select 'submit data'</h2>");
```

You write out the data entry form for the user:

```
    out.println("<FORM action=\"/S41/form\" method=\"POST\">");
    out.println("  <INPUT TYPE=\"text\" NAME=\"query\" " +
                " size=\"60\" />");
```

```
        out.println("  <BR />");
        out.println("  <INPUT TYPE=\"submit\" NAME=\"doit\" " +
                    " VALUE=\"submit data\" />");
        out.println("  <INPUT TYPE=\"HIDDEN\" NAME=\"product\"" +
                    " VALUE=\"0\" />");
        out.println("</FORM>");
```

You get the text query text, and if the user typed anything into this text input field, you pass the text string to the method `UP()` in class `Str` (in the library for this example in `S41/WEB-INF/lib`) and write the returned string to the web page:

```
        String query = req.getParameter("query");
        if (query != null && query.length() > 0) {
            String s = demo.Str.UP(query);
            out.println("<p>query string converted to upper case: " +
                        s + "</p>");
        }
        out.println("</body>");
        out.println("</HTML>");
        return;
    }
```

The example library source code and JAR file can be found in the `S41/WEB-INF/lib` directory and subdirectories. You can look at the code—I will not discuss it here.

The entry form in Solution 40 used a GET request. In the `FormServlet`, I used a POST request to avoid seeing all the parameters in the URL for the page. The following screen shot shows the example servlet *FormServlet*:

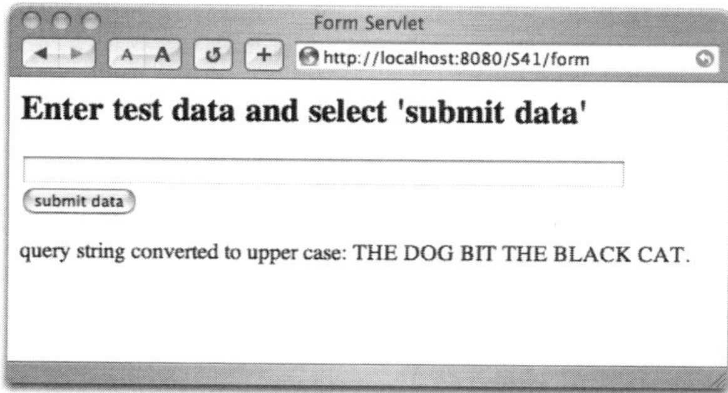

NOTE Notice how your web applications look tidier when the user does not see the parameters encoded in the URL. I use GET requests during development in order to see all parameters in the URL field of my browser, and then I switch to POST requests after testing my web applications.

SOLUTION 42

Performing Custom Servlet Initialization

PROBLEM You want to take a Java application and publish it as a web application. Your application has a long startup time.

SOLUTION You will use a servlet initialization method to perform up-front initialization before clients connect to your servlet. The servlet initialization method will use a separate work thread.

I will show you two useful techniques in this solution: using a thread in a servlet and using an initialization method. The `PrimeServlet` example allows you to enter an integer in a web form and then prints out whether this is a prime number or not. A utility library that I wrote provides the class `CheckPrime` in the package primes. This class needs to precalculate a large array of prime numbers. This library is located in `S42/WEB-INF/lib`.

NOTE The algorithm that you use for testing a number for being prime is simple: you precalculate the list of starting prime numbers (skipping `1`): `2`, `3`, `5`, `7`, `11`, `13`, `17`, etc. Then, you consider any number to be prime if it is not evenly divisible by any of the precalculated prime numbers. This check fails if the number you are testing is greater than the square of the largest prime number that you precalculate.

The servlet initialization method will use a separate thread to precalculate the starting list of prime numbers. This is important to allow the servlet container and servlet to start promptly without waiting for the cache of starting prime numbers to be calculated.

Implementing the Prime Number Servlet

The `PrimeServlet` lets you type in numbers and then tells you if the number is a prime number. If the number is not a prime number, then a prime factor for the number is printed out. The `PrimeServlet` looks similar to the `FormServlet` seen in Solution 41, with the following changes:

You implement a servlet `init()` method that starts a separate work thread.

The work thread creates an instance of the `CheckPrime` class. The class constructor for the `CheckPrime` class takes a while to run because it caches the first 5000 prime numbers.

When handling the form data, you first check to see if the reference to the instance of `CheckPrime` is not null and that the cache in this object is ready for use.

The following code snippet shows the `PrimeServlet` class definition:

```
public class PrimeServlet extends HttpServlet {

    public void doGet(HttpServletRequest req,
                      HttpServletResponse res)
        throws ServletException {
      doPost(req, res);
    }

    public void doPost(HttpServletRequest req,
                       HttpServletResponse res)
        throws ServletException {
      PrintWriter out = null;
      try {
          out = res.getWriter();
      } catch (Exception e2) {
      }
      res.setContentType("text/html");
```

You need to output the HTML to implement a prime number query form:

```
      out.println("<html><head><title>Prime Servlet</title>" +
                  "</head><body>");
      out.println(
        "<h2>Enter test data and select 'submit data'</h2>");
      // print out the HTML FORM to the output stream:
      out.println(
        "<FORM action=\"/S42/prime\" method=\"POST\">");
      out.println(
        " <INPUT TYPE=\"text\" NAME=\"query\" size=\"60\" />");
      out.println("  <BR />");
      out.println("  <INPUT TYPE=\"submit\" NAME=\"doit\"" +
                  " VALUE=\"check prime\" />");
      out.println("</FORM>");

      String query = req.getParameter("query");
```

You need to check that the text form item does contain text:

```
      if (query != null && query.length() > 0) {
          try {
```

The following statement will throw an error on an incorrect number format:

```
              long number = Long.parseLong(query);
```

Because a separate work thread is initializing the prime cache, you must first check if the caching of prime numbers is complete:

```
                if (checkPrime==null ||
                    checkPrime.cacheReady() == false) {
                    out.println("<h2>Prime Number Cache is not" +
                                " initialized - try again</h2>");
                } else {
```

Because the caching of prime numbers is complete, you can test to see if the number that the user types in is a prime number:

```
                    long primeFactor = checkPrime.check(number);
                    if (primeFactor == 0) {
                        out.println("<h2>" + number +
                                    " is a prime number</h2>");
                    } else {
                        out.println("<h2>" + number +
                                    " is a not prime number. " +
                                    "A prime factor is " +
                                    primeFactor + "</h2>");
                    }
                }
            } catch (Exception ee) {
```

Note that if the user types in an illegal number format, they will see an error like this on the returned web form page:

Servlet error: java.lang.NumberFormatException: For input string: "12a34".

```
                out.println("<p>Servlet error: " + ee + "</p>");
            }
        }
        out.println("</body>");
        out.println("</HTML>");
        return;
    }
```

The reference to an instance of the class `CheckPrime` is initially `null`—you want to create an instance inside the work thread to avoid blocking the creation of this servlet:

```
    primes.CheckPrime checkPrime = null;
```

The servlet `init()` method creates an instance of the inner thread work class and then immediately returns. Note that the servlet container calls the `init()` method so that a servlet can perform application-specific initialization:

```
    public void init(ServletConfig config)
           throws ServletException {
        System.out.println("entering PrimeServlet.init(...)");
        super.init(config);
```

```
        (new CachePrimesThread()).start();
        System.out.println("  leaving with PrimeServlet.init()");
    }
```

The inner class `CachePrimesThread` creates a new instance of the class `CheckPrime` in a separate work thread to avoid blocking the creation of the servlet. Note that if the user tries to test a number for being a prime before this object is done initializing, they'll receive a warning to try again.

```
    class CachePrimesThread extends Thread {
        public void run() {
            checkPrime = new primes.CheckPrime();
            checkPrime.initCache();
        }
    }
}
```

If the user types in a number that is not a prime, this web application prints out a prime factor of the number. The following screen shot shows my web browser while running the prime number checking web application:

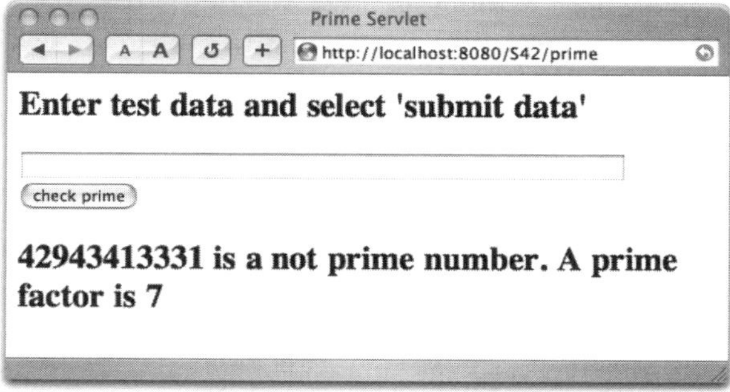

In this example, I typed the number 42943413331 into the text entry form and then clicked the Check Prime submit button on the form.

Configuring the Prime Number Servlet

The `web.xml` file for the `PrimeServlet` is similar to the configuration files in Solutions 40 and 41 except that you tell the Tomcat servlet container to preload this servlet; that is, to initialize the servlet when Tomcat starts up and to not wait until the first user accesses the servlet:

```
<?xml version="1.0" encoding="ISO-8859-1"?>

<!DOCTYPE web-app
    PUBLIC "-//Sun Microsystems, Inc.//DTD Web Application 2.3//EN"
    "http://java.sun.com/dtd/web-app_2_3.dtd">
```

```
<web-app>
 <servlet>
  <servlet-name>PrimeServlet</servlet-name>
   <servlet-class>PrimeServlet</servlet-class>
   <load-on-startup> 1 </load-on-startup>
  </servlet>

  <servlet-mapping>
      <servlet-name>PrimeServlet</servlet-name>
      <url-pattern>/prime</url-pattern>
  </servlet-mapping>
</web-app>
```

NOTE In the last section of Solution 40, I discussed the life cycle of servlets. Because the `web.xml` file for the `PrimeServlet` web application specified the "load at startup" option, the servlet container will load this class and call its `init()` method as soon as the servlet container is started.

This example servlet shows a common implementation pattern: you have a Java application class (in this example, `CheckPrime`) that you wish to "publish" as a web application. You design a web input form to provide the API of your application class with required parameters, call the API method of your class, and display the results on the client web browser.

NOTE For my work, if the Java application that I want to "publish" as a web application is large with a long initialization process, I almost always use a servlet to publish it and use the servlet's `init()` method to initialize my application. However, if my Java applications are implemented as simple JavaBeans with no long initialization process, then I use JSPs with JavaBeans, as you will see in Solution 47.

SOLUTION 43

Using Cookies and Session Data for Personalizing a Website

PROBLEM You want users of your web applications to have a personalized experience based on user profiles and previous interactions with your site.

SOLUTION You will use cookies and session data.

Cookies and session data have similar uses: to maintain user state data while users are using your web application. Session data is only valid during one session using your web application. If, for example, the user kills their browser and restarts it, the session data is lost. On the other hand, if you set an expiration time for a cookie, the user can log off, restart the browser, etc., and as long as the expiration time for the cookie has not been reached, then the browser will send the cookie data back to the server.

The example servlet `UserServlet` puts form data into both session and cookie data. You can experiment with the effects of restarting your browser when experimenting with this servlet to see that cookie data is persistent (if an expiration time was set for the cookie) while session data is not. As seen in Solutions 40, 41, and 42, you start by extending the class `HttpServlet`:

```
import javax.servlet.http.*;
import javax.servlet.ServletException;
import java.io.PrintWriter;
import java.util.Enumeration;

public class UserServlet extends HttpServlet {
```

You can write a `doGet()` method that simply uses the `doPost()` method in order to support both GET and POST requests:

```
    public void doGet(HttpServletRequest req,
                      HttpServletResponse res)
           throws ServletException {
        doPost(req, res);
    }

    public void doPost(HttpServletRequest req,
                       HttpServletResponse res)
           throws ServletException {
        PrintWriter out = null;
        try {
            out = res.getWriter();
        } catch (Exception e2) {
        }
        res.setContentType("text/html");
        out.println("<html><head><title>User Servlet</title>" +
                    "</head><body>");
        // check session data:
        out.println("<H2>Current Session Data</H2>");
```

You can get the current session data from the request object and get an enumeration of all available attribute names in the session object:

```
        HttpSession session = req.getSession();
        Enumeration enum = session.getAttributeNames();
```

```
out.println("<UL>");
while (enum.hasMoreElements()) {
    String name = (String) enum.nextElement();
    String value = (String) session.getAttribute(name);
    out.println("  <LI>" + name + " : " + value +
                "</LI>");
}
out.println("</UL>");
// check cookie data:
```

You can get an array of cookies from the request object. This object will be null if there are no available cookies. Here you can look at the attributes of each available cookie:

```
Cookie[] cookies = req.getCookies();
out.println("<H2>Cookie Data</H2>");
if (cookies != null) {
    for (int i = 0; i < cookies.length; i++) {
        String comment = cookies[i].getComment();
        String domain = cookies[i].getDomain();
        String value = cookies[i].getValue();
        String name = cookies[i].getName();
        String path = cookies[i].getPath();
        out.println("<h3>" + name + " has value: " +
                    value + "</h3>");
        out.println("comment: " + comment + ", domain: "
                    + domain + ", path: " + path);
    }
}
// print out the HTML FORM to the output stream:
```

The following HTML form is similar to those used in Solutions 40, 41, and 42 with the addition of a SELECT element:

```
out.println("<FORM action=\"/S43/user\" "+
            "method=\"GET\">");
out.println(" <SELECT NAME=\"Hobbies\" size=5>");
out.println("  <OPTION VALUE=\"movies\">" +
            "movies</OPTION>");
out.println("  <OPTION VALUE=\"music\">music</OPTION>");
out.println("  <OPTION VALUE=\"cooking\">cooking" +
            "</OPTION>");
out.println("  <OPTION VALUE=\"hiking\">" +
            "hiking</OPTION>");
out.println("  <OPTION VALUE=\"reading\">reading" +
            "</OPTION>");
```

```
            out.println("  </SELECT>");
            out.println("  <INPUT TYPE=\"text\" NAME=\"name\"" +
                        "  size=\"60\" />");
            out.println("   <BR />");
            out.println("  <INPUT TYPE=\"submit\" NAME=\"doit\"" +
                        "  VALUE=\"enter name\" />");
            out.println("</FORM>");

            String name = req.getParameter("name");
            if (name != null && name.length() > 0) {
                // make a new cookie:
                Cookie cookie = new Cookie("name", name);
                // if you do not set an age, then the cookie will not
                // be availablein a future session:
                cookie.setMaxAge(3600); // 1 hour
```

The default age for a cookie is negative, which means that the cookie is only available during a single session. Setting the age to zero deletes the cookie. Here, you set the age for this cookie to one hour:

```
                res.addCookie(cookie);
                // add session data:
```

You can also add data directly to a session attribute. In this case, you are only adding a string value. You will, in general, find it useful to also use Java collection objects as attribute values:

```
                session.setAttribute("name", name);
            }
            String hobby = req.getParameter("Hobbies");
            if (hobby != null) {
                System.out.println("hobby: " + hobby);
                // make a new cookie:
                Cookie cookie = new Cookie("hobby", hobby);
                cookie.setMaxAge(3600); // 1 hour
                res.addCookie(cookie);
                // add session data:
                session.setAttribute("hobby", hobby);
            }
            out.println("</body>");
            out.println("</HTML>");
            return;
        }
    }
```

The following screen shot was taken of my web browser when running this servlet:

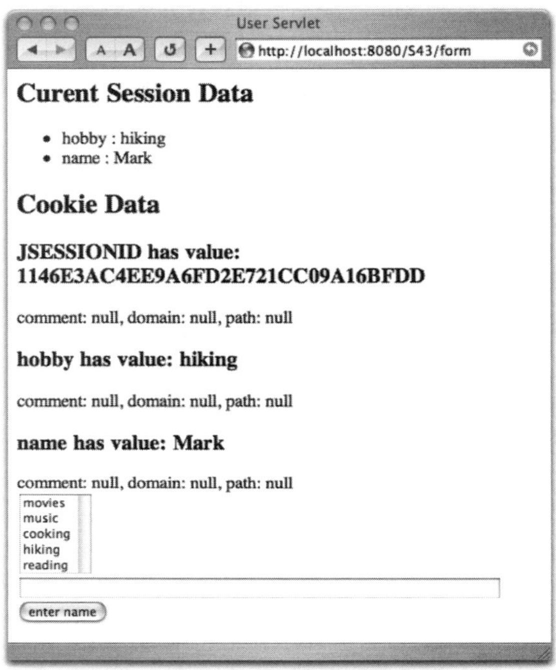

NOTE In Solution 46 while covering JSPs, I will use session data again in managing user login forms.

SOLUTION 44

Handling Runtime Errors

PROBLEM You need to handle errors that occur in your servlets.

SOLUTION You insulate your users: they will not see low-level server side runtime errors. They will see high-level errors that let them know that something went wrong.

If you do not add any specific error handling code to your Java servlets, then when errors occur your users will see Java trace-backs in their web browser. While these trace-backs will undoubtedly be fascinating to you the developer, they will probably confuse the users of your web applications.

We will look at two techniques: adding error handling specifications to the `web.xml` file and catching errors inside servlet code.

Adding Error-Page Elements to *web.xml*

The example servlet `ErrorServlet` is used to generate a "page not found" error. Here is the `doPost()` method for this servlet:

```
public void doPost(HttpServletRequest req,
                   HttpServletResponse res)
        throws ServletException {
    PrintWriter out = null;
    try {
        out = res.getWriter();
    } catch (Exception e2) {
    }
    res.setContentType("text/html");
    out.println(
       "<html><head><title>Error Servlet</title></head><body>");
    // print out the HTML FORM to the output stream:
    out.println(
```

You specify a nonexisting action target so the servlet will generate an error when the user hits this form submit button:

```
        "<FORM action=\"/S44/doesnotexist\" method=\"GET\">");
    out.println(" <INPUT TYPE=\"submit\" NAME=\"doit\"" +
                " VALUE=\"try to go to non-existing URL\" />");
    out.println("</FORM>");
    out.println("</body>");
    out.println("</HTML>");
    return;
}
```

If you run this servlet and click the form submit button, you will see an error similar to this in your browser:

```
HTTP Status 404 - /S44/doesnotexist
type Status report
message /S44/doesnotexist
description The requested resource (/S44/doesnotexist) is not available.
Apache Tomcat/4.1.18-LE-jdk14
```

If you want your users to see a custom page for this type of error, you can add the following to the `web.xml` configuration file for this web application:

```
<error-page>
  <error-code>404</error-code>
  <location>/notfound.html</location>
</error-page>
```

If any HTML errors of type 404 (that is, page not found errors) occur while running a servlet, this addition to the end of the `web.xml` file will cause Tomcat to display your custom HTML page, in this case, the file `notfound.html`.

You can test this servlet using the URL:

```
http://localhost:8080/S44/error
```

You should see an input form with a submit button labeled "try to go to non-existing URL". If you click this submit button, the servlet container should redirect you to the following page:

Handling Errors in Servlet Code

As you saw in the last section, handling standard HTML errors is as simple as adding `error-code` elements to the `web.xml` file for your application. I prefer a different approach for handling Java runtime exceptions (although these can also be caught using `exception-type` elements in your `web.xml` files): using `try/catch` code blocks and printing meaningful error messages back to the client's web page.

The servlet for this section that I use to demonstrate several techniques for handling errors is `JavaErrorServlet`. Here is the `doPost()` method for this servlet:

```
public void doPost(HttpServletRequest req,
                   HttpServletResponse res)
       throws ServletException {
    PrintWriter out = null;
    try {
        out = res.getWriter();
    } catch (Exception e2) {
    }
```

```
        res.setContentType("text/html");
        out.println("<html><head><title>Java Error " +
                    "Servlet</title></head><body>");
        out.println("<h2>Generate a Java Arithmetic Exception</h2>");
        try {
            int i = 10;
            int j = 0;
            int k = i / j;
```

The servlet will never get to the following statement because a divide by zero error will be thrown while executing the previous statement:

```
            out.println("10 / 0 = " + k);
        } catch (Exception ee) {
```

Because a Java runtime error occurred, you want to print a meaningful error message while handling runtime errors:

```
            out.println("An error occurred in the servlet: " + ee);
        }
        return;
    }
```

When the runtime error is thrown, the following printout is sent to the user's browser:

```
An error occurred while running the servlet: java.lang.ArithmeticException: / by
zero
```

If you wanted the user to see a trace-back, you could add the following line of code inside the `try/catch` code block:

```
ee.printStackTrace(out);
```

This would print a standard Java error trace-back to the output stream for the response object.

You can test this servlet using the URL:

```
http://localhost:8080/S44/javaerror
```

The following screen shot shows my web browser after the servlet error occurred:

Handling Redirections

The last demo servlet you use in this section is `RedirectionServlet`. This servlet uses the `setRedirect()` method call on the response object to redirect the user to an alternative URL. Although this is a general purpose technique, you can use redirects to handle errors. Here is the `doPost()` method for this servlet:

```
public void doPost(HttpServletRequest req,
                   HttpServletResponse res)
       throws ServletException {
    PrintWriter out = null;
    try {
        out = res.getWriter();
    } catch (Exception e2) {
    }
    res.setContentType("text/html");
    out.println("<html><head><title>Redirect Demo " +
                "Servlet</title></head><body>");
    out.println("<h2>User will not see this - page will " +
                "redirect</h2>");
    try {
```

You use the `sendRedirect()` method on the response object to redirect the browser to an alternative URL. This method call can throw an error, so you place it in a `try/catch` code block:

```
        res.sendRedirect("test.html");
    } catch (Exception ee) {
        out.println("Error trying to set redirect to test.html: "
                    + ee);
    }
    return;
}
```

You can test this servlet using the URL:

`http://localhost:8080/S44/redirect`

Your browser should be redirected to the page at `http://localhost:8080/s44/test.html`.

Java ServerPages (JSPs)

SOLUTION 45

Using JSP Declarations and Directives

PROBLEM You want to get started using JSPs.

SOLUTION I will introduce JSP declarations and directives using a simple example. I will also cover the use of style sheets and configuring and installing JSPs.

Solutions 45 through 49 on JSPs will be easier to use and understand if you have worked through Solutions 40 through 44 on servlets. After covering the basics of JSPs, I will discuss how a JSP container managers JSPs.

A First JSP Example

The directory `S45` contains the following files:

S45/ Main directory for the Solution 45 example.

S45/site.css Cascading style sheet for this example.

S45/footer.jsp A JSP file that contains common footer information for a website or individual web page.

S45/header.jsp A JSP file that contains common header information for a website or web page.

S45/index.jsp Default page for the context `/S45`. This file includes the file `header.jsp`, a simple input form, a few lines of embedded Java code, and the file `footer.jsp`.

S45/WEB-INF/ Top-level web information directory.

S45/WEB-INF/classes/ Any compiled Java classes used by JSPs for this web application can go in this directory.

S45/WEB-INF/lib/ Any JAR library files used by JSPs for this web application can go in this directory.

S45/WEB-INF/lib/m.sh A shell script to compile the Java source files in the demo subdirectory and put the compiled class files in the file `str.jar`.

S45/WEB-INF/lib/str.jar Contains compiled Java classes used in the `index.jsp` JSP.

S45/WEB-INF/lib/demo/ Source directory for Java classes.

S45/WEB-INF/lib/demo/Str.java A simple string utility class.

The servlet examples that you saw earlier in this book had a simple look to them because I was demonstrating how servlets work. In the JSP examples, I introduce the use of style sheets. Style sheets allow you to specify custom formatting for HTML tags like <p>. If you use the same style sheet throughout your web application, you can quickly change the look of your web application simply by modifying the style sheet. The following code snippet shows the contents of the file `site.css`:

```
<style type="text/css">
  body { color: black; background: white; }
  p { color: black; background: red; }
</style>
```

This is a simple style sheet—I am changing only the display characteristics of the <body> and <p> tags: I am setting the foreground and background colors.

NOTE Dave Raggett has written a fine tutorial on using cascading style sheets at `www.w3.org/MarkUp/Guide/Style`. Read this tutorial and have fun experimenting with changing the look of your JSP-based web applications.

The following code snippet shows the contents of the header file `header.jsp`:

```
<html>
<header>
    <title>JSP Demo</title>
    <link type="text/css" rel="stylesheet" href="site.css">
</header>
<body>
```

I find it convenient to use separate header and footer files for my JSP pages. Usually the header and footer files stay unchanged and the main page (in this case, `index.jsp`) is shorter and more convenient to maintain. The only HTML element in the header that you might not be familiar is the <link> element that specifies which cascading style sheet you are using. Here I used a local filename, `site.css`, but this could also be a URL to a style sheet on the Web.

NOTE JSP containers automatically detect changes in JSP files and recompile them (more on this later). However, JSP containers do not check the date stamp on included files. If I do change an included header, footer, or cascading style sheet file, I either restart Tomcat or I "touch" all JSP files in a web application, which causes Tomcat to recompile all the JSP files in my web application.

The footer file `footer.jsp` is simple in this example:

```
<br />
<br />
<i>Example footer for JSP example</i>
</body>
</html>
```

I often implement menus in my web applications using an HTML table containing a row of links. I usually place this "menu" in my header include file. The default file for this web application is `index.jsp`; the following code snippet shows the contents of this file. The first line in the file is a JSP page directive that allows you to add to the CLASSPATH for loading other Java classes. The directory `S45/WEB-INF/classes` is on the CLASSPATH by default, as are the contents of any Jar files in the directory `S45/WEB-INF/lib`; the following statement specifies that I am going to use the class `Str` in package `demo` on this JSP:

```
<%@ page import = "demo.Str" %>
```

The page directive sets attributes for the entire page. In addition to the import attribute, you can set other attributes; the most commonly used are `language` (default to "java"), `session` (default to "true"), `autoFlush` (default to "true"), `isThreadSafe` (default to "true"), and `errorPage`. The following statement is an `include` directive to include the contents of the file `header.jsp`:

```
<%@include file="header.jsp"%>
```

The following seven lines contain plain HTML:

```
<h2>Enter test data and select 'submit data'</h2>

<FORM action="/S45/index.jsp" method="POST">
  <INPUT TYPE="text" NAME="query" size="60" />
  <BR />
  <INPUT TYPE="submit" NAME="doit" VALUE="submit data" />
</FORM>
```

You can embed Java code in JSP pages by wrapping the code in <% and %>:

```
<%
    String query = request.getParameter("query");
    if (query != null && query.length() > 0) {
        String upperCase = Str.UP(query);
%>
```

The variables `request`, `response`, and `session` are automatically defined for you to use on JSPs; here, I am calling the `getParameter()` method on the `request` object to get any text that the user has typed into the HTML input form. You can also embed Java expressions wrapped in <%= and %>; in this example, I insert the value of the Java local variable *`upperCase`*:

```
<p>Entered string converted to upper case: <%=upperCase%></p>
<%
```

```
    }
%>
<%@include file="footer.jsp"%>
```

The following screen shot shows this JSP:

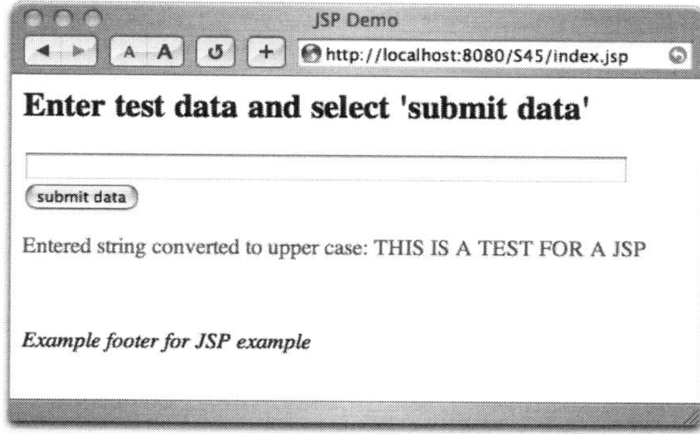

You can also embed Java expressions between `<%!` and `%>` tags. For example, here is HTML with an embedded Java expression to get the value of a parameter `query`:

```
<p>
   The query parameter is <%! request.getParameter("query") %>
</p>
```

Life Cycle of JSPs

In Solutions 40 and 42, you looked at the life cycle of Java servlets, specifically the servlet `init()` method and the servlet `destroy()` method. The JSP container automatically writes Java servlets for you using your JSP files as input. The JSP container places generated Java code and compiled class files in the `TOMCAT/work` directory; for example, the generated files for the project for Solution 49 are as follows:

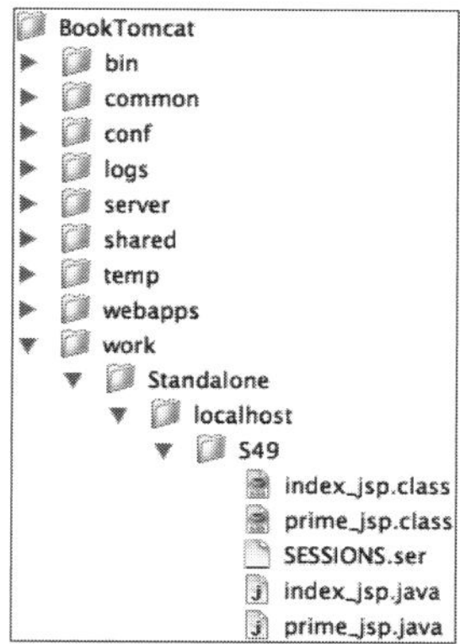

Here, I show the files you will be using later in Solution 49 because this example is the most complex JSP example in this book. This file layout is specific to Tomcat—other JSP containers may use different directory layouts.

When you write JSP files, it is possible to specify your own `init()` and `destroy()` methods that the JSP container will copy over to generated Java servlet classes; for example:

```
<%!
public void jspInit(){
// initialization code here
}

public void jspDestroy() {
// tear down code here
}
%>
```

The JSP container will copy these methods (changing the names to `init()` and `destroy()`) to the generated servlet code. In Solution 42, you used custom servlet initialization; you can do exactly the same thing in JSPs. Whenever a JSP container has to load a generated class for a JSP, the container also calls the `JspInit()` method.

You should understand that using JSPs instead of servlets is no less efficient than using servlets at runtime. JSPs are only converted to Java servlets and compiled when a JSP has a newer file time stamp than the automatically generated class files, so there is a one-time expense whenever a JSP file is edited.

SOLUTION 46

Handling Login Forms

PROBLEM You need to force users to log in before using your web application.

SOLUTION I will provide an example login form written in JSPs. You will use a placeholder Java class `LoginDB` in this example that you can replace with code using JDBC to access your own database.

The files used for this solution are similar to the files and directory structure for Solution 45—please refer back to Solution 45 for a file/directory listing and explanation.

The S46/WEB-INF/lib/database directory contains a placeholder Java class LoginDB:

```
package database;
public class LoginDB {
    public static boolean checkLogin(String account, String password) {
        if (Math.random() < 0.5) return true;
        return false;
    }
}
```

In your web application, you should rewrite this class using JDBC (see Solutions 34 through 39) to see if a user's account name and password are in a local database. Here, the method checkLogin() returns true or false to indicate whether the login is OK or failed. For testing purposes, I wrote this test method to randomly accept an account name and password about half the time.

The JSP file index.jsp contains an input form that has another JSP page loginok.jsp as the action target. You will look at the file loginok.jsp later.

```
<%@include file="header.jsp"%>

<h2>Please login</h2>
```

You can use session data to see if a previous login attempt failed. This attribute is set on the loginok.jsp page. Print out a message if a previous login attempt failed:

```
<%
   if (session.getAttribute("login") != null) {
%>
       <p>Previous login attempt failed</P>
<%
   }
%>
```

In most of the previous servlet and JSP examples in this book, form action targets pointed back to the same page; here you want to go to the loginok.jsp page after the user enters account and password and clicks the Login submit button:

```
<FORM action="loginok.jsp" method="POST">
  Account:
  <INPUT TYPE="text" NAME="account" size="60" />
  <BR />
  Password:
  <INPUT TYPE="text" NAME="password" size="60" />
  <BR />
  <INPUT TYPE="submit" NAME="doit" VALUE="Login" />
</FORM>
<%@include file="footer.jsp"%>
```

The file `loginok.jsp` uses the stub class `LoginDB` in the package `database`. The following code snippets show the contents of the file `loginok.jsp`:

```
<%@ page import = "database.LoginDB" %>

<%@include file="header.jsp"%>
```

You first get the account and password parameters from the request object. I mentioned before that JSP pages have Java variables predefined for the `request`, `response`, and `session` objects:

```
<%
   String account = request.getParameter("account");
   String password = request.getParameter("password");
```

Because the `checkLogin()` method is static, you do not need to create an instance of the `LoginDB` class; you can just directly call the static method:

```
if (LoginDB.checkLogin(account, password) == false) {
   // login failed:
```

If the login fails, then set the session attribute `login` to `fail` and use the `sendRedirect()` method on the `response` object:

```
   session.setAttribute("login", "fail");
   response.sendRedirect("index.jsp");
} else {
```

If the login is OK, then set session data for other pages in your web application to use to make sure that the user has logged in and not simply bookmarked a URL inside your web application:

```
      session.setAttribute("login", "ok");
   }
%>

<p>You are logged in.</p>

<%@include file="footer.jsp"%>
```

The following screen shot shows the initial login form:

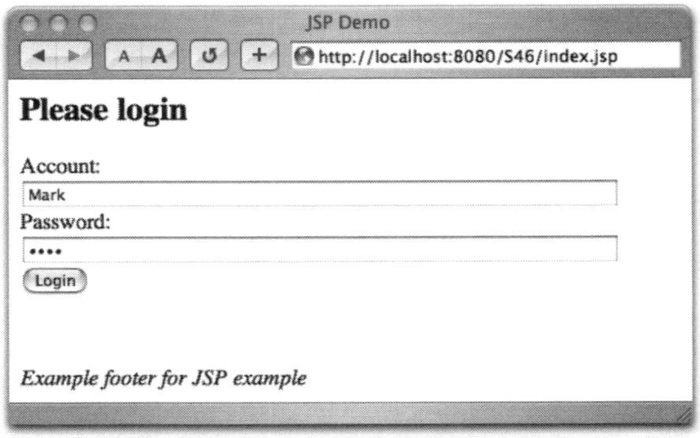

NOTE Notice that in this example I am using http POST requests instead of GET requests. This is important because using GET requests leaves user's account names and passwords in a browser's history list. For a more secure login system you should also consider using HTTPS instead of HTTP. The Tomcat server supports HTTPS.

The following screen shows a failed login attempt:

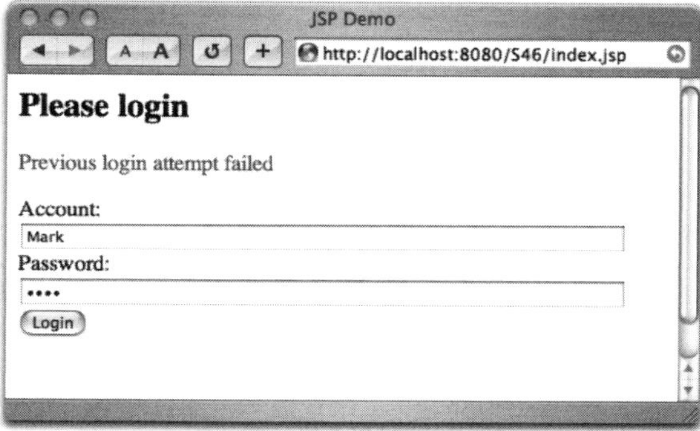

The following screen shows a successful login:

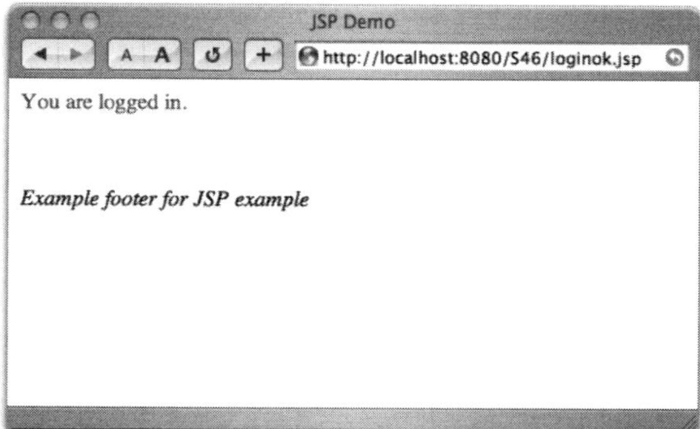

The example for this solution is fairly simple. If you are just getting started writing JSP-based web applications, you can copy this example in order to get a quick start on your development. Solution 49, in which I introduce you to Struts, offers good alternatives for using "plain" JSPs. I usually recommend the use of plain JSPs (as in this example) for small projects and the use of Struts for large web application projects.

SOLUTION 47

Using JavaBeans with JSPs

PROBLEM You have existing JavaBeans that you would like to use in web applications.

SOLUTION You will use JSP directives for using JavaBeans.

The JavaBean component model and JSPs are a great combination. Ideally, JavaBeans are used to implement what is often called "business logic" of your application, and JSPs are used to handle the presentation. In practice, JSPs unfortunately also tend to get bloated with Java code blocks, but at least these code blocks are specific to handling the presentation to the user, control navigation through a web application, etc.

The package `beans` contains two example JavaBeans for the example in this solution: `DateBean` and `MemoryUseBean`. The source code to these beans is in the directory `S47/WEB-INF/lib/beans`. The implementation of both classes is short enough to list here. The `DateBean` class will be used to demonstrate accessing `JavaBean` properties from a JSP:

```
package beans;
import java.util.Date;
public class DateBean {
    // properties:
    private String timeZoneName = "'not set'";
    public Date getDate()  {
        return new Date();
    }
    public String getTimeZoneName() { return timeZoneName; }
    public void setTimeZoneName(String name) {
        timeZoneName = name;
    }
}
```

The bean class `MemoryUseBean` has three public methods that I will call directly in the example `index.jsp` JSP:

```
package beans;
public class MemoryUse {
    Runtime runtime = null;
    public MemoryUse() {
      runtime = Runtime.getRuntime();
```

```
    }
    public String getFreeMemory() {
      return "Free memory: " + runtime.freeMemory();
    }
    public String getMaxMemory() {
      return "Max memory: " + runtime.maxMemory();
    }
    public String getTotalMemory() {
      return "Total memory: " + runtime.totalMemory();
    }
}
```

NOTE When Tomcat is started, it loads the JAR files in the `lib` subdirectories of all the webapps context directories (for example, `S47/WEB-INF/lib`, etc.). If you recompile the code and rebuild any of these JAR files, Tomcat will not "notice" this. You must restart Tomcat for code changes to take effect. I will cover the use of the ant build tool in "Automating Development with Ant, jUnit and XDoclet" with examples for building and deploying JSP-based web applications.

The following listing shows the example JSP `index.jsp`. The first thing to notice is that you do not need to use a `<% page import="beans.DataBean, beans.MemoryUseBean" />` statement:

```
<%@include file="header.jsp"%>
```

Instead of the page import JSP statement, you will use the `<jsp:usebean />` statement. The use bean statement replaces the page import statement and assigns symbolic names to newly created instances of the two JavaBean classes that you are using:

```
<jsp:useBean id="date" class="beans.DateBean" />
<jsp:useBean id="mem"  class="beans.MemoryUseBean" />
<h2>Directly Calling JavaBean Methods</h2>
<h4>Memory Use for the JVM Running Tomcat</h4>
```

Here, you are directly calling methods on the two JavaBean instances that the `<jsp:useBean />` statements created:

```
<p> <%=mem.getFreeMemory() %> </p>
<p> <%=mem.getMaxMemory() %> </p>
<p> <%=mem.getTotalMemory() %> </p>
```

You can also use the `<jsp:getProperty />` statement to get any JavaBean property; in this case you access properties from the `DateBean`:

```
<h2>Experiments with JavaBean Properties</h2>
<h4>
    Current Date is
```

```
        <jsp:getProperty name="date" property="date" />
    </h4>
    <h4>
        The time zone is
        <jsp:getProperty name="date" property="timeZoneName" />
    </h4>
```

You can use the `<jsp:setProperty />` statement to call any set property method on a JavaBean:

```
<jsp:setProperty name="date" property="timeZoneName" value="Arizona Time" />
```

I repeat the display of information from the instance of the DateBean to show that the time zone name property was changed:

```
<h4>
    Current Date is
    <jsp:getProperty name="date" property="date" />
</h4>
<h4>
    The time zone is
    <jsp:getProperty name="date" property="timeZoneName" />
</h4>
<%@include file="footer.jsp"%>
```

The following screenshot shows this JSP in my web browser:

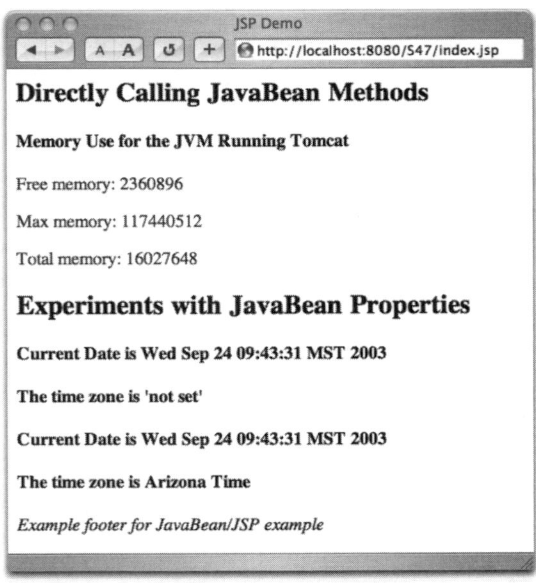

The easy integration of JavaBean components and JSPs is no accident: the JSP architecture was designed to work with JavaBeans. Although I will continue with more advanced techniques for building web applications (that is, more JSP techniques, Struts, and Enterprise Java Beans [EJBs]), this solution gives you a foundation for solving most simple web application problems. The combination of JavaBeans, JSPs, and the free Tomcat server allows you, the Java developer, to inexpensively and quickly build web applications out of existing Java application code.

SOLUTION 48

Handling User Sessions

PROBLEM You want to keep track of a user's navigation history during a session using your web application.

SOLUTION I will use three interlinked JSPs to show how to keep navigation history in a JSP session object.

The example for this solution uses three JSPs that each have links to the other two JSPs as seen in this diagram:

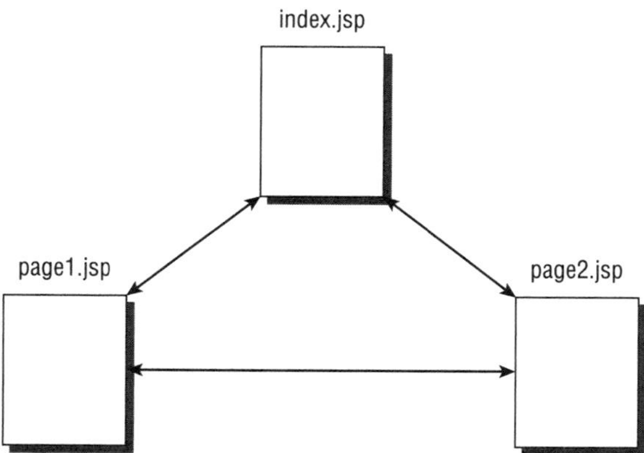

Each time a user clicks a link to navigate to another linked page in this example, a navigation history will be updated in the session object for the web application. A fourth include file JSP `history.jsp` prints out the current navigation history; this file is included in the other three JSPs to avoid repeating common JSP code.

The files `index.jsp`, `page1.jsp`, and `page2.jsp` are all very similar, so you will only look at `index.jsp` here. Start by importing the `java.util.ArrayList` class:

```
<%@ page import = "java.util.ArrayList" %>
```

As before, you place common header information in a separate include file:

```
<%@include file="header.jsp"%>
```

Each of the files `index.jsp`, `page1.jsp`, and `page2.jsp` has a different header so you will know which page you are on while running this demo; for example the file `index.jsp` contains:

```
<h2>index.jsp</h2>
```

You need links to the other two pages in this example; here, the file `index.jsp` has links to `page1.jsp` and `page2.jsp`:

```
Go to page <a href="page1.jsp">page1.jsp</a>
<br />
Go to page <a href="page2.jsp">page2.jsp</a>
<br />
```

Because JSPs are compiled by the JSP container into Java servlets, you can use as many comments as you want with no runtime performance penalty:

```
<!-- If an ArrayList to hold navigation history
     is not already in the session data, add one:
-->
```

The following Java code gets the array list used to store navigation history from the session data by getting the value of the attribute `"history"`. If this attribute does not yet exist, you can simply create a new array list—it will later be saved back to session data:

```
<%
    ArrayList al = (ArrayList)session.getAttribute("history");
    if (al == null) {
        al = new ArrayList();
    }
    al.add("index.jsp");
    session.setAttribute("history", al);
%>
```

The include file `history.jsp` does the work of adding the history list to the web page returned to the user's browser; you use the JSP include directive to insert the contents of `history.jsp`:

```
<%@include file="history.jsp"%>
```

The other linked files, `page1.jsp` and `page2.jsp`, are very similar; you can read their source from the directory `S48`. The JSP `history.jsp` accesses the history list and prints it out. The following code snippet shows the contents of the file `history.jsp`:

```
<!-- Include file to add history list output -->
<%
    al = (ArrayList)session.getAttribute("history");
    if (al != null) {
        out.println("<h3>Navigation History List</h3>");
        for (int i=0, size=al.size(); i<size; i++) {
            out.println("" + al.get(i) + "<br />");
        }
    }
%>
```

The following illustration shows my browser while running this example web application:

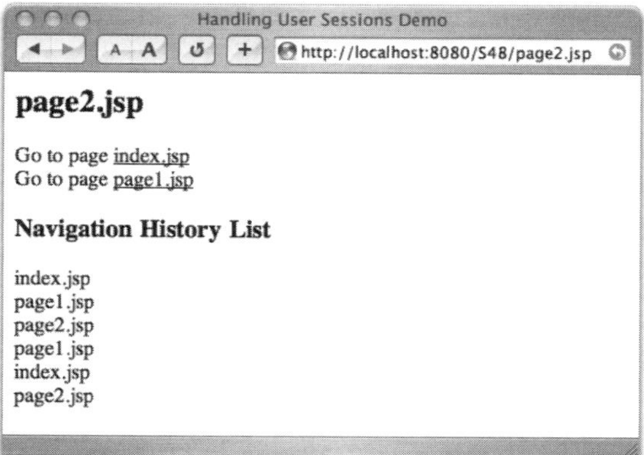

This figure shows that the page `page2.jsp` is currently shown and the navigation history is `index.jsp -> page1.jsp -> page2.jsp -> page1.jsp -> index.jsp -> page2.jsp`.

NOTE In this example, I kept user session data in a simple array list collection object. For most web applications that track what a user is doing, it is better to design your own Java class that encapsulates all necessary data about a user and what they are doing while running the web application. As in Solution 47, you would use a JavaBean.

SOLUTION 49

Using the Struts Tag Libraries and MVC Architecture

PROBLEM You have a large web application project and you want to keep it manageable.

SOLUTION You will go through a long learning curve for using the Struts MVC architecture and tag libraries. Using Struts, at least initially, has a high setup overhead. For large projects you will save time in the long run using Struts with your JSP web applications.

If I were to try to cover Struts in detail, this "10-minute solution" would turn into a "500-minute solution." Instead, I will get you up to speed on using Struts using a short, clear Struts example web application that uses just two Struts tag libraries (html and bean) and introduces you to the Model View Controller (MVC) architecture of Struts.

I will start with an overview of the example Struts web application that (like earlier servlet and JSP examples in this book) allows a user to first login and then interactively test numbers to see if they are prime numbers. I will follow this up with a brief Struts tutorial. After you understand the design and architecture of Struts, it will be much easier to understand the implementation of the example Struts web application later in this solution.

NOTE After you work through the S49 example and get comfortable with the subset of Struts that I introduce you to, I recommend that you try "cloning" my Struts example and replace the prime number application with one of your own projects. At first, try to just use just my Struts framework. This will make you feel comfortable enough with the basics of using Struts to tackle larger scale applications that use the full range of available Struts tag libraries.

Overview of the Struts Example Web Application

Struts-based web applications have a specific directory structure with mandatory configuration files and library files. Understanding how the example Struts application is laid out will help you in the next section in which I will introduce you to Struts. The following illustration shows the directory layout that you will use in the S49 example:

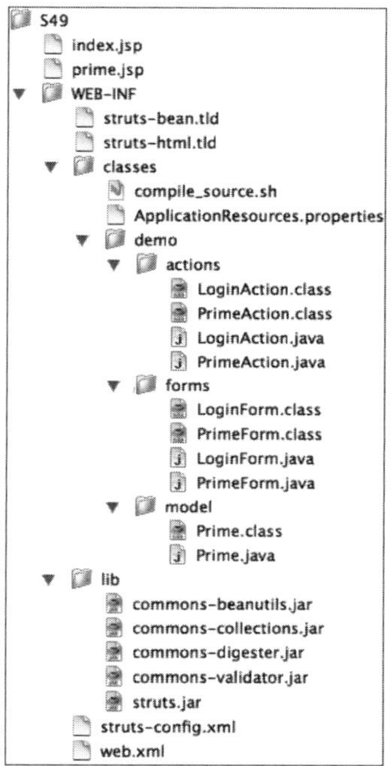

The JSP files `index.jsp` and `prime.jsp` both contain HTML input forms. The Java classes `LoginForm` and `PrimeForm` contain instance variables that correspond to values on the HTML input forms. The Struts servlet uses set methods in these classes to populate data in these classes. The Java classes `LoginAction` and `PrimeAction` are responsible for controlling navigation to other web pages; these classes also have form data available and can use model (application-specific) classes. The class `Prime` is an application-specific class. The `lib` directory contains required utilities for using Struts. The files with TLD extensions are tag library definition files (in this example, I use only two tag libraries: bean and html). The `struts-config.xml` and `web.xml` files are used to configure the Struts action servlet.

NOTE You notice that I have both the Java source and class files in the `S49/WEB-INF/classes` subdirectories with a shell script for compiling the Java source files. This is the simplest possible development setup. "Automating Development with Ant, jUnit and XDoclet" covers the ant build tool. I will provide an ant example for building and deploying a Struts application there.

The file `ApplicationResources.properties` contains mappings of key names to text strings that are displayed on JSPs. For reference, I list the contents of this file here:

```
#titles
index.title=Struts test
prompt.username=Please enter your name
prompt.password=Enter any password
prompt.number:Please enter a number
button.login=Login
button.check.prime=Check for prime

#errors
error.bad.username=Must enter a user name
error.bad.password=Must enter a password
error.bad.number.format=Bad number format
```

Getting Up to Speed

The configuration files web.xml and `struts-config.xml` are read by the Struts controller when your Struts-based web application is initialized by a JSP container. While you will see in later sections that part of writing Struts-based web applications is writing subclasses of Struts action forms and Struts actions, the heart of using Struts is designing the navigation for the web application (which I will do in the next section) and specifying data that allows the Struts controller servlet to control your application. The Struts controller is written for you, and the controller class is included in the `struts.jar` file. You need to write the `struts-config.xml` file, configure servlet parameters in the `web.xml` file, write your Struts action form and action classes and then write the JSPs that use the Struts tag libraries.

Struts is a Model View Controller (MVC) based system. "Model" refers to an application-specific object model—the classes and instances of these classes that are used in your application. In the S49 example, the class `Prime` represents the model. The model classes have nothing to do with either the user's view of the system or any controller functionality—they are application specific and can be reused in other non-MVC applications. "View" refers to the visual representation of the system to the user. You will use JSPs to implement the View component. The controller is responsible for mediating between the view and the model.

If you have an interesting Java application that you want to expose as a web-based application, then think of the core application classes as the model. In the S49 example, the model application is trivial and implemented in the single class `Prime`. I will introduce you to Struts by first showing how to configure the controller using the `struts-config.xml` and `web.xml` files. I will cover the navigation details for the S49 example in the next section; for now it enough to know that there are two web pages, one for login and one for entering numbers.

The following illustration shows a high-level view of how the Struts controller manages browser requests, uses the action classes that you define for your application, and returns information to the client browser.

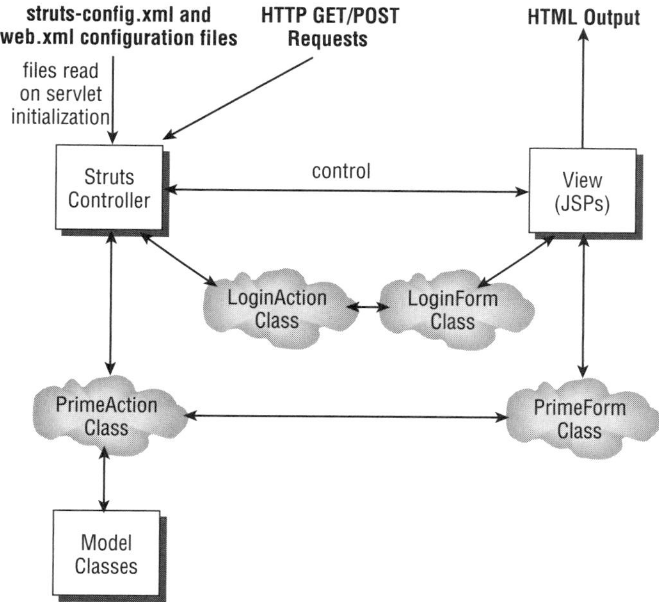

After the Struts controller servlet is initialized using the two configuration files, it is ready to mediate between the view and model components. The controller servlet uses the form classes to hold data entered on HTML input forms; these form classes often have behavior for checking form input values. You will see later how errors are logged and handled using Struts facilities in the html and bean tag libraries. In the example systems, user login information is not checked against a database; the `LoginAction` class merely checks that the user typed in some data for both username and password. The `PrimeAction` class uses the model class `Prime`.

NOTE The website `http://rollerjm.free.fr/pro/Struts11.html` has UML diagrams by Jean-Michel Garnier for the main Struts controller classes. This site is a great resource for digging into the architecture of the Struts implementation.

As you will see in later sections, writing the form and action classes is fairly simple; you will want to use the example classes in the S49 example as a template when you write your first Struts web applications.

I think configuring the Struts controller servlet is the most difficult part of Struts to understand; so I will tackle the hardest thing first. The follow code snippet shows the complete `struts-config.xml` file that you use in the S49 project. The first few lines specify that this is an XML file and specify the DTD for this XML file:

```
<?xml version="1.0" ?>

<!DOCTYPE struts-config PUBLIC
  "-//Apache Software Foundation//DTD Struts Configuration 1.1//EN"
  "http://jakarta.apache.org/struts/dtds/struts-config_1_1.dtd">
```

The top level element is `struts-config`. The first subelement `data-sources` is left empty because I am not using a database in the example web application.

```
<struts-config>

  <data-sources>
  </data-sources>
```

In this example, I am not using a database so the data-sources element is empty. However, if you need to use a database, the following XML is used to specify data source properties:

```
<data-sources>
    <data-source>
      <set-property property="autoCommit"
                     value="true"/>
      <set-property property="driverClass"
                     value="org.gjt.mm.mysql.Driver"/>
      <set-property property="password"
                     value="pa23k4k56k"/>
      <set-property property="url"
                     value="jdbc:mysql://localhost:3306/test"/>
      <set-property property="user"
                     value="testuser"/>
    </data-source>
  </data-sources>
```

To use this data source, you would do the following:

```
DataSource dataSource = servlet.findDataSource(null);
Connection connection = dataSource.getConnection();
```

There are two form beans used in this example: one for the data on the login form and one for the data on the prime number test form. The `name` attribute assigns a symbolic name to the form bean and the `type` attribute specifies a Java class name including package information:

```
<form-beans>
  <form-bean name="loginForm"
             type="demo.forms.LoginForm"/>
  <form-bean name="primeForm"
             type="demo.forms.PrimeForm"/>
</form-beans>
```

The global forwards element allows you to specify zero or more global names to URL path mappings. In large web applications, it is useful to be able to refer to forward mappings by name in action classes and avoid using physical filenames for JSPs.

```
<global-forwards>
  <forward name="prime" path="/prime.jsp"/>
</global-forwards>
```

The Struts controller uses action mappings to determine which action classes to call for action paths specified in web forms.

```
<action-mappings>
```

An action path is specified as the action attribute in HTML forms:

```
<action path="/login"
```

The `type` attribute is the fully package qualified class name for the action class, in this case, the login action class:

```
type="demo.actions.LoginAction"
```

The `name` attribute is the symbolic name of the corresponding action form:

```
name="loginForm"
```

The `scope` attribute can specify a request of session scope:

```
scope="request"
```

The `input` attribute specifies which URL to redirect to if there are any errors when the Struts servlet calls the methods in your form and action classes. In this example, if there are any errors found in the login action class (for example, no data entered for either account name or password), then the user is simply redirected back to the `index.jsp` page, which contains the login HTML form. You will see later when you look at the `index.jsp` file how to handle errors in a standard way using the Struts tag libraries.

```
input="/index.jsp">
```

The `forward` element specifies the path that the Struts controller servlet should redirect to if there are no errors in the execute method of the login action class:

```
  <forward name="showPrime" path="/prime.jsp"/>
</action>
```

The action mapping for the prime number checking page is similar to the login page (`index.jsp`) except that the user is always brought back to the `prime.jsp` page whether or not there are any errors found while running the execute method of the prime action class:

```
<action path="/prime"
        type="demo.actions.PrimeAction"
        name="primeForm"
        scope="request"
        input="/prime.jsp">
  <forward name="showPrime" path="/prime.jsp"/>
```

```
    </action>
  </action-mappings>
```

The messages-resources element is used to specify the name of the file containing the text resources. This example assumes the use of the English language (an English "locale") but it is very straightforward to support multiple languages by providing multiple resource files.

```
    <message-resources parameter="ApplicationResources" null="false" />
  </struts-config>
```

This struts-config.xml file is fairly simple because the example web application uses only two web form pages. This configuration file can get long and complex for large web applications.

The web.xml configuration file for this example is similar to the configuration files you used when writing servlets but with a few extra elements added (copy this as-is for your projects):

```
<?xml version="1.0" ?>

<!DOCTYPE web-app
    PUBLIC "-//Sun Microsystems, Inc.//DTD Web Application 2.3//EN"
    "http://java.sun.com/dtd/web-app_2_3.dtd">

<web-app>
```

The servlet element specifies the use of the Struts action servlet; this is the controller in the MVC architecture (copy this as-is for your projects):

```
<servlet>
  <servlet-name>action</servlet-name>
  <servlet-class>
      org.apache.struts.action.ActionServlet
  </servlet-class>
  <init-param>
    <param-name>application</param-name>
    <param-value>ApplicationResources</param-value>
  </init-param>
  <init-param>
```

This servlet reads the struts-config.xml file that you just looked at (copy this as-is for your projects):

```
    <param-name>config</param-name>
    <param-value>/WEB-INF/struts-config.xml</param-value>
  </init-param>
```

You need to ensure that the servlet/JSP container initializes this servlet when the container starts up. The higher the startup number, the lower the startup priority. In this case, you do not care if other servlets are preloaded before this servlet (copy this as-is for your projects).

```
    <load-on-startup>2</load-on-startup>
  </servlet>
```

You need to specify that all URL requests ending in `.do` are handled by the Struts action servlet (copy this as-is for your projects):

```
<servlet-mapping>
  <servlet-name>action</servlet-name>
  <url-pattern>*.do</url-pattern>
</servlet-mapping>
```

You might want to change the welcome file list. This list contains one or more files that are the starting files used for a web application. In this case, I specify just one file so if the user specifies a URL with just the web application context (for example, `http://localhost:8080/S49`), this file will be opened first.

```
<welcome-file-list>
  <welcome-file>index.jsp</welcome-file>
</welcome-file-list>
```

You must specify Tag Library Definition (TLD) files for each tag library that you will be using:

```
  <taglib>
    <taglib-uri>/WEB-INF/struts-bean.tld</taglib-uri>
    <taglib-location>/WEB-INF/struts-bean.tld</taglib-location>
  </taglib>
  <taglib>
    <taglib-uri>/WEB-INF/struts-html.tld</taglib-uri>
    <taglib-location>/WEB-INF/struts-html.tld</taglib-location>
  </taglib>
</web-app>
```

Writing the two configuration files for your web application forces you to address up-front issues of site navigation options, which tag libraries you are using, etc. Once the configuration is complete, the remaining components of a Struts-based application can be divided easily among different team members.

User Interactions with the Example Struts Web Application

Although I covered Struts configuration for the S49 example in the last section, I assumed some knowledge of the web application page layout and navigation in defining the `struts-config.xml` file. I will discuss the layout and navigation in some detail in this section. As mentioned in the last section, there are only two web pages with data entry forms in this example:

index.jsp This is the login form page. The login form contains fields name and password.

primes.jsp This is the prime number testing form page. This form contains a number field.

The navigation is simple: if the data entered for login is not valid, the user is brought back to the login page. Once the user enters valid login data (which in this example is any data at all), the user is shown the prime number testing page. Regardless of any errors (for example, entering an illegal number format), the user is always brought back to the prime number testing page. If the user has previously entered a number, the results of testing that number appear at the top of the page above the number entry form.

The following illustration is a UML activity diagram that shows navigation options for the example Struts-based web application:

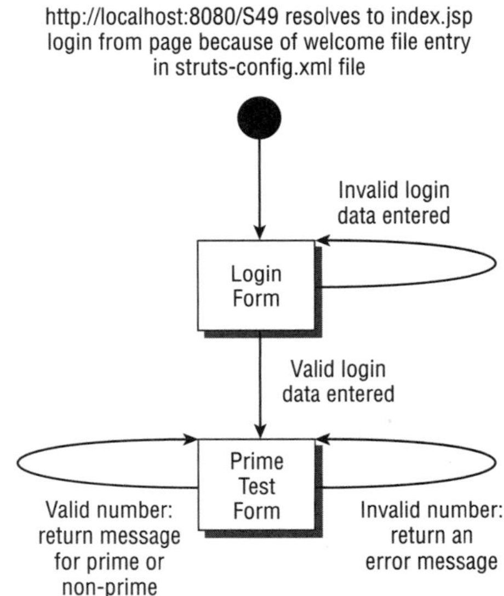

Mapping HTML Forms to Java: Struts Forms Classes

Struts forms classes are derived from the Struts abstract class `ActionForm`. Form classes look like JavaBean classes: they contain nonpublic property definitions with get/set methods for reading and writing these parameters. Additionally, you will define two extra methods not seen in plain JavaBeans:

validate() This method is called by the controller (that is, the Struts action servlet) to validate data the user entered on the form corresponding to this class.

reset() This method resets parameters to their default values. This method is also called directly by the Struts action servlet.

The following code snippet shows the `LoginForm` class (import statements removed for brevity):

```
public final class LoginForm extends ActionForm {
```

Define the two parameters that correspond to the data entry form elements on the `index.jsp` page:

```
private String username = null;
private String password = null;
```

You need JavaBean style get/set methods for both parameters:

```
public String getUserName() {
    return (this.username);
}
public void setUserName(String username) {
    this.username = username;
}
public String getPassword() {
    return (this.password);
}
public void setPassword(String password) {
    this.password = password;
}
```

The `validate()` method assumes that the Struts action servlet has used the `setUserName()` and `setPassword()` methods to set the username and password parameters from data the user entered on the login form before calling this method:

```
public ActionErrors validate(ActionMapping mapping,
                             HttpServletRequest request) {
```

You will always create an instance of the `ActionErrors` class to use as a return value. These errors can be displayed on the target JSP. You will display any errors in the `index.jsp` file that you will look at in a later section.

```
    ActionErrors errors = new ActionErrors();
    if ((username == null) || (username.length() < 1))
        errors.add("userName",
                   new ActionError("error.bad.username"));
    if ((password == null) || (password.length() < 1))
        errors.add("password",
                   new ActionError("error.bad.password"));
    return errors;
}
```

The argument in the constructor calls for `ActionError` key strings that are used to look up print strings in the `ApplicationResources.properties` file. The `reset()` method is used by the Struts action servlet to reset parameters to default values:

```
    public void reset(ActionMapping mapping,
                      HttpServletRequest request) {
        this.username = null;
        this.password = null;
    }
}
```

The form class for the `prime.jsp` number enter page is listed in the following code snippet:

```
public final class PrimeForm extends ActionForm {
```

Here, you only need one parameter to represent the number enter field on the `prime.jsp` page:

```
private String number = null;
public String getNumber() {
    return (this.number);
}
public void setNumber(String number) {
    this.number = number;
}

public ActionErrors validate(ActionMapping mapping,
                             HttpServletRequest request) {
    ActionErrors errors = new ActionErrors();
```

For the S49 example, you don't detect any errors in the form class for entering numbers—for now, accept anything the user types in. However, the action class (that you will see in the next section) for the prime input form will perform error checking before a number is tested for being a prime:

```
        return errors;
    }
    public void reset(ActionMapping mapping,
                      HttpServletRequest request) {
        this.number = null;
    }
}
```

Writing Struts Action Classes

The action classes that you write as part of your Struts-based web applications control the view part of the MVC architecture. Before your action classes transfer control to a view page they have the opportunity to access form entry data, use model JavaBeans, etc.

The following code snippet shows the implementation of the login action class (with import statements not shown for brevity):

```
public final class LoginAction extends Action {
```

The `execute()` method is called by the Struts action servlet to control the view part of the web application. This control is performed by selecting the JSP to transfer to and setting session data that can be displayed by the target JSP.

```
public ActionForward execute(ActionMapping mapping,
                             ActionForm form,
                             HttpServletRequest request,
                             HttpServletResponse response)
    throws Exception {
```

You will get the username and password from the form object (this data was added automatically to the session data by the Struts servlet after calling public methods of your `LoginForm` class):

```
String userName=null;
String password=null;
if (form != null){
    userName = ((LoginForm) form).getUserName();
    password = ((LoginForm) form).getPassword();
}
```

If the user did not enter any text in either the username or password fields, then forward the user back to the `"login"` target (which is mapped to `index.jsp` in the `struts-config.xml` file). In a real web application, you would want to use a model class here that used a local database to verify login information.

```
if (userName == null || userName.length() < 1) {
    return (mapping.findForward("login"));
}
if (password == null || password.length() < 1) {
    return (mapping.findForward("login"));
}
```

If the login data was OK, then you want to save the username in the session data object:

```
request.getSession().setAttribute("userName", userName);
```

Since there are no errors, you want to return a mapping to the "prime" target (this is mapped to the `prime.jsp` page in the `struts-config.xml` file):

```
        return mapping.findForward("prime");
    }
}
```

The following code snippet show the implementation of the prime number test action class:

```
public final class PrimeAction extends Action {

    public ActionForward execute(ActionMapping mapping,
                                 ActionForm form,
                                 HttpServletRequest request,
                                 HttpServletResponse response)
        throws Exception {
```

You will get the string value from the number entry form on the `prime.jsp` page:

```
String number=null;
if (form != null){
    number = ((PrimeForm) form).getNumber();
}
```

You will use the model class `demo.model.Prime` to test the number for being a prime number. First, though, you will make sure the string value is a valid number format:

```
int num = -12345;
try {
    num = Integer.parseInt(number);
} catch (Exception ee) {
```

You are using a session attribute `"primeResults"` to store either an error message (which you set here) or the prime or not-prime result (which is set later):

```
request.getSession().setAttribute("primeResults",
               ""+number+" is not a valid number");
```

Since an error occurred, immediately forward the user back to the `"prime"` target (that is, the `prime.jsp` page). The error message will be displayed by `prime.jsp` instead of the results of a prime number test.

```
    return mapping.findForward("prime");
}
```

The following code is executed if there were no errors in converting the number string to an integer. You want to place a result string in session data for display by `prime.jsp`:

```
if (new Prime().isPrime(num)) {
    request.getSession().setAttribute("primeResults",
                          "" +  num + " is a prime");
} else {
    request.getSession().setAttribute("primeResults",
                          "" +  num + " is not a prime");
}
```

You now want to forward the user back to the `"prime"` target (that is, the `prime.jsp` page).

```
        return mapping.findForward("prime");
    }
}
```

Notice that you never have to refer to physical JSPs; that is, you do not hard code `prime.jsp` in the Java source file. Instead you use a symbolic name `"prime"` that is configured in `struts-config.xml` to reference `prime.jsp`.

Writing JSPs for a Struts Web Application

Struts use JSPs for the view part of the MVC architecture. I have already covered JSPs in Solutions 45 through 48. Now I introduce the use of Struts tag libraries in JSPs. The following code snippets show the `index.jsp` file that contains the login form:

```
<%@ page language="java" %>
```

The following two statements specify the URI for the TLDs for the bean and html tag libraries. The prefix names can be anything you want; they specify the XML namespace for the two tag libraries that you will use on this page. The use of the names "bean" and "html" is a standard choice.

```
<%@ taglib uri="/WEB-INF/struts-bean.tld" prefix="bean" %>
<%@ taglib uri="/WEB-INF/struts-html.tld" prefix="html" %>
```

Instead of simply using a HTML <html> element here, you use the html element defined in the html tag library:

```
<html:html>
  <head>
        <title>
```

The message tag in the bean tag library reads the text string from the application resources and writes the text for the specified key to the generated HTML output stream. You should avoid placing literal string constants in your Struts JSPs; using the message tag makes it easier to later add internationalization support.

```
            <bean:message key="index.title"/>
        </title>
  </head>

<body>
  <h2>Struts Taglib Test - Login Form</h2>
```

You want to define an input form here to allow users to type in their username and password. However, before you handle the input form, you need to think about error handling. Remember that when you implemented the `LoginForm` class that you checked the string input values to make sure the user entered some input text. Specifically, you already had code in the `LoginForm` class to add action errors if the user did not type any text in for the username and password; to refresh your memory, here is the Java code for adding errors to the action errors collection:

```
public ActionErrors validate(ActionMapping mapping,
                             HttpServletRequest request) {
    ActionErrors errors = new ActionErrors();
```

```
        if ((username == null) || (username.length() < 1))
            errors.add("userName",
                       new ActionError("error.bad.username"));
        if ((password == null) || (password.length() < 1))
            errors.add("password",
                       new ActionError("error.bad.password"));
        return errors;
    }
```

Now, back to the `index.jsp` file: the following JSP code that uses the html and bean tag libraries checks for error messages stored in the action errors collection; if any exist they are displayed in a red colored font:

```
<html:messages id="message">
     <font color="red">
       <bean:write name="message"/>
     </font>
     <br />
</html:messages>
```

You are using two bits of Struts tag library magic here. First, the `messages` tag in the html tag library requires a message ID attribute. In this case, I specified the default attribute value to retrieve any action errors collected by the last action form (in this case the class `demo.form.LoginForm`) to be executed. The second bit of magic that is performed by the Struts tag libraries involves the `write` tag in the bean tag library: specifying the value of the name attribute as `"message"` causes any action errors to be written to the HTML output stream. The following screen shows what happens now if I try to login without specifying a username:

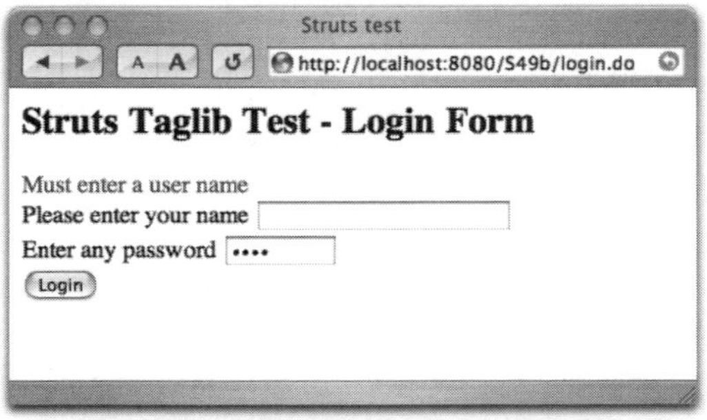

Now, you get redirected back to the login form (on the page `index.jsp`) and a message "Must enter a user name" is displayed in red font.

While there are several ways to handle errors in Struts web applications, the method that I used here is my favorite: have your form classes add errors to the action error collection that is returned from the `validate()` method. Then use the JSP code previously listed.

Now that you have handled the display of any errors from a previous login attempt, you are ready to add an input form in the file `index.jsp` in which the user can enter their username and password data. You should notice that you do not use a standard HTML form element. Rather, you need to use the form tag in the html tag library in order to interact properly with the Struts action servlet. The action `"/login"` is mapped in the `struts-config.xml` file to the action class `demo.action.LoginAction`:

```
<html:form action="/login" focus="userName">
```

The focus of this form is set to the `"username"` property defined next. Once again, you should avoid placing string literals like `"Login name:"` in your JSPs; here, I again use the message tag in the bean tag library:

```
<bean:message key="prompt.username"/>
```

You use the `text` tag in the html tag library for entering text instead of a plain HTML text element:

```
<html:text property="userName" size="22" maxlength="22"/>
<br />
<bean:message key="prompt.password"/>
```

The `password` tag is like the `text` tag except that it does not echo the characters typed by the user. You should also use the `redisplay` attribute and set it to false so that the password that the user types does not show up if a user uses the `"show source"` option on their web browser:

```
<html:password property="password" size="9" maxlength="9"
               redisplay="false"/>
<br />
```

You should use the `submit` tag in the html tag library in order to properly interact with the Struts servlet:

```
<html:submit property="submit" >
```

Once again, you should avoid using string literals, so you use the `message` tag in the bean tag library to specify the text field for the submit button:

```
          <bean:message key="button.login"/>
    </html:submit>
  </html:form>

</body>
</html:html>
```

There are a few things to be careful of when writing the JSP-based view component; the most important is to remember to properly nest the tag library tags. Not closing tags properly or forgetting to use tags from the tag libraries instead of regular HTML elements will cause strange runtime problems that are sometimes difficult to track down (I speak from experience).

NOTE In the Struts example project in this solution I did not use JSP include file directives because the JSPs were simple. In a production system, I recommend that you aggressively "factor out" common code like the error message display code shown above, tag library statements, etc. into separate files and include them as needed in other JSPs. This will reduce the overall line count of your JSP files and make maintenance simpler.

The following code snippets show the contents of the file `prime.jsp`. This example uses some embedded Java script code. As in the `index.jsp` file, you specify Java as the scripting language and define URIs and XML namespace prefixes for the bean and html tag libraries:

```
<%@ page language="java" %>

<%@ taglib uri="/WEB-INF/struts-bean.tld" prefix="bean" %>
<%@ taglib uri="/WEB-INF/struts-html.tld" prefix="html" %>

<html:html>
  <head>
        <title>
           <bean:message key="index.title"/>
        </title>
  </head>

<body>
  <h1>Hello <%= session.getAttribute("userName") %></h1>
```

The following Java code gets the session data attribute "primeResults" that was set in the class `PrimeAction` and displays it:

```
<%
   String primeResults =
          (String)session.getAttribute("primeResults");
   if (primeResults != null)
       out.println("<b>"+primeResults+"</b>");
%>

<h2>Enter a number</h2>
```

This displayed information will either be an error message if the last number entered was not a legal numeric format, or it will be the results of testing the last entered number. After displaying the previous results (or an error message), you use a html tag library form tag to get a number form the user:

```
  <html:form action="/prime" focus="number">
    <bean:message key="prompt.number"/>
    <html:text property="number" size="12" maxlength="12"/>
    <br />
```

```
      <html:submit property="submit" >
           <bean:message key="button.check.prime"/>
      </html:submit>
    </html:form>

  </body>
  </html:html>
```

NOTE I am not using cascading style sheets in this Struts example because I am trying to make it as simple as possible and still introduce the key ideas for using Struts. In a production system, I would strongly recommend the use of style sheets (see Solution 45).

Running the Example Web Application

I assume that you have unzipped the file `part10.zip` in your TOMCAT `webapps` directory that created the S49 subdirectory for this example web application. You can reference the URL `http://localhost:8080/S49` that is mapped (via the welcome page list in `web.xml`) to the `index.jsp` page. The following illustration shows this login page:

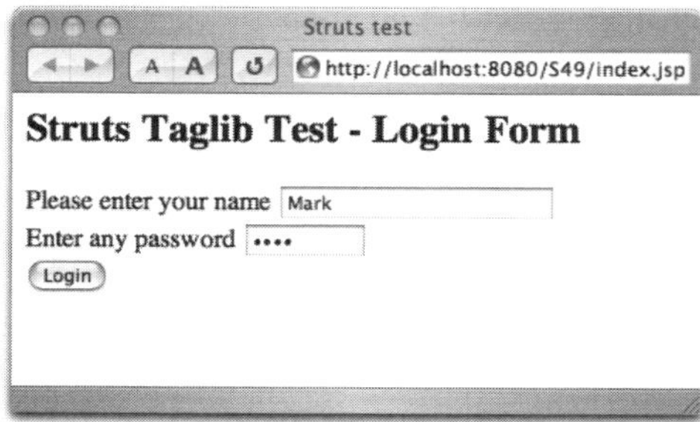

The following illustration shows the prime number test entry page:

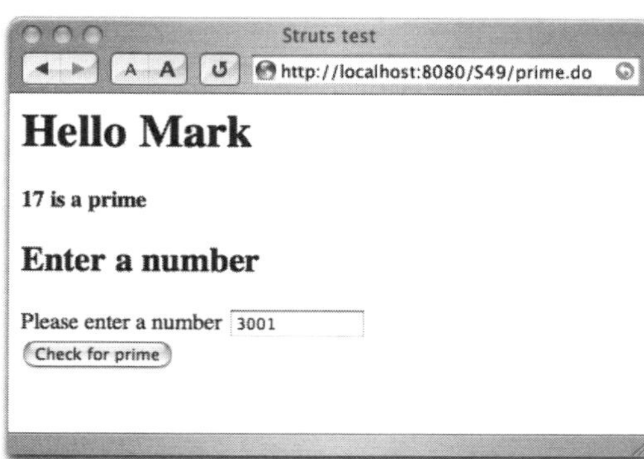

NOTE In Automating Development with Ant, jUnit and XDoclet, I will cover the use of the ant tool. I will give an example of an ant build file for building and deploying Struts-based web applications to a Tomcat web server and servlet/JSP container.

Further Study

You now have a good understanding of the Struts MVC architecture and you know how to write form and action classes, but you have only been introduced to two Struts tag libraries (html and bean). I have just scratched the surface in introducing the Struts tag libraries. You should check out the logic, nested, and tile tag references on the Apache Jakarta Struts site: `http://jakarta.apache.org/struts/`.

There are other useful Struts tag libraries and Sun Microsystems' Java Standard Template Libraries (JSTL). If you search the web, you will also find many useful tag libraries written by individuals and organizations.

If you have worked completely through this rather long "10-minute solution," you have learned a lot of new material. Definitely time to take a break. When you want to learn more about using Struts, the official Struts website has a very complete reference for using Struts at `http://jakarta.apache.org/struts/userGuide/`.

Enterprise JavaBeans (EJBs)

SOLUTION 50

Using Stateless Session EJBs to Develop Web Applications

PROBLEM You want to use the EJB Java Enterprise Component Model to write web applications.

SOLUTION You will install the JBoss EJB container and write a stateless session EJB and example client.

Writing and deploying EJBs has the reputation of being complex and difficult. While it is true that writing Java Enterprise systems is huge subject that I do not attempt to completely cover in this book, I am going to show you a few shortcuts for deploying simple applications as EJBs. Part of the magic of this simple approach is using ant and XDoclet. I will cover these topics separately in Solutions 54 and 57, where I will show you how to write generic ant build files for building and deploying different types of EJBs. You will see shortly that if you use XDoclet style JavaDoc tags in a Java application class, you will be done coding your EJB!

TIP You will notice in Solutions 50 through 53 that I do not explain how EJBs work. I concentrate on showing you how to easily write the commonly used types of EJBs using XDoclet tags. As you start to use EJBs to build web applications, you will want to read at least a few of the detailed EJB tutorials on the Web.

In Solutions 50 through 53, I concentrate on showing you a few relatively simple EJB implementation techniques. EJB components are standardized reusable enterprise components. While EJBs are fairly portable between EJB containers, the configuration of EJBs is container specific. You will use the free and open source JBoss EJB container for Solutions 50 through 53.

NOTE You use ant to build and deploy EJBs to the JBoss container. Solution 57 provides details for building and deploying EJBs to JBoss. Solution 54 covers installing and using ant. Solutions 50 through 53 concentrate on writing EJBs; these solutions use ant build files, so you will need to have ant installed as per the directions in Solution 54.

You should download JBoss bundled with Tomcat from the website `www.jboss.org`. Installing JBoss is simple as unzipping the distribution file. Running JBoss is simple; for Linux, Mac OSX, and Unix, change directory to the `JBOSS/bin` directory and type:

```
/run.sh
```

For Windows, change directory to the `JBOSS/bin` directory and type:

```
run.bat
```

This starts JBoss in the default mode that includes Java Messaging System (JMS) support that you will need in Solution 52 and the built-in default database hsql. You should have JBoss running while you work through Solutions 50 through 53 and Solutions 54 and 57.

The JBoss group makes money to support their activities by selling documentation for the free JBoss software. JBoss developer Andreas Schaefer has written a very good "JBoss 3.0 Quick Start Guide" that is free and which you should download when you get the JBoss/Tomcat bundle. If you start using JBoss for deploying web applications, I suggest you consider purchasing additional documentation from the JBoss developers.

NOTE EJBs are very portable between EJB containers. The examples in this book are tailored to JBoss, ant, and XDoclet. However, except for minor changes to the ant `build.xml` file for the EJBs in this book, they are likely to run with little or no modifications in other EJB containers.

You should permanently set the environment variable `JBOSS_HOME` to the full directory path to your JBoss installation. This environment variable must be set in order for both the client build scripts and the ant EJB build scripts to work. The `JBOSS_HOME` environment variable should not include the bin directory—it should point to the main JBoss installation directory.

Introduction to Session EJBs

EJBs are the component model for Java enterprise development. As a Java programmer, you are familiar with the JavaBean component model that supports private data with public GET/SET methods. Stateless session EJBs are like regular JavaBeans that live in an EJB container and expose some or all of their public methods to both local and remote clients. You will see in Solution 51 that Container Managed Persistent (CMP) EJBs are also like regular JavaBeans except that the EJB container takes over responsibility for persisting them in a database.

The example in this solution uses stateless session EJBs. As the name implies, a stateless session EJB does not maintain any state information between calls to its public API. This is in contrast to stateful session EJBs that support a series of API calls from a single client and maintain state while the session is open. Stateless session EJBs are much more efficient because multiple clients can share a single stateless EJB.

Although you can code stateless EJBs with member variables, you should keep in mind that the EJB container is likely reusing the same bean for multiple clients, so member data may not be consistent or relevant in the face of use by multiple clients. The message is clear: stateless session EJBs are best used for atomic operations where all required data is passed in through API arguments.

You will see in Solution 51 that Container Managed Persistent EJBs are uniquely identified by a primary key that maps an EJB to a row in a specific database table. Stateful session EJBs are somewhat like persistent EJBs except that they do not have a primary key and the state that they maintain is transient—the state is not in general backed up to a persistent store (for example, a relational database).

Implementing a Stateless Session EJB Using XDoclet Tags

Stateless session EJBs do not maintain state between uses: they are used to provide access to objects that implement application-specific APIs. Writing EJBs from scratch is a bit of work: besides writing the application-specific class, there are several other classes that provide support for behaving like an EJB. The good news is that you are going to use XDoclet JavaDoc-like tags to specify EJB configuration information, and the XDoclet ant task will automatically generate the required boilerplate EJB support classes for you. The news gets even better: you will see in Solution 57 how a single ant `build.xml` file can be reused for building and deploying different EJBs by just changing one parameter at the top of the `build.xml` file (if you are curious, this is the name to be given to the EAR deployment file). The file extension "EAR" is usually used for JAR archive files used to deploy EJBs to JBoss. I will deal with the required ant build file in Solution 57. To run the example for this solution, I assume that you have JBoss installed and have ant and XDoclet configured as per the instructions in Solution 54. Here, I will just cover the Java programming techniques for session EJBs.

I will briefly cover the directory layout used for the EJB in this solution. The example directory `parts_12_13_src` contains the EJB examples for this book as well as the ant build files that use XDoclet ant tasks. The example for this solution is in the subdirectory `session`. The following illustration shows a clean source directory structure with no build files (you can always "clean out" this directory by running `ant clean` in the `session` directory):

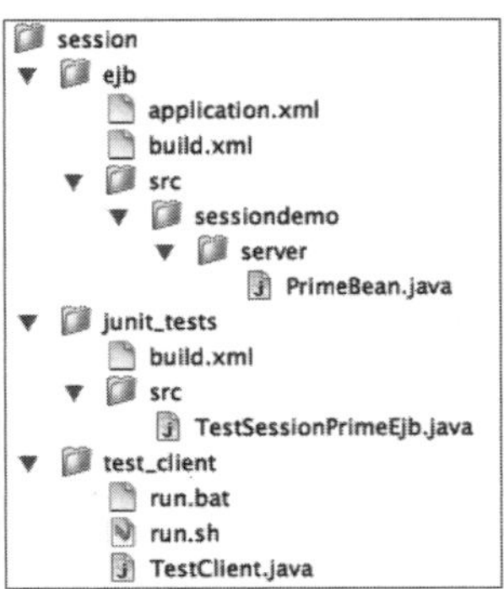

The XML files `application.xml` and `build.xml` files will be discussed in Solution 57 when I show you how to use ant and XDoclet to build and deploy EJBs to the JBoss server. The source code to the EJB and the XDoclet tags are contained in the file `PrimeBean.java`. The subdirectory `junit_tests` contains JUnit material that will be used in the example for Solution 58. You will look at the test client `TestClient.java` later in this solution. The script files for the test client (`run.bat` and `run.sh`) will also be discussed later.

The following code snippets show the implementation of the application-specific EJB class `PrimeBean`. The XDoclet tags defined in the comments are very important: without these tags the XDoclet ant task will not know how to both automatically generate the EJB boilerplate classes and know how to deploy this EJB to JBoss. The naming of the class is also important: for the ant build files (see Solution 57) to work correctly, any classes that you want to build and deploy as EJBs must end in "Bean".

Another requirement for using the `build.xml` file for ant and XDoclet is that the package that a EJB is in must have the last package name equal to `server`—if you change this protocol, then you will have to edit the ant build file. The top-level package names can be anything you want; in this case, you place the class `PrimeBean` in the package `sessiondemo.server` and import the EJB session bean base class `SessionBean`:

```
package sessiondemo.server;
import javax.ejb.SessionBean;
```

When using XDoclet, the `@ejb:bean` tag must appear in the JavaDoc comments for the class implementing the application-specific behavior for a session EJB. The `type` is set to `"Stateless"` indicating a session (nonpersistent) EJB. The `name` attribute should be set to the class name. The attribute `jndi-name` specifies the name that clients of this EJB will use to get a local interface for instances of this EJB class. You will use this `jndi-name` value later when writing a client for this EJB:

```
/**
 * @ejb:bean type="Stateless"
 *           name="PrimeBean"
 *           jndi-name="ejb/PrimeBean"
 *
 * @author markw@markwatson.com
 */
public abstract class PrimeBean implements SessionBean {
```

Any methods that you want to expose to clients of this EJB must use the `@ejb:interface-method` tag. There are three possible view types: local, remote, and both. *Local* refers to use only inside the EJB container (for example by use by other EJBs). *Remote* refers to the use of remote clients. Both refers to implementing both local and remote interfaces. The `view-type` value "both" is the default. I set the value to "remote" because I was only interested in supporting remote clients. In any case, the @ejb:interface-method tag is mandatory:

```
/**
 * @ejb:interface-method view-type="remote"
 */
```

The public method checkPrime() will be available for use by remote clients:

```
    public boolean checkPrime(long number) {
        if (number < 3) return false;
        long half = number / 2;
        for (long i=3; i<half; i+=2) {
            if ((number/i)*i == number) return false;
        }
        return true;
    }
}
```

This is it! This small class using XDoclet tags and a generic ant build file is all you need to write to implement a session EJB. You have probably heard that EJBs are difficult to develop and deploy. Using Aspect Oriented Programming (AOP) as implemented by XDoclet takes the pain away from using EJBs. You will see in Solution 57 that managing the ant and XDoclet build and configuration files is also easy to do.

NOTE You saw a few XDoclet tags used in the example transient session EJB example in this solution. You will be introduced to other EJB-specific tags in later solutions. This website has a complete reference for EJB specific XDoclet tags: http://xdoclet.sourceforge.net/tags/ejb-tags.html. A reference for JBoss-specific tags can be found at: http://xdoclet.sourceforge.net/tags/jboss-tags.html.

In the PrimeBean EJB, I specified a jndi-name value of ejb/PrimeBean. You will see in the next section how to use this name to look up this EJB in the JBoss naming service and obtain a local interface for using the EJB running in the JBoss EJB container. This is similar to using RMI and CORBA (see Solutions 30 through 33).

Implementing a Session EJB Client

Implementing EJB clients is simple: you need to look up the desired EJB using a Java Naming Server, build a local interface to the remote object, and then use the local interface as if it were a local object in the same JVM. This is similar to using RMI and CORBA (see Solutions 30, 31, 32, and 33). This example is specific to the JBoss server. The following code snippets implement a test client. You will need access to the InitialContext and Context classes for obtaining a local interface for the remote EJB; you will use a hash table to set JBoss specific environment parameters for the naming service:

```
import javax.naming.InitialContext;
import javax.naming.Context;
import java.util.Hashtable;
```

The following are local interface stubs for the remote object. You may have noticed that these interfaces do not exist in the example directory—that is because they will be automatically generated by the XDoclet ant tasks that you will see in Solution 57.

```
import sessiondemo.interfaces.PrimeBean;
import sessiondemo.interfaces.PrimeBeanHome;

public class TestClient {

    public static void main(String[] args){
        try {
```

You use a hash table to put environment parameters specific to the JBoss naming service. The following parameters work for JBoss running on the same computer (notice the `"localhost"` value—that could be replaced by an absolute IP address or the domain name of a remote server):

```
Hashtable env = new Hashtable();
env.put(Context.INITIAL_CONTEXT_FACTORY,
        "org.jnp.interfaces.NamingContextFactory");
env.put(Context.PROVIDER_URL, "localhost:1099");
env.put("java.naming.factory.url.pkgs",
        "org.jboss.naming:org.jnp.interfaces");
```

You use these parameters for getting an initial context for accessing the JBoss server's JNDI naming service:

```
InitialContext lContext = new InitialContext(env);
```

You use this initial JNDI naming context to look up a home interface for a remote `PrimeBean` object. You should notice that the JNDI lookup name is identical to the `jndi-name` attribute for the `@ejb:bean` tag that you saw in the last section:

```
PrimeBeanHome lHome =
  (PrimeBeanHome) lContext.lookup( "ejb/PrimeBean" );
```

Finally, you can now get a local interface for the remote object. You should note that `PrimeBean` is the interface `sessiondemo.interfaces.PrimeBean` and not the implementation of the remote EJB class:

```
PrimeBean primeBean = lHome.create();
for (long i=3; i<2000; i++) {
```

Here you can use the local interface as if you had an instance of the real implementation class available:

```
        if (primeBean.checkPrime(i)) {
            System.out.println("" + i +
                               " is a prime number");
        }
    }
```

The following call cleans up the connection to the remote object:

```
                primeBean.remove();
            } catch( Exception e ){
                e.printStackTrace();
            }
        }
    }
```

This example showed a standalone client using a remote EJB. EJB clients are frequently other EJBs, servlets, and JSPs. For EJBs, servlets, and JSPs running in the JBoss/Tomcat server, you should make sure to specify the `@ejb:interface-method` view-type attribute as either `"local"` or `"both"` when you write your EJB implementation class using XDoclet tags.

After you read Solutions 54 and 57 (so you can build and deploy the PrimeBean EJB), you can compile and run this client using the scripts `run.sh` (for Mac OS X, Linux, and Unix) and `run.bat` (for Windows). Discussing these scripts is useful; here is the `run.sh` script:

```
javac -classpath .:$JBOSS_HOME/client/jbossall-client.jar:../ejb/build/session_
demo.jar *.java
java -classpath .:$JBOSS_HOME/client/jbossall-client.jar:$JBOSS_HOME/client/
log4j.jar:../ejb/build/session_demo.jar TestClient
```

Note that each of these commands should appear on one line (please ignore the line wrap). I assume that you have set the environment variable `JBOSS_HOME` to the top level JBoss installation directory. I am using both the JBoss client JARs and the `session_demo.jar` file that you will build in Solution 57.

WARNING My apologies if it is confusing having to refer forward to Solutions 54 for installing ant and XDoclet and to Solution 57 for learning how to use ant and XDoclet to support EJB development. I try to keep solutions in this book short and focused on teaching one specific technique (when possible), so splitting the Java coding aspects of EJBs from the ant and XDoclet build and deployment techniques seemed reasonable.

Although the code example in this section is for a standalone Java client (that is, a client running in a remote JVM, which is different from JVM running the JBoss server), you will use the same code when accessing EJBs in other EJBs and servlets/JSPs running in the JBoss/Tomcat server. The only difference is that if the EJB client code is running in the JBoss server, you do not need to set up the environment before getting a naming context:

```
InitialContext lContext = new InitialContext();
```

In the code example, you passed a hash table with environment settings for the JBoss JNDI naming service to the `InitialContext` constructor—this is not required when running inside the JVM for the JBoss server.

NOTE The directory `parts_13_13_src/junit_tests` contains JUnit tests that you will look at in Solution 58.

SOLUTION 51

Using Container Managed Persistent EJBs to Simplify Database Access

PROBLEM You want to use a database in your web application.

SOLUTION You will use Container Managed Persistence (CMP) EJBs.

Container Managed Persistence (CMP) EJBs take the hassles out of saving the state of EJBs to a relational database. Using CMP also allows your web applications to take advantage of performance enhancements in an EJB container for managing database connection pools, and so on. The example in this solution uses a simple customer database table and a short Java class `CustomerBean` that uses XDoclet tags to provide information for automatically generating the boilerplate code for CMP EJBs.

WARNING You will be surprised how simple it is to write CMP EJBs for the JBoss platform. However, you will be relying on XDoclet to write a lot of code, so you must be careful when using this solution as a development template when you write your own CMP EJBs: the XDoclet tags that are in the example `CustomerBean` class drive this automatic code generation. I will cover XDoclet in Solution 57.

Introduction to Persistent EJBs

You are probably familiar with storing data in relational databases. I covered the use of JDBC in Solutions 34 through 39. Persistent EJBs are simply a way to map Java objects to rows in a database table; a CMP EJB is a persistent EJB that is identified by a primary key that maps to a primary key in a database table.

I will not cover Bean Managed Persistence (BMP) in this book with code examples. BMP is more difficult to implement but offers the advantage of being able to use data in more than one database table to persist the state of a single EJB. As an example, you might have a customer table and an order table. A single unique customer might have placed many orders so there is a one-to-many relationship between a customer table and an order table. You might want a single persistent EJB to maintain state of both a specific customer and all of the orders that the customer has placed.

A persistent EJB may be shared by many clients. For example, several applications might want access to the EJB that represents customer Mary Smith in the database. I will show you in Solution 53 how to use transactions that can avoid simultaneous modification of shared data and provide atomic database operations.

You will see in the next section that the EJB container manages all database access for CMP EJBs: you will not see any JDBC calls embedded in the example code. This makes CMP EJBs very portable because their persistence does not rely on any specific database product. When you use an EJB container like JBoss, you can change the underlying database; for example, you might want to develop a large web application with many EJBs and servlets/JSPs using JBoss with the default built in Hypersonic hsql database and then deploy using either JBoss and Postgress (or MySQL), or move to a commercial web application server using a commercial database product like Oracle.

Database Tables and CMP EJBs

CMP EJBs utilize a database for saving the state of EJBs. The JBoss EJB container will automatically create required tables in the default database for any deployed CMP EJBs. For the example in this solution, I will assume a database table CustomerBean is available with the following columns:

id A unique string identifier (primary key)

name A customer's name

email The customer's e-mail address

As you will see later, this table will be automatically created the first time the example CMP EJB `CustomerBean` is deployed to JBoss. (The example CMP EJB does not explicitly specify a database table name, so the EJB container creates a table with the same name as the EJB.) The JBoss server contains a default database server Hypersonic hsqldb. To make your setup as easy as possible for this solution, you will use this default database server. JBoss and hsql provide a command-line database client that you will find useful to check the contents of database tables, clear all rows from a table, and so on. In order to start the database client, run JBoss and then reference the URL `http://localhost:8080/jmx-console` to bring up the default JBoss management console. On this web page, click the link labeled `service=Hypersonic` and then go to the bottom of the web page and look for a form button labeled void startDatabaseManager() and click the Invoke button. A Java applet should start that contains a text input form in the center top of the window. The following illustration shows this applet running on a Mac OS X desktop:

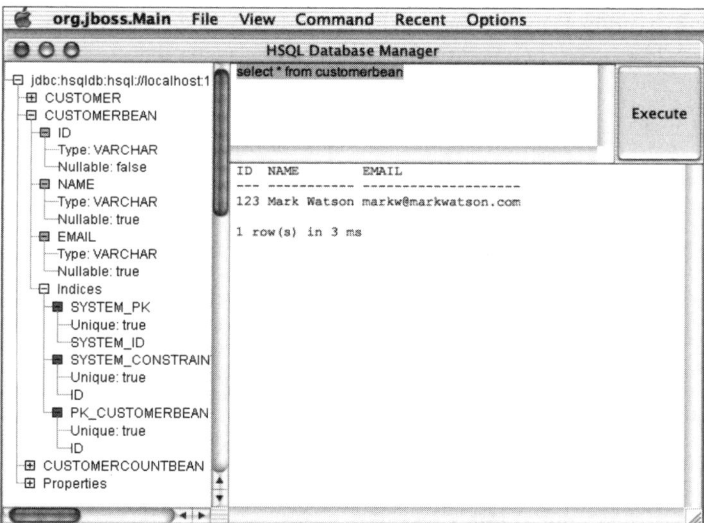

In this figure, I just typed **`select * from customerbean`** and clicked the Execute button. The menus for this applet allow full control over the hsql database built-in to the JBoss server.

Implementing the CustomerBean CMP EJB

CMP EJBs are more complex than session beans (see Solution 50). I will make the example CMP EJB example `CustomerBean` as simple as possible and still show you what you need to do to write your own CMP beans for your web applications. The following code snippets show the complete implementation of the `CustomerBean` class. As in the session EJB example in Solution 50, the CustomerBean class must be in a package ending in `.server` (the ant build file assumes this packaging scheme because the "server" package name is converted to "interface" when automatically generating the Java interfaces for a EJB):

```
package containerdemo.server;
import javax.ejb.*;
```

You need to define six attributes for the `@ejb:bean` tag. The `type` attribute is set to `CMP` to indicate to the XDoclet ant task that this is a Container Managed Persistence EJB. The attribute `cmp-version` will default to the value "1.1", but I like to use the newest CMP standard. The `name` attribute can be anything, but I like to set the value to the class name. The `jndi-name` attribute value will be used by clients of this EJB to find it using a JNDI naming service. The `primary-field` attribute is used to provide information about which field is the primary key field; when the container automatically creates the database table CustomerBean (if required), this will be the primary key for the database. The `view-type` attribute is set to the default value `"both"` (it could be set to `"remote"` or `"local"`):

```
/**
 * @ejb:bean type="CMP"
 *           cmp-version="2.x"
 *           name="CustomerBean"
 *           jndi-name="ejb/CustomerBean"
 *           primkey-field="id"
 *           view-type="both"
 *
```

I set the transaction type to `"Required"` because I will also use this EJB in the transaction example in Solution 53:

```
 * @ejb.transaction type="Required"
 *
```

The `@ejb:pk` tag is used to specify the Java class used for the primary key:

```
 * @ejb.pk class="java.lang.String"
 *
```

The following XDoclet tag is JBoss specific and specifies the primary field name and the column name (this example would work without this tag):

```
 * @jboss.cmp-field field-name="id" column-name="id"
 *
```

The following is a standard JavaDoc tag and will be ignored by the XDoclet ant task:

```
 * @author markw@markwatson.com
 */
public abstract class CustomerBean implements EntityBean {
```

NOTE Stateless session EJBs in Solution 50 implemented the SessionBean interface. You should note that CMP EJBs implement a different interface: the EntityBean interface.

The following five methods must be defined, but for this example they can be empty methods:

```
public void setEntityContext(EntityContext c) { }
public void ejbActivate() { }
public void ejbLoad() { }
public void ejbStore() { }
public void ejbRemove() { }
```

The method `ejbCreate()` is called by an EJB container when creating a new instance of a CMP EJB. The `@ejb.create-method` tag flags this method as a create method so the XDoclet ant task will add this method to the automatically generated `CustomerBeanHome` class:

```
/**
 * @ejb.create-method

 */
public String ejbCreate(String id, String name, String email)
       throws javax.ejb.CreateException {
```

I added the following check on the ID length because I will use this EJB in Solution 53. I will want to be able to force a runtime exception when creating this EJB and showing you how to use transactions:

```
if (id.length() < 1)
    throw new Exception("zero length id");
```

The following three methods are used to fill in values for fields. The EJB container will create a new row in the CustomerBean database table after this method is called, so you need to populate the values that will be written to the database:

```
setId(id);
setName(name);
setEmail(email);
```

Although many people return the primary key value, returning null also works:

```
    return null;
}
```

The container calls `ejbPostCreate` immediately after calling `ejbCreate()` (and before writing a new row in the table CustomerBean):

```
public void ejbPostCreate(String id, String name,
                          String email)
       throws javax.ejb.CreateException {
    // would set Container Managed Relations (CMR) fields
       // here (if we were using them)
}
```

The following six methods are defined to be abstract (the XDoclet ant task will generate actual implementations of these methods in the required subclasses of this abstract class) and all use two XDoclet tags to specify that they are public interface methods and specify the database table column name used for persistence:

```
/**
  * @ejb.persistence column-name="id"
  * @ejb.interface-method
  * @ejb.persistent-field
  */
public abstract void setId(String id);

/**
  * @ejb.persistence column-name="id"
  * @ejb.interface-method
  * @ejb.persistent-field
  */
public abstract String getId();

/**
  * @ejb.persistence column-name="name"
  * @ejb.interface-method
  * @ejb.persistent-field
  */
public abstract String getName();

/**
  * @ejb.persistence column-name="name"
  * @ejb.interface-method
  * @ejb.persistent-field
  */
public abstract void setName(String name);

/**
  * @ejb.persistence column-name="email"
  * @ejb.interface-method
  * @ejb.persistent-field
```

```
     */
    public abstract String getEmail();

    /**
     * @ejb.persistence column-name="email"
     * @ejb.interface-method
     * @ejb.persistent-field
     */
    public abstract void setEmail(String email);
```

With a few additions (that is, the methods starting with `ejb`), this class is a Plain Old Java Object (POJO) that defines fields and GET/SET methods for those fields. The good news is that the slight overhead of supplying required `ejb` methods and the standard XDoclet tags for CMP EJBs allows POJO classes to be trivially turned into persistent data object classes for web applications. In the next section, you will see how to write a test client for this CMP EJB and get a better idea of how to use CMP EJBs.

NOTE You will see in Solution 53 how an EJB container provides support for transactions in client EJBs that use CMP EJBs. This will help convince you that EJBs are a powerful and relatively simple to use technology for building robust and efficient web applications.

Implementing a Test Client

In this section, you will see how to write remote clients that use CMP EJBs and also get a better understanding of how CMP EJBs work. In this example, you will create a customer object by specifying the primary key for the desired customer, change fields in a customer object, persist these changes back to the database, create new customers in the database (by creating a new `CustomerBean` EJB), and delete customers from the database.

NOTE The following example assumes that there is a row in the CustomerBean database table with a primary key `"123"`. You should create a row using the hsql applet that I showed you earlier; for example, execute the following SQL command: `insert into customerbean values ('123', 'Mark', 'mark@cc.com')`.

The following import statements are used to access both standard Java classes (the naming context and initial context classes and the hash table utility class) and the interface `CustomerBean` and class `CustomerBeanHome` generated automatically for you by the XDoclet ant task:

```
import javax.naming.InitialContext;
import javax.naming.Context;
```

```
import java.util.Hashtable;

import containerdemo.interfaces.CustomerBean;
import containerdemo.interfaces.CustomerBeanHome;

public class TestClient {

    public static void main(String[] args){
        try {
```

As you saw in the client example in Solution 50, you need to set up environment parameters for the remote JBoss JNDI naming service:

```
Hashtable env = new Hashtable();
env.put(Context.INITIAL_CONTEXT_FACTORY,
        "org.jnp.interfaces.NamingContextFactory");
env.put(Context.PROVIDER_URL, "localhost:1099");
env.put("java.naming.factory.url.pkgs",
        "org.jboss.naming:org.jnp.interfaces");
InitialContext lContext = new InitialContext(env);
```

Creating a home interface from a JNDI lookup will allow you to later create a local interface for the remote EJB:

```
CustomerBeanHome lHome =
    (CustomerBeanHome)
     lContext.lookup( "ejb/CustomerBean" );
```

Now, you will try to find a customer in the database with a primary key of `"123"` (if you did not create a row with this primary key, comment out this part of the example):

```
CustomerBean customerBean =
   lHome.findByPrimaryKey("123");
```

You can get fields from the remote EJB using the local interface:

```
String name = customerBean.getName();
String email = customerBean.getEmail();
System.out.println("Name: " + name + ", email: "
                   + email);
```

You can also change a field value and persist this change back to the database:

```
customerBean.setEmail(email+".com");
System.out.println("Modified email in database: "
                   + customerBean.getEmail());
```

If you do not change the value back to the original value, then the database will be permanently modified:

```
customerBean.setEmail(email);
```

You can also create a new customer in the database:

```
lHome.create("222","Carol","carol@cc.com");
```

As an example, you can fetch this new object back out of the database:

```
customerBean = lHome.findByPrimaryKey("222");
name = customerBean.getName();
email = customerBean.getEmail();
System.out.println("New customer: name: " + name
                   + ", email: " + email);
```

Use the remove() method if you want to remove a customer object from the database:

```
            customerBean.remove();

        } catch( Exception e ){
            e.printStackTrace();
        }
    }
}
```

As you see from this example, except for a little hassle getting local interfaces for remote objects, once you have a local interface you can use a remote object as if it were a local object in the same JVM.

The directory parts_12_13_src/container/test_client contains scripts for both Windows and Linux/MacOS X/Unix for compiling and running this example client program; here is the Linux script:

```
javac -classpath .:$JBOSS_HOME/client/jbossall-client.jar:../ejb/build/
container_managed_demo.jar *.java
java -classpath .:$JBOSS_HOME/client/jbossall-client.jar:$JBOSS_HOME/client/
log4j.jar:../ejb/build/container_managed_demo.jar TestClient
```

Both of these commands should each appear on one line—the lines wrap here because of limited page width. You need to have built and deployed the CustomerBean EJB and started the JBoss server before running this test client.

You Want to Manually Use JDBC in Your EJBs

Because I am trying to make the use of EJBs as simple as possible, I am not using Bean Managed Persistence (BMP) or Bean Managed Transactions in this book. That said, it is useful to show you how to get a JDBC connection for the default JBoss database server inside any EJB:

```
InitialContext lContext = new InitialContext();
DataSource dataSource = (DataSource)lContext.lookup("java:/DefaultDS");
System.out.println("dataSource="+dataSource);
java.sql.Connection conn = dataSource.getConnection();
```

```
Statement stmt = conn.createStatement();
ResultSet rs = stmt.executeQuery("select * from customerbean");
while (rs.next()) {
     String id = rs.getString(1);
     String name = rs.getString(2);
     System.out.println("id="+id+", name="+name);
}
conn.close();
```

I have not shown error handling code in this snippet.

SOLUTION **52**

Using Message-Driven EJBs for Asynchronous Processing

PROBLEM You want web application code in EJBs to interact asynchronously with other EJBs.

SOLUTION You will use message-driven EJBs and learn how to use the Java Messaging Service.

Message-Driven EJBs (MDBs) use the Java Messaging Service (JMS) to support transaction-aware asynchronous communication between EJBs in a EJB container and with remote clients. Although I will not go into too much detail in this book, it is the combination of automatic support for transactions and JMS-based asynchronous messaging that makes MDBs such a powerful tool for building large-scale robust web applications.

Short Introduction to JMS

JMS provides fault-tolerant asynchronous message delivery. The JBoss system provides a built-in JMS facility that you will use in this solution.

NOTE If you want to use JMS in standalone Java applications, I recommend the open source Joram JMS implementation that you can download from `http://joram.objectweb.org`. More information on JMS can be found at `http://java.sun.com/products/jms/`.

Used either as part of a J2EE-compliant server or (with Joram or commercial JMS systems) in standalone Java applications, asynchronous messaging allows you to efficiently communicate between components of large-scale systems. Asynchronous messaging is an important technique for dealing with long running services: services can accept a message, perform the required work, and then accept the next available message.

JMS works in two primary modes: sending messages to a message queue and allowing other programs to register as listeners, and using publish and subscribe. Message queues have a specific JNDI name—listeners can look up message queues and process available messages. For publish subscribe, JNDI names specify topics.

NOTE I will only use message queues in this example, not publish and subscribe.

JMS servers are usually configured in either a persistent mode or a higher performance non-persistent mode. In persistent mode, all message traffic is immediately logged to the file system to enable recovery in the event of server crashes (assuming that the file system remains intact). Running in persistent mode makes it simpler to design distributed systems that are robust in the face of server crashes, network partitions, and so on.

Defining JMS Message Queues in JBoss

For the MDB example, you will need one message queue. Although JBoss sets up several test message queues by default, I will show you how to create a new queue. There are several ways to create message queues in JBoss:

- Use the management console to create temporary message queues that last only while the JBoss server is running.
- Edit the existing `JBOSS/server/default/deploy/jbossmq-destinations-service.xml` file and add new elements for your message queues.
- Create a new XML file in the directory `JBOSS/server/default/deploy` that ends with `-service.xml` and contains elements for your message queues.

You can access the management console by using the URL `http://localhost:8080/jmx-console`. I don't recommend using this technique for creating message queues, however, because you have to manually create the queues every time you restart the JBoss server. In the discussion that follows, I will assume that you are simply adding new queue definition elements at the end of the file `jbossmq-destinations-service.xml` (add the new `<mbean>` elements before the closing `</server>` tag at the end of the file.

Here is a listing of the end of this file after I added the new queue name definition elements to define a queue name `CheckPrime`:

```
<!-- MLW: added for Java 10 minute solutions book examples: -->
    <mbean code="org.jboss.mq.server.jmx.Queue"
```

```
        name="jboss.mq.destination:service=Queue,name=CheckPrime">
        <depends optional-attribute-name="DestinationManager">
           jboss.mq:service=DestinationManager
        </depends>
     </mbean>
</server>
```

If the JBoss server is already running, you should stop it and restart it so this configuration change takes effect. You will access this message queue by doing a JNDI naming lookup using the name `/queue/CheckPrime`.

Implementing a Message-Driven EJB for Determining Prime Numbers

A Message-Driven EJB (MDB) is a stateless session EJB that acts as a JMS message listener. The EJB container invokes the bean whenever a message is available on a registered queue or topic.

MDBs are very different from other types of EJBs: they do not have a home class of a local interface. Instead they receive incoming messages from a message queue through a simple mechanism: the EJB container calls the `onMessage()` method of an MDB when there are available messages on its queue.

You will notice something different in this EJB: no XDoclet tags! The ant build file for this example is very different from the build file used for Solutions 50 and 51 (session and CMP EJBs) because it does not use the XDoclet ant task. I will cover the ant build file for this example MDB in Solution 57.

```
package message.prime;

import javax.ejb.*;
import javax.jms.*;
import javax.naming.*;
```

The class `PrimeMessageBean` implements two interfaces: `javax.ejb.MessageDrivenBean` and `javax.jms.MessageListener`. The `MessageDrivenBean` interface defines two method signatures: `ejbRemove()` and `setMessageDrivenContext()`. The `MessageListener` interface defines the method signature `onMessage()`:

```
public class PrimeMessageBean
    implements MessageDrivenBean, MessageListener {
```

The method `onMessage()` is called with a `javax.jms.Message` object containing the incoming message:

```
public void onMessage(Message msg) {
```

The class `Message` provides a uniform API for all types of JMS messages. This method is written to handle the `Message` subclass `TextMessage` so you cast the argument to a TextMessage object:

```
TextMessage textMessage = (TextMessage)msg;
try {
```

You will not use this value in this example, but I wanted to show you how to get the name of the requestor who sent this message. In this example, no response is returned explicitly to the sender, although you will later configure this MDB (in Solution 57) to automatically acknowledge message receipt to the JMS server:

```
        String requestorName =
            textMessage.getStringProperty("requestorName");
        System.out.println("Requestor name: " +
                           requestorName);
```

You will get the text from the message and parse it as a long integer. It is common for JMS message listeners to accept work, do the work, and have no further explicit communication with the requestor. In this example, you print out a result to the JBoss default output log (this output appears in the command window where you run the JBoss server):

```
        String numberText = textMessage.getText();
        long num = -1;
        try {
            num = Long.parseLong(numberText);
            System.out.println(" Number: " + num);
            System.out.println(" Prime status: " +
                               checkPrime(num));
        } catch (Exception e) {
            System.out.println(" Number: " + numberText +
                     " is not a valid number format.");
        }
    }
    catch(JMSException ex) {
        ex.printStackTrace();
    }
}
```

The following method simply checks for prime number status:

```
private boolean checkPrime(long number) {
    if (number < 3) return false;
    long half = number / 2;
    for (long i=3; i<half; i+=2) {
        if ((number/i)*i == number) return false;
    }
    return true;
}
```

In this example, the `ejbRemove()` method does not have to do anything when the EJB container removes this object after it is no longer needed:

```
        public void ejbRemove() {
        }
```

The `setMessageDrivenContext()` method is required; you do not use the context in this example:

```
        public void setMessageDrivenContext(MessageDrivenContext ctx){
            this.ctx = ctx;
        }
        private MessageDrivenContext ctx;
    }
```

This example MDB does not directly acknowledge to the requestor that it has executed the requested action. This is common in JMS applications where messages delivered are assumed to be guaranteed. Ideally, if the server running this MDB crashes (for example) while the `onMessage()` method is executing the desired action, the JMS server will resend the message at a later time (depending on how the JMS server is configured).

Implementing a Test Client Application

MBD clients can be EJBs or servlets/JSPs running in the same application server or external client programs executing in remote JVMs. The example program in this section (the class `TestClient`) is a standalone Java program that runs in a remote JVM:

```
import javax.naming.InitialContext;
import javax.naming.Context;
import java.util.Hashtable;
import javax.jms.*;

public class TestClient {

    public static void main(String[] args){
        try {
```

Because this program is not running inside the same JVM as the JBoss server, you need to set up the environment to access the remote JBoss JNDI server (in this case, running on `localhost`—the same computer):

```
            Hashtable env = new Hashtable();
            env.put(Context.INITIAL_CONTEXT_FACTORY,
                    "org.jnp.interfaces.NamingContextFactory");
            env.put(Context.PROVIDER_URL, "localhost:1099");
            env.put("java.naming.factory.url.pkgs",
                    "org.jboss.naming:org.jnp.interfaces");
            InitialContext lContext = new InitialContext(env);
```

The example MDB is configured (in Solution 57) to use the message queue CheckPrime, so the JNDI lookup name is queue/CheckPrime:

```
Queue queue =
   (Queue)lContext.lookup("queue/CheckPrime");
```

You need a queue connection factory; this is similar to getting a home interface when accessing session and CMP EJBs:

```
QueueConnectionFactory qcf =
   (QueueConnectionFactory)
    lContext.lookup("ConnectionFactory");
```

You do not need the lookup context once you have a queue connection factory, so the context can be closed:

```
lContext.close();
```

Here you create a queue connection. This is similar to getting a connection to a database:

```
QueueConnection qc = qcf.createQueueConnection();
```

You create a session that can be used to group a batch of outgoing messages and commit them all at one time:

```
QueueSession qs = qc.createQueueSession(true, 0);
```

You now create a queue sender that can be used to send messages to a message queue:

```
QueueSender qsend = qs.createSender(queue);
```

The example MDB expects a text message so you create one and set the text field:

```
TextMessage msg = qs.createTextMessage();
msg.setText("13");
```

Here you are only sending one message. It is sometimes useful to batch up many messages and then commit them all at one time:

```
qsend.send(msg);
```

The message is actually sent only when the commit() method on the queue sender is called:

```
qs.commit();
```

You should free resources by closing the queue connection when you are done with it:

```
            qc.close();
          } catch( Exception e ){
            e.printStackTrace();
          }
      }
  }
```

If you are using a standalone JMS server with standard (that is, not running in an EJB container) Java applications, you will use similar code. The directory `parts_12_13_src/message/test_client` contains scripts for both Windows and Linux/MacOS X/Unix for compiling and running this example client program; here is the Linux script:

```
javac -classpath .:$JBOSS_HOME/client/jbossall-client.jar:$JBOSS_HOME/client/
jbossmq-client-client.jar *.java
java -classpath .:$JBOSS_HOME/client/jbossall-client.jar:$JBOSS_HOME/client/
log4j.jar:$JBOSS_HOME/client/jbossmq-client-client.jar TestClient
```

Both of these commands should each appear on one line—the lines wrap here because of limited page width. You need to have built and deployed the `PrimeMessageBean` EJB and started the JBoss server before running this test client.

SOLUTION 53

Using Container Managed Transactions for Database Integrity

PROBLEM You want to use CMP EJBs and want either all actions using these EJBs to occur, or none.

SOLUTION You will use the transaction support built-in to EJB containers.

I discussed database transactions in Solution 38 where you bound multiple JDBC update requests into single transactions for "all or nothing" changes to a database. In this solution, you will do something similar except that you do not directly use JDBC—you use CMP EJBs that indirectly access the database under management of the EJB container. You will use JBoss for this example, but the Java code in this solution should be portable to other EJB containers.

Implementing Container Managed Transactions in an EJB

You will develop a stateless session EJB in this section using XDoclet tags. This example EJB uses the `CustomerBean` CMP EJB from Solution 51. In this example, you will create three new customer objects that are persisted to the database table CustomerBean. If any of these three operations fail, then none of the three new customers will be created.

WARNING This example will fail if the customers are already in the database table CustomerBean, so you should use the JBoss Hypersonic hsql applet and execute the following SQL statement: `delete from customerbean`. This will clear all data from this table. You need to run this update before running the test client in the next section.

This session EJB is similar to the session example in Solution 50 with just a few changes to support transactions. As in Solutions 50 and 51, the package for this class must end in `.server` because the ant build file relies on this packaging scheme:

```
package transactiondemo.server;

import javax.ejb.*;
import javax.naming.*;
import javax.jms.*;
import java.rmi.RemoteException;

import java.util.*;
```

The following two interfaces were created when building the example CMP EJB in Solution 51:

```
import containerdemo.interfaces.CustomerBean;
import containerdemo.interfaces.CustomerBeanHome;
```

The `@ejb:bean` XDoclet tag specifies that the EJB container is responsible for handling transactions. The EJB container will consider a rollback necessary if the method `testTransaction()` throws either an `EJBException` or any exception that is a subclass of `EJBException`:

```
/**
 * @ejb:bean type="Stateless"
 *           name="TransactionBean"
 *           jndi-name="ejb/TransactionBean"
 *           transaction-type="Container"
 *
 * @author markw@markwatson.com
 */
public abstract class TransactionBean implements SessionBean {
```

You use the XDoclet `@ejb:transaction` tag to specify that transactions are required when executing this method:

```
/**
 * @ejb:interface-method view-type="remote"
 * @ejb:transaction type="Required"
 */
public void testTransaction() throws EJBException {
  try {
     InitialContext lContext = new InitialContext();
```

Because you are going to use the CMP EJB from Solution 51, you need to create a home interface for this `CustomerBean` EJB that can be used to create all three new customers:

```
CustomerBeanHome lHome =
  (CustomerBeanHome)lContext.lookup("ejb/CustomerBean");
```

For a test, initially create two new customers; this will not fail as long as the database table CustomerBean had all rows deleted before calling this method:

```
lHome.create("222","Carol","carol@cc.com");
lHome.create("227","Julie","julie@cc.com");
```

If you uncomment the following line, then a customer with a zero length ID field will be created, but this will throw an exception:

```
    //lHome.create("", "Mary", "mary@cc.com");
    lHome.create("229","David","david@cc.com");
} catch (Exception e) {
```

The code in this `catch` block will be executed if any errors occurred while trying to create the new customers in the database. Note that I am throwing an `EJBException`; this is a flag to the EJB container that an error occurred that requires a rollback. If you throw, for example, a plain `Exception`, then the rollback will not work.

```
          throw new EJBException("Transaction failed: " + e);
        }
      }
}
```

As you see in this simple example, using container managed transactions is simple as long as the CMP EJBs are configured to also use container managed transactions. To refresh your memory, here is the relevant XDoclet tag used in Solution 51 when writing the `CustomerBean` CMP EJB:

```
* @ejb.transaction type="Required"
```

Implementing a Test Client

The test client gets a local interface for a remote `TransactionBean` EJB and calls the method `testTransaction()`. If the remote EJB throws an exception, then the exception will be returned to the client and a stack trace will be printed—if there is an error, no customers will be added to the database.

The following code snippets are from the file `parts_12_13_src/transaction/test_client/TestClient.java`:

```
import javax.naming.InitialContext;
import javax.naming.Context;
```

```
import java.util.Hashtable;

import transactiondemo.interfaces.TransactionBean;
import transactiondemo.interfaces.TransactionBeanHome;

public class TestClient {

    public static void main(String[] args){
        try {
```

You must set up the parameters to access a remote JBoss JNDI service:

```
Hashtable env = new Hashtable();
env.put(Context.INITIAL_CONTEXT_FACTORY,
        "org.jnp.interfaces.NamingContextFactory");
env.put(Context.PROVIDER_URL, "localhost:1099");
env.put("java.naming.factory.url.pkgs",
        "org.jboss.naming:org.jnp.interfaces");
InitialContext lContext = new InitialContext(env);
```

You use a context lookup to get a home interface for the remote EJB class:

```
TransactionBeanHome lHome =
     (TransactionBeanHome)
     lContext.lookup("ejb/TransactionBean");
```

You get a local interface for the remote object and call the `testTransaction()` method:

```
            TransactionBean transBean = lHome.create();
            transBean.testTransaction();
        } catch( Exception e ){
            e.printStackTrace();
        }
    }
}
```

The directory `parts_12_13_src/transaction/test_client` contains scripts for both Windows and Linux/MacOS X/Unix for compiling and running this example client program; here is the Linux script:

```
javac -classpath .:$JBOSS_HOME/client/jbossall-client.jar:../ejb/build/
transaction_demo.jar *.java
java -classpath .:$JBOSS_HOME/client/jbossall-client.jar:$JBOSS_HOME/client/
log4j.jar:../ejb/build/transaction_demo.jar TestClient
```

Each of these commands should appear on one line—the lines wrap here because of limited page width. You need to have built and deployed the `TransactionBean` EJB and started the JBoss server before running this test client.

EJB Wrap Up

Writing and deploying EJBs has a perhaps justified reputation for being difficult. In Solutions 50 through 53 I tried to take a "show you how to do it" rather than "how does this work?" approach to introducing you to EJBs. Using XDoclet tags is certainly a large help; for session and persistent beans this saves you the work of writing "home" and "remote" Java interfaces. I will cover the required ant and XDoclet XML configuration files for these EJB solutions in Solution 57. After reading Solution 57, you should be able to augment your web applications by using stateless session and Container Managed Persistence EJBs. Using JSPs for presentation and EJBs for "business logic" is a common design pattern and implementation strategy for medium to complex web applications.

If you do use EJBs in your projects, eventually you will have to learn how EJBs work, how the EJB container manages the life cycle of different types of EJBs, and so on. It is likely that you will eventually want to use bean managed persistence EJBs in order to use one-to-many database table mappings in some EJBs.

I recommend that you start to use EJBs the "easy way" with the generic ant build scripts in Solution 57 and the example EJBs in Solutions 50 through 53 as implementation templates. This will get you started quickly. After you have taken this short cut and used EJBs in practical applications, you will much more easily understand the specifications and documentation for EJB containers and different types of EJBs.

Ant, JUnit, and XDoclet

SOLUTION 54

Installing Ant, JUnit, and XDoclet

PROBLEM You want to use the ant, JUnit, and XDoclet Java programming tools.

SOLUTION I will provide you with download URLs and advice on setting up your development environment so you can easily use ant, JUnit, and XDoclet.

First you need to visit the following websites and download the latest stable versions of ant, JUnit, and XDoclet:

`ant.apache.org`

`www.junit.org`

`xdoclet.sourceforge.net`

Install all three tools in the same directory on your system. This configuration makes sense because you will only run JUnit and XDoclet as ant tasks (discussed in Solutions 55 through 58). I have a directory `bin` on all of my development systems (Mac OS X, Linux, and Windows 2000). I place this `bin` directory on my PATH environment so any scripts (that is, files ending with `.sh` (or no extension) for Mac OS X and Linux or ending with `.bat` for Windows 2000) placed in the `bin` directory can be run from any directory. The following illustration shows the layout of a `bin` directory set up to use JUnit and XDoclet with ant:

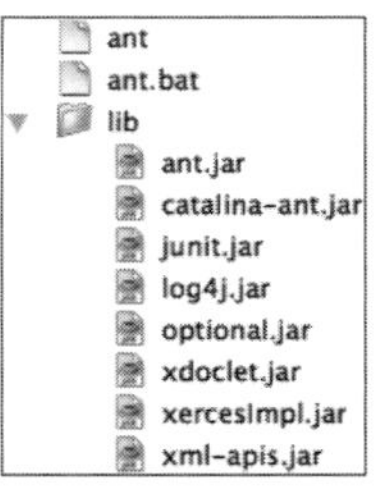

NOTE Actually, my `bin` directory has more command-line scripts; for example: Apache Axis SOAP, ZEUS (see Solution 12), etc. command-line tools.

In the `lib` directory in the previous illustration, the JAR files `ant.jar`, `optional.jar`, `xercesImpl.jar`, `log4j.jar`, and `xml-apis.jar` are required by ant. You get the file `junit.jar` from the JUnit download. The `xdoclet.jar` file is from the XDoclet distribution in the `lib` directory. You can copy the file `catalina-ant.jar` (this will be required for Solution 56) from your Tomcat installation from the directory `TOMCAT/server/lib`.

My top-level `bin` directory in the previous illustration contains a shell script ant that I copied without modification from the ant download distribution. For Mac OS X, Linux, or Windows, there is one more thing that you must do: set the environment variable *ANT_HOME* to the full directory path to your `bin` directory (or whatever you name it). For my Mac OS X system, I have *ANT_HOME* set to `/Users/markw/bin`. For Windows 2000, I have `ANT_HOME` set to `c:\ant`. It is also a good idea to have the *JAVA_HOME* environment variable set to the directory path for your Java Development Kit (JDK).

NOTE A copy of my `bin` directory set up for ant, XDoclet, JUnit, and hot deployment to Tomcat is available in the ZIP file `bin.zip` on the website supporting this book. Using a copy of my bin directory will help ensure that you don't have problems running the ant, XDoclet, JUnit, and Tomcat hot deploy examples in this book. However, you might want to get the latest JAR files form the project websites in order to have the latest versions.

You can perform a preliminary test on your ant installation by putting your new `bin` directory on your *PATH* environment variable and typing **ant**—you should get a warning:

```
Buildfile: build.xml does not exist!
Build failed
```

This error is okay (for now). Ant always expects to find by default a build script named `build.xml` in the current directory. Using ant with the examples in Solutions 55 through 58 will further test your installation.

SOLUTION 55

Using Ant

PROBLEM You want to start using ant in your Java development projects.

SOLUTION I will show you the basics of using ant.

The ant build tool uses scripts written in XML to control the builds, deployments, and tests during development. Additionally, it is possible to customize ant by writing scripts using the Bean Scripting Framework (BSF) language and writing custom ant task definitions in Java. I do not cover either scripting or custom task definitions in this book. You can find more information by searching the web for "ant BSF scripts" and "writing ant custom tasks."

Ant was developed as part of the Apache project and is the de facto standard for building most medium and large-scale Java applications.

Why Use Ant?

Using ant saves time for you as a developer. While it is easy enough to compile and run small Java programs using the command `javac` and `java` tools, you will save time by automating as many development related activities as possible. You will learn the basics of using ant in this solution. In Solutions 56, 57, and 58 you will learn how to use ant to streamline your development process for building and deploying servlets and JSPs to Tomcat, running XDoclet to automatically generate EJB boilerplate classes and deploying EJBs to JBoss, and automating the unit testing process with JUnit.

Using Ant with Java IDEs

In order to get the benefits of Java code completion, class refactoring, and so on, most Java developers at least occasionally use an IDE. I usually use the commercial product IntelliJ for most of my Java development and occasionally use the free NetBeans and Eclipse IDEs. The good news is that all of these IDEs support the use of ant. More information on obtaining and using these IDEs with ant is available at the websites `www.intellij.com`, `www.netbeans.org`, and `www.eclipse.org`. There is also an ant build utility for Emacs and JDE.

If you use ant to control building, deploying, and testing your projects, then different developers on your team can use different IDEs and everyone will still have the same standard build process. While IDEs in general save development time, it is also great to have the flexibility to simply use your favorite text editor and command-line ant tools.

A Simple Ant Project Example

I will introduce using ant with a very simple project. The ant example projects for this solution are in a ZIP file, `ant_demos.zip`, on the website for this book. Your first demo project is in a subdirectory `demo1`. Your goals for this project are to:

- Keep Java source code separate from compiled class files.
- Automate the compile process.

- Automate the test process (but not using JUnit, which I will cover in Solution 58).
- Automate cleaning up the project directories (that is, deleting compiled files and the working directory `build`).

While the example Java code for this project is not important (it is trivial), you should pay some attention to the directory structure used. The following illustration shows the directories for a clean project directory:

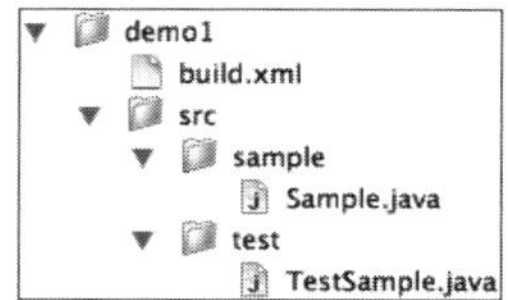

The `build.xml` file is the input to the ant program. The directory `src` contains two java packages `sample` and `test`; each package contains one Java source file. After building this project, there will be a new directory called `build` that contains the compiled class files for both packages:

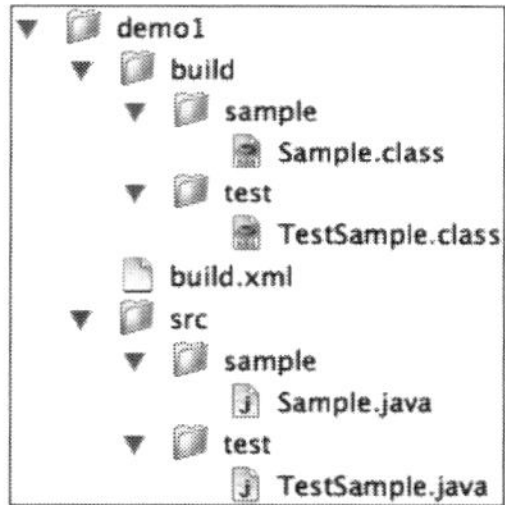

While it is not as important for small projects, it is very important for large projects that you keep compiled class files separate from source files. This will be especially important when you start using XDoclet in Solution 57.

The following code snippets show the entire contents of the file `build.xml` with comments:

```
<?xml version="1.0"?>
```

The top-level element for ant build files is `<project>`. The attribute `name` is an arbitrary name that you give your project, the attribute `default` is the default build target, and the attribute `basedir` is the home directory for the project (which is almost always the directory in which the `build.xml` file is located):

```
<project name="sample" default="test" basedir=".">
```

The first build target is `"compile"`:

```
<target name="compile">
```

The first task for this target is to create the subdirectory `build` if it does not already exist:

```
<mkdir dir="build"/>
```

The second task is to compile all files in a specified directory and recursively compile files in subdirectories. The attribute `destdir` specifies the top-level directory in which the compiled class files are placed (in their proper packages). The attribute `debug` controls the generation of debug-enabled class files (for example, with source line numbers, etc.). The attribute `optimize` controls Java byte code optimization:

```
<javac destdir="build"
       debug="on"
       optimize="on">
```

The element `src` is used to specify the top-level source code path:

```
      <src path="src"/>
   </javac>
</target>
```

The second build target defined in this file is `"test"`. This target depends on the target `"compile"` that you just looked at. Running the `"test"` target will automatically run the `"compile"` target first:

```
<target name="test" depends="compile">
```

You use the ant `<java>` task to run arbitrary Java compiled code. The attribute `fork` has allowed values of `"no"` and `"yes"`. Setting `fork` to `"yes"` runs the specified Java program in a new JVM. The attribute `failonerror` is used to control if ant aborts on any runtime errors when the specified program is executed. The attribute `classname` is used to specify the class with the public static main method to be called. The attribute `classpath` is used to set the CLASSPATH for running the program. (You will see in later examples how to use external JAR files, etc.) Here, the desired CLASSPATH is the `build` subdirectory. The `<arg>` element can be used to pass command-line arguments to the Java program that you are running with the Java ant task; for example, you can set a Java property using `<arg line="-Ddemomode" />`:

```
<java fork="no" failonerror="yes"
         classname="test.TestSample"
         classpath="build">
        <arg line=""/>
   </java>
</target>
```

The last build target defined in this file is `"clean"`. This target deletes the `build` subdirectory and recursively all subdirectories and files.

```
   <target name="clean">
      <delete dir="build"/>
   </target>
</project>
```

The following output shows the ant "test" target that first runs the target "compile":

```
markw% ant test
Buildfile: build.xml

compile:
    [mkdir] Created dir: /Users/markw/Content/Java_10_minute_solutions/ant_
demos/demo1/build
    [javac] Compiling 2 source files to /Users/markw/Content/Java_10_minute_
solutions/ant_demos/demo1/build

test:
     [java] result = 3

BUILD SUCCESSFUL
Total time: 5 seconds
```

Because the build target "test" is the default build target, I did not need to specify test as a command-line argument. The first target "compile:" shows output from two ant tasks: [mkdir] and [javac]. The second target "test:" shows the output form the ant task [java].

After building and testing this project, you can clean up the project directory by running the clean ant target:

```
markw% ant clean
Buildfile: build.xml

clean:
   [delete] Deleting directory /Users/markw/Content/Java_10_minute_solutions/
ant_demos/demo1/build

BUILD SUCCESSFUL
Total time: 3 seconds
```

TIP Although writing ant build files is fairly easy, I usually copy one of my old build files for new similar projects. There are just a few general types of projects that I tend to use ant for, over and over again: simple programs like this demo, applications that build and use JAR files, Tomcat servlet and JSP projects, and JBoss-hosted EJB projects. I copy and reuse my own build files and make tiny modifications as required instead of starting from scratch when I start a new project.

An Ant Project Making and Using Jar Files

I will use another simple project to show you how to make your ant build files more flexible. The goals for this project are to:

- Specify application-specific configuration data at the top of a build file to facilitate reusing build files for future projects.

- Build an application JAR file.
- Use the application JAR file in a test application.

The subdirectory `demo2` contains the files for this project. The following illustration shows the directory layout with a clean project:

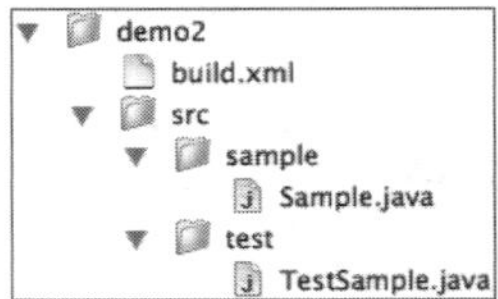

This looks like the directory structure for the first simple demo. After using the ant build file for this new project (which you will look at later), the directory structure looks like the following illustration:

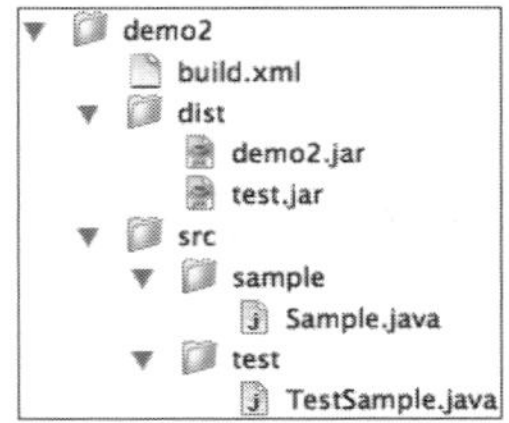

You should notice two things: a new temporary working subdirectory `dist` contains a JAR file `demo2.jar` that contains all of the application classes for this project (one, in this case). This JAR file does not contain the test case. The working directory `build` is not seen in this illustration because it is deleted after the output JAR files are created in the `dist` directory. The following code snippets show the complete contents of the `build.xml` file for this new project:

```
<?xml version="1.0"?>

<project name="sample" default="test" basedir=".">
```

This ant build file can be reused for other projects if you change the following two ant property elements as appropriate:

```
 <!--  NOTE: THE FOLLOWING LINES SHOULD BE EDITED FOR YOUR PROJECT:  -->
 <property name="root.project.name" value="demo2"/>
 <property name="test.class" value="test.TestSample"/>

<!-- NOTE: THE REST OF THIS FILE CAN PROBABLY REMAIN UNCHANGED FOR YOUR NEW
PROJECTS -->
```

You create a filename for the application JAR file from the root `project name` property:

```
<property name="jar.module" value="${root.project.name}.jar"/>
```

It is often useful to define one or more CLASSPATHs that include required directories of compiled class files and paths to JAR files. You will use the path with ID `"test.path"` when running the test program later in this file in the `"test"` target.

```
<path id="test.classpath">
    <pathelement location="dist/${jar.module}"/>
    <pathelement location="dist/test.jar"/>
</path>
```

This is the same target definition that you saw in the first example: recursively compile all Java files in the `src` directory and subdirectories and put the compiled class files in the `build` directory:

```
<target name="compile">
   <mkdir dir="build"/>
   <javac destdir="build"
          debug="on"
          optimize="on">
      <src path="src"/>
   </javac>
</target>
```

The `"makejar"` target depends on the `"compile"` target.

```
<target name="makejar" depends="compile">
```

You use the `<mkdir>` ant task to create the `dist` subdirectory if it does not already exist:

```
    <mkdir dir="dist"/>
```

You use the `jarfile` attribute in the `<jar>` ant task to specify the output JAR file; here you place the output JAR file in the `dist` subdirectory:

```
    <jar jarfile="dist/${jar.module}">
```

You use the `<fileset>` ant task to create a set of files that will be placed in the output JAR file:

```
    <fileset dir="build">
```

You use one or more `<include>` ant tasks to specify files; here, the "**" pattern matches any level of nested subdirectories, so this `<include>` task creates a set of all compiled class files in the `build` directory and in subdirectories in the `build` directory:

```
        <include name="**/*.class"/>
```

It is often useful to exclude files that have been identified by `<include>` tasks. Here, you are asking for all compiled class files except for those in the `test` subdirectory:

```
      <exclude name="test/*.class"/>
    </fileset>
  </jar>
```

Because you have build JAR files for both the application and the `test` class, you can clean up the development directory by deleting the `build` directory:

```
    <delete dir="build"/>
</target>
```

The `"test"` target depends on the `"makejar"` target, which depends on the `"compile"` target:

```
<target name="test" depends="makejar">
```

Instead of specifying a `classpath` attribute as you did in the first ant demo project, you can now use the CLASSPATH ID defined earlier in this build file:

```
<java fork="no" failonerror="yes"
      classname="${test.class}">
    <classpath refid="test.classpath"/>
```

As in the first ant demo project, this test program requires no command-line arguments:

```
            <arg line=""/>
        </java>
    </target>

    <target name="clean">
        <delete dir="build"/>
        <delete dir="dist"/>
    </target>

</project>
```

You can reuse this build file for new projects by copying it and changing the two properties at the top of the file. In specifying a CLASSPATH ID, you can also specify directories in addition to JAR files; for example:

```
<path id="another.test.classpath">
    <pathelement location="build"/>
</path>
```

The following output is from running the default ant target `"test"`:

```
markw% ant
Buildfile: build.xml

compile:
    [mkdir] Created dir: /Users/markw/Content/Java_10_minute_solutions/ant_
demos/demo2/build
    [javac] Compiling 2 source files to /Users/markw/Content/Java_10_minute_
solutions/ant_demos/demo2/build
```

```
makejar:
      [jar] Building jar: /Users/markw/Content/Java_10_minute_solutions/ant_
demos/demo2/dist/demo2.jar
      [jar] Building jar: /Users/markw/Content/Java_10_minute_solutions/ant_
demos/demo2/dist/test.jar
   [delete] Deleting directory /Users/markw/Content/Java_10_minute_solutions/
ant_demos/demo2/build

test:
     [java] result = 3

BUILD SUCCESSFUL
Total time: 4 seconds
```

More Ant Build Techniques

This solution should get you started using ant. In Solution 56, I will show you how to use ant and a Tomcat-specific ant task definition for hot deploying servlets and JSPs to a running Tomcat server—this will save you a lot of development time because you can avoid restarting Tomcat to test new versions of web applications. In Solution 57, I will show you how to use the XDoclet ant task definitions to build EJB web applications and hot deploy them to the JBoss server. In Solution 58, I will show you how to use the JUnit testing framework in ant.

SOLUTION **56**

Using Ant for JSP/Struts Tomcat Projects

PROBLEM You want to start using ant for your JSP/Struts Tomcat development projects.

SOLUTION I will show you how to configure Tomcat to enable the web management application and how to use an ant task for hot deploying web applications to Tomcat.

In the example for this solution I will repackage the JSP/Struts example from Solution 49 and add ant build and deployment support. In Solutions 45 through 49, the build setup I used was too simple for real development: simply keeping all Java source files, JSP files, etc. in the Tomcat `webapps` deployment subdirectories for these solutions. In those JSP solutions, I concentrated on showing you coding techniques. Now that you have been introduced to ant build files in Solution 55, it is time to set you up with a flexible ant build file for building, hot deploying, and hot undeploying web applications to a running Tomcat server. In the example for this solution I will use the most complex JSP example in this book: the JSP Struts example from Solution 49.

In Solution 54, you installed ant, XDoclet, JUnit, and the Tomcat hot deployment ant task. For hot deployment to work, you also need to edit the Tomcat configuration file `TOMCAT/config/tomcat-users.xml` and add an element like the following before the ending `</tomcat-users>` tag:

```
<user name="brady"   password="n2a1t88w"
      roles="standard,manager,admin" />
```

You will probably not want to name your new manager user `"brady"` (the name of my baby parrot), and you will want to use a different password. Later in this solution, you will see where you need to edit the `build.xml` ant script to set the Tomcat manager username and password.

There are many ways to set up web application projects using ant. I am going to show you the method that I like to use because it is simple, easy to understand, and easy to adapt to other JSP-based web applications. While my method works well in my development environment, I urge you to also study other people's ant build files, gather ideas, and be creative in building ant build environments that both save you manual effort in your development and increase your enjoyment of developing web applications.

In designing my JSP ant build setup, I had several goals in mind:

- Separation of Java and JSP source code from compiled and temporary build files
- Clear layout for required web application configuration files
- Automatic hot deployment and undeployment from a running Tomcat server

I like to have a subdirectory `resources` that contains the web application's `WEB-INF` directory with all required files except for compiled Java class files and the source code to the JSPs. I keep the JSPs in the subdirectory `jsp` and the Java application source files in the directory `src`. The following illustration shows a clean development directory that you can get from the zip file `ant_jsp_struts.zip` on the website for this book.

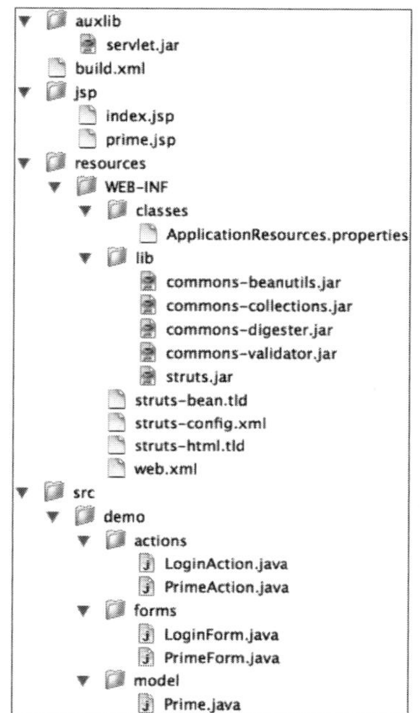

This illustration shows a clean project (you can always get the project back to this state by running `ant clean`). During the build process, a subdirectory `build` is created that holds a copy of all compiled code, JSPs, required Struts library files, and configuration files. A second working subdirectory `dist` is created for the web application WAR file.

TIP Using this build setup for your own JSP/Struts-based web applications is simple: replace the contents of the source directory with your own application classes, replace the JSP files in the subdirectory `jsp` with the JSP files for your application, and edit the first few lines of the `build.xml` files to change the project name and set valid Tomcat username and password property values to support hot deployment.

The following code snippets show the contents of the ant `build.xml` file:

```
<?xml version="1.0"?>
```

When you reuse this ant build script for your own JSP/Struts web applications, you will want to change the project name:

```
<project name="struts_demo" default="dist" basedir=".">
```

You will also want to change the following three property values. The `project.name` property is used for both naming the WAR file and defining the Tomcat web application context name; for example, this web application can be used by accessing the URL `http://localhost:8080/struts_demo`.

```
<property name="project.name" value="struts_demo"/>
<property name="tomcat.username" value="brady"/>
<property name="tomcat.password" value="n2a1t88w"/>
```

You probably do not need to change the management URL unless you have Tomcat running on a different computer from your development machine.

```
<property name="tomcat.manager.url"
          value="http://localhost:8080/manager"/>
```

You should not have to change any of the remaining lines in this build file when reusing it for your projects. Next, you set a local CLASSPATH used for compiling your Java application classes. There are three paths that you need on your CLASSPATH: the output directory where the compiled Java class files will be written, all the Struts JAR files, and the contents of the directory `auxlib`, which in this case is the `servlet.jar` file:

```
<path id="local.classpath">
   <pathelement location="build/WEB-INF/classes"/>
   <fileset dir="build/WEB-INF/lib">
      <include name="*.jar"/>
   </fileset>
   <fileset dir="auxlib">
      <include name="*.jar"/>
   </fileset>
</path>
```

The `prepare-dirs` ant build target simply creates the subdirectory `build` and copies the contents of both subdirectories `resources` and `jsp` into `build`:

```
<target name="prepare-dirs">
   <mkdir dir="build"/>
   <copy todir="build">
      <fileset dir="resources"/>
   </copy>
   <copy todir="build">
      <fileset dir="jsp"/>
   </copy>
</target>
```

The `compile` ant build target recursively compiles all Java source files in the directory `src` and any subdirectories of `src` and places the compiled class files in the build `WEB-INF` classes directory.

You are using the local CLASSPATH that has the Struts JAR files, the `servlet.jar` file, and your previously compiled application classes:

```
<target name="compile" depends="prepare-dirs">
   <javac destdir="build/WEB-INF/classes"
          debug="on"
          optimize="on"
          classpathref="local.classpath">
      <src path="src"/>
   </javac>
</target>
```

The `dist` ant build target creates the subdirectory `dist` and creates the output war file in this new directory. The entire contents of the directory `build` is copied into this war file:

```
<target name="dist" depends="compile">
   <mkdir dir="dist"/>
   <jar jarfile="dist/${project.name}.war" basedir="build"/>
</target>
```

The `clean` ant build target simply deletes the directories `dist` and build:

```
<target name="clean">
   <delete dir="dist"/>
   <delete dir="build"/>
</target>
```

The `deploy` ant build task uses the Tomcat management web services interface to hot deploy this web application to a running Tomcat server. You will need the absolute path name to the war file for this web application; you use the ant task `pathconvert` to convert a relative path name to an absolute path name. You need to explicitly set the `dirsep` attribute for this build file to work on Windows and Linux/Mac OS X/Unix systems. After converting the path, you can use the ant `echo` task to print out the full path name. I often use `echo` for "debugging" my ant build scripts and, in this case, I decided to leave the `echo` task in this script after I got it working. You can use the ant `taskdef` task to define a new ant task. In this case, you need to use the `InstallTask` class, and here you give the task the name `"deploy-to-tomcat"`. Next, you use this new task to do the actual hot deployment. The attribute `path` specifies the web context. The attribute `url` is the Tomcat management web service URL. The attribute `war` contains a fully qualified JAR URL for the war file:

```
<target name="deploy" depends="dist">
   <pathconvert property="absolute.war.file.path" dirsep="/">
      <path>
         <pathelement location="dist/${project.name}.war" />
      </path>
```

```
    </pathconvert>
    <echo>
      "Absolute war file path: ${absolute.war.file.path}"
    </echo>
    <taskdef name="deploy-to-tomcat"
             classname="org.apache.catalina.ant.InstallTask" />
    <deploy-to-tomcat path="/${project.name}"
                      url="${tomcat.manager.url}"
                      username="${tomcat.username}"
                      password="${tomcat.password}"
              war="jar:file:/${absolute.war.file.path}!/" />
  </target>
```

This last ant build task (`deploy`) will fail if this web application is already deployed. You use the `undeploy` ant build task to hot undeploy this web application. When I develop web applications, I edit source files as needed and do an "`ant undeploy`", followed by an "`ant deploy`". You might want to create a separate ant target that depends on "`undeploy`" and then "`deploy`" to collapse these last two steps. I prefer keeping them separate.

```
    <target name="undeploy" depends="dist">
       <taskdef name="undeploy-from-tomcat"
                classname="org.apache.catalina.ant.RemoveTask" />
       <undeploy-from-tomcat path="/${project.name}"
                             url="${tomcat.manager.url}"
                             username="${tomcat.username}"
                             password="${tomcat.password}" />
    </target>

  </project>
```

Writing web applications with JSPs (with perhaps the Struts framework as used in this example) is a powerful technique for writing web applications. Using ant build scripts to build and hot deploy your web applications takes the manual effort out of your development process and lets you concentrate on presentation (the JSPs) and your business logic (JavaBeans, deployed EJBs, etc.).

Combining JSPs and EJBs

In addition to using JavaBeans to build JSP-based web applications, you will also sometimes want to use EJBs either directly from your JSPs, or better, from JavaBean business objects that are used in your JSPs. One thing that you do not want to do is to create huge monolithic projects that build all required EJBs and the client web application. Both JavaBeans and EJBs are component architectures. The value of using components like JavaBeans and EJBs is that they are developed, tested, and maintained separately.

If you are combining JSPs and EJBs, you will likely use JBoss (or another EJB container of your choice). The following discussion assumes the use of JBoss. I will cover JBoss deployment in some detail in Solution 57. As a result, an ant build file for a combined JSP and EJB project will contain a property specifying the file path to your JBoss server deployment and not use the Tomcat hot deployment ant task. I will discuss combining JSPs and EJBs further at the end of Solution 57.

SOLUTION 57

Using Ant and XDoclet for EJB/JBoss Projects

PROBLEM You want to use ant and XDoclet to facilitate EJB/JBoss development.

SOLUTION I will show you how the ant scripts for Solutions 50 through 53 (coding EJBs with XDoclet tags) work and how to set up your own projects.

You saw how to write the Java code for EJBs in Solutions 50 through 53. In this solution, I am going to show you how to use ant build files for two distinct types of EJB projects:

- Message-Driven EJBs (MDBs) that are written without XDoclet tags.
- Session- and container-managed persistent EJBs that utilize XDoclet tags to automatically generate home and remote interfaces.

I have an ant build file that I use for XDoclet EJB projects and another that I use for non-EJB projects. Except for changing a few property values at the top of the ant build file, the `build.xml` files are identical in Solutions 50 and 51; the ant build file for Solution 53 has one extra line specifying the path to the client JAR file for Solution 51.

This means you can use the two build files that I use for XDoclet and non-XDoclet EJB projects, and with trivial changes, use them in your projects. While you should feel free initially to use these build files without digging too deeply into how they work, eventually you will want to use ant in your own creative ways to automate and speed up your own Java development process. In the next two sections, I will go into detail about how these two generic ant build files work.

Generic Ant *build.xml* File for XDoclet-Based EJBs

The material in this solution is specific to the JBoss EJB container, but it is also relevant to using other types of servers. You will see that deploying web application WAR and EAR files is simpler using the JBoss/Tomcat bundle than just using Tomcat. This will make the ant build file simpler, at least for deployment. However, using the XDoclet ant tasks is fairly complex. Using XDoclet tags made the EJB examples in Solutions 50, 51, and 53 simple because you did not have to write home and remote interfaces. Here, you will see both how the XDoclet ant tasks create these interfaces for you and how they handle much of the complexity of creating EJB XML configuration files.

WARNING As noted in Solutions 50, 51, and 53, my EJB ant build process relies on a couple assumptions: all EJB classes must end with `"Bean"`, and all EJB classes must be in a package ending with `".server"`. The following ant build file depends on these assumptions.

The `build.xml` files for XDoclet-based EJBs are found in the following example directories:

- `parts_12_13_src/session` (Solution 50)
- `parts_12_13_src/container` (Solution 51)
- `parts_12_13_src/transaction` (Solution 53)

Here, you will just look at the `build.xml` file for stateless session EJBs:

```
<?xml version="1.0"?>
```

For your projects, you will want to change the project name. I set the default ant build target to `"options"` which prints out a list of all available build targets in this file. A good alternative for a default target is `"deploy"`.

```
<!--  NOTE: CHANGE THE PROJECT NAME FOR YOUR PROJECT:  -->

<project name="session_demo" basedir="." default="options">
```

When you reuse this ant build file for your XDoclet-based EJB projects, it is likely that the only thing that you need to change is the root project name property:

```
<!-- NOTE: THE REST OF THIS FILE CAN REMAIN UNCHANGED
     FOR YOUR NEW PROJECTS
-->
    <property name="root.project.name"
              value="${ant.project.name}"/>
    <property name="ear.file" value="${root.project.name}.ear"/>
    <property name="jar.module" value="${root.project.name}.jar"/>
```

You will need to set the property JBOSS_HOME on your development system to point to the top-level JBoss installation directory. The following two property elements access the system-wide environment values and then the value of the JBOSS_HOME system environment variable:

```
<property environment="env"/>
<property name="jboss.home" value="${env.JBOSS_HOME}"/>
```

The JBoss server has three standard configurations: minimal contains only JNDI, logging, and dynamic loading facilities; default contains all possible JBoss services except multiple server clustering options and RMI using CORBA IIOP; and all contains all possible services. Except for experimenting with JBoss, I always use the default server option, so I hardcode this option into my ant build files:

```
<property name="dir.jboss.deploy"
          value="${jboss.home}/server/default/deploy"/>
```

The following local CLASSPATH setting contains all required JAR files and compiled application class files:

```
<path id="local.classpath">
    <pathelement location="build"/>
    <pathelement location="auto-generated-source-code-build"/>
    <pathelement location="${ant.home}/lib/xdoclet.jar"/>
    <pathelement path="${jboss.home}/client/jboss-j2ee.jar"/>
    <pathelement
          path="${jboss.home}/client/jnp-client.jar"/>
    <pathelement
          path="${jboss.home}/client/jboss-client.jar"/>
    <pathelement path="${jboss.home}/lib/jboss-jaas.jar"/>
    <pathelement path="${jboss.home}/lib/ext/jboss.jar"/>
    <pathelement path="${jboss.home}/lib/jmxri.jar"/>
    <pathelement path="${jboss.home}/client/jndi.properties"/>
    <pathelement location="${ant.home}/lib/log4j.jar"/>
    <pathelement location="${ant.home}/lib/ant.jar"/>
</path>
```

The following default ant build target simply prints out other build options using the echo ant task:

```
<target name="options" description="print out build options">
    <echo>Options:</echo>
    <echo>
      ant deploy  - completely generate code, compile and
      deploy to JBoss</echo>
    <echo>ant undeploy  - undeploy from JBoss</echo>
    <echo>
      ant clean  - remove all generated and compiled
```

```
        files - get a clean system
    </echo>
</target>
```

Because you are using XDoclet, the build process creates several working build directories and lots of files. The `clean` ant build target deletes all generated code, compiled class files, and the application EAR file. Note that the second delete task also removes the deployed EAR file from the JBoss server—this hot undeploys the EJB. You should comment out the second delete task if you do not want an `"ant clean"` to also undeploy your EJB:

```
<target name="clean" description="cleans everything">
    <delete dir="build"/>
    <delete dir="${dir.jboss.deploy}/${ear.file}"/>
    <delete dir="auto-generated-source-code"/>
    <delete dir="auto-generated-source-code-build"/>
    <delete dir="distribution"/>
</target>
```

The build process requires five working directories:

```
<target name="make.working.dirs">
    <mkdir dir="build"/>
    <mkdir dir="auto-generated-source-code-build"/>
    <mkdir dir="auto-generated-source-code"/>
    <mkdir dir="distribution"/>
    <mkdir dir="auto-generated-source-code/ejb/META-INF"/>
</target>
```

The `undeploy` ant build task simply removes the EJB ear file from the JBoss deployment directory; this hot undeploys the EJB:

```
<target name="undeploy"
     <delete file="${dir.jboss.deploy}/${ear.file}"/>
</target>
```

The `generate.ejb` ant build task uses the XDoclet ant task to generate the home and remote interfaces:

```
<target name="generate.ejb">
    <taskdef name="ejbdoclet"
             classname="xdoclet.ejb.EjbDocletTask">
```

The JAR file for the XDoclet task is on the local CLASSPATH:

```
        <classpath refid="local.classpath"/>
        </taskdef>
```

The `ejbdoclet` task performs a lot of work for you; I will go through the attributes explaining the purpose of each:

```
    <ejbdoclet
```

The default EJB specification is 1.1, but I prefer using the newer specification:

```
ejbspec="2.0"
```

You must specify the output directory for the automatically generated Java code:

```
destdir="auto-generated-source-code"
```

The local CLASSPATH contains all class and JAR files for running this task:

```
classpathref="local.classpath"
sourcepath="src">
```

The subtask `packageSubstitution` is used to switch package names in the generated code from ending with `".server"` to ending with `".interfaces"`. The client test applications in Solutions 50, 51, and 53 use these generated interface files to obtain home and local interfaces for the EJB:

```
<packageSubstitution packages="server"
                     substituteWith="interfaces"/>
```

The `ejbdoclet` task will process all Java source files in the `src` directory (and subdirectories) ending with `"Bean.java"`:

```
<fileset dir="src">
    <include name="**/*Bean.java"/>
</fileset>
```

Instruct the `ejbdoclet` task to generate home, remote, and session interfaces:

```
<homeinterface/>
<remoteinterface/>
<session/>
```

Specify the relative directory path for the automatically generated EJB deployment description file:

```
<deploymentdescriptor
  destdir="auto-generated-source-code/ejb/META-INF"/>
```

Specify the relative directory path for the JBoss deployment descriptor and options:

```
        <jboss
            version="3.0"
            xmlencoding="UTF-8"
            destdir="auto-generated-source-code/ejb/META-INF"
            validatexml="true"/>
    </ejbdoclet>
</target>
```

The `ejbdoclet` task created automatically generated Java code and deployment descriptors. The `compile.ejb` ant target compiles these automatically generated classes:

```
<target name="compile.ejb"
        depends="make.working.dirs, generate.ejb">
```

First, you compile all application classes in the `src/**` server directory:

```
    <javac srcdir="src" destdir="build">
        <classpath refid="local.classpath"/>
        <include name="**/server/"/>
    </javac>
```

Next, you compile the automatically generated classes:

```
    <javac srcdir="auto-generated-source-code"
           destdir="auto-generated-source-code-build">
        <classpath refid="local.classpath"/>
        <include name="**/*"/>
    </javac>
</target>
```

The `jar.ejb.server` builds a JAR file containing compiled code and configuration data files:

```
<target name="jar.ejb.server" depends="compile.ejb">
    <jar jarfile="build/${jar.module}">
        <fileset dir="auto-generated-source-code-build">
            <include name="**/*"/>
        </fileset>
        <fileset dir="build">
            <include name="**/server/"/>
        </fileset>
```

You need to include both the JBoss configuration data and the EJB configuration data in the meta information:

```
        <metainf
           dir="auto-generated-source-code/ejb/META-INF/"
           includes="ejb-jar.xml,jboss.xml"/>
     </jar>
</target>
```

The ear ant build target packages the EJB EAR file, the library JAR files, and the required application configuration file (more on this later) in the EJB EAR file:

```
<target name="ear" depends="jar.ejb.server">
    <ear earfile="build/${ear.file}"
         appxml="application.xml">
        <fileset dir="build" includes="${jar.module}"/>
    </ear>
</target>
```

The `deploy` ant target simply has to copy the EJB ear file to the JBoss server deployment directory. JBoss will "notice" a new ear file and hot deploy it for you.

```
    <target name="deploy" depends="ear">
        <copy file="build/${ear.file}"
              todir="${dir.jboss.deploy}"/>
    </target>

</project>
```

This ant build file is fairly generic (I use it for all of my XDoclet-based EJB development). You did have to edit one property for new projects:

```
<property name="root.project.name" value="session_demo"/>
```

There is one more change that you must make for new projects: editing the `application.xml` file. Here is the `application.xml` that matches this `build.xml` file:

```
<?xml version="1.0" encoding="UTF-8"?>

<!DOCTYPE application PUBLIC
          '-//Sun Microsystems, Inc.//DTD J2EE Application 1.3//EN'
          'http://java.sun.com/dtd/application_1_3.dtd'>

<application>
    <display-name>Session EJB Demo</display-name>
    <module>
        <ejb>session_demo.jar</ejb>
    </module>
</application>
```

I highlighted in bold font the two changes you need to make: changing the EJB display name and setting the name of the EJB ear filename. You should notice that the strings `session_demo` must match in both the `build.xml` and `application.xml` files.

After you deploy this EJB to JBoss, you can run the sample test client as per the instructions in Solution 50.

Generic Ant *build.xml* File for EJBs That Do Not Use XDoclet

The Message-Driven EJB (MDB) developed in Solution 52 did not use XDoclet because MDBs do not need home and remote interfaces. While this makes the ant build file a little simpler, you will have to manually create both the `jboss.xml` and `ejb-jar.xml` configuration files. You also need to manually edit the `jndi.properties` file. The following illustration shows the directory layout and files in a clean state. You can always get back to a clean development state by running `ant clean`.

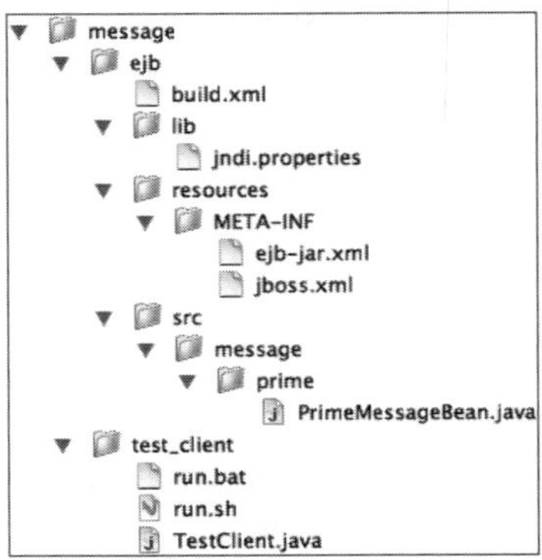

Before going into any details on the ant build file, I want to show you the changes that you will need to make to the `jndi.properties`, `ejb-jar.xml`, and `jboss.xml` files when you reuse this project for your own MDB projects. The following code snippet shows the contents of the file `jndi.properties`:

```
java.naming.factory.initial=
   org.jnp.interfaces.NamingContextFactory
java.naming.factory.url.pkgs=org.jboss.naming:org.jnp.interfaces
java.naming.provider.url=localhost
```

The first two properties will have to be changed if you are not using JBoss. The third property must be changed if you run JBoss in a clustering mode and the naming service is on a different host computer.

The following code snippet shows the contents of the `ejb-jar.xml` file with changes that you need to make for your own projects in bold font:

```
<?xml version="1.0" encoding="UTF-8"?>
<!DOCTYPE ejb-jar PUBLIC "-//Sun Microsystems, Inc.//DTD Enterprise JavaBeans
2.0//EN" "http://java.sun.com/dtd/ejb-jar_2_0.dtd">

<ejb-jar >

   <description>Example MDB</description>
   <display-name>Prime MDB</display-name>

   <enterprise-beans>
      <message-driven >
         <description>example</description>
         <display-name></display-name>
```

```
            <ejb-name>message/prime</ejb-name>
            <ejb-class>message.prime.PrimeMessageBean</ejb-class>
            <transaction-type>Container</transaction-type>
            <message-driven-destination>
               <destination-type>javax.jms.Queue</destination-type>
               <subscription-durability>
                  NonDurable
               </subscription-durability>
            </message-driven-destination>
            <security-identity>
                <run-as>
                    <role-name>Server</role-name>
                </run-as>
            </security-identity>
         </message-driven>
      </enterprise-beans>

      <assembly-descriptor >
        <security-role>
            <role-name>Server</role-name>
        </security-role>
        <container-transaction>
          <method>
            <ejb-name>message/prime</ejb-name>
            <method-name>*</method-name>
          </method>
          <trans-attribute>Required</trans-attribute>
        </container-transaction>
      </assembly-descriptor>
   </ejb-jar>
```

Most of the indicated changes are obvious: changing the display name, EJB name, and EJB class. The other change is critical:

```
<subscription-durability>
    NonDurable
</subscription-durability>
```

The other possible value is `Durable`, in which case message traffic is logged to persistent storage so you will not lose messages if the server crashes. The following code snippet shows the contents of the file `jboss.xml` with text that you will change for your projects in bold font:

```
<?xml version="1.0" encoding="UTF-8"?>
<!DOCTYPE jboss PUBLIC "-//JBoss//DTD JBOSS//EN" "http://www.jboss.org/j2ee/dtd/
jboss.dtd">

<jboss>
   <enterprise-beans>
```

```
        <message-driven>
            <ejb-name>message/prime</ejb-name>
            <destination-jndi-name>
                queue/CheckPrime
            </destination-jndi-name>
        </message-driven>
    </enterprise-beans>
</jboss>
```

Here, you would want to change the EJB name and JNDI lookup name as appropriate for your MDB projects.

The following listing shows the contents of the ant `build.xml` file. If you reuse this in your MDB projects, the only change you need to make is the project name (in bold font in this listing):

```
<?xml version="1.0"?>

<!-- NOTE: CHANGE THE PROJECT NAME FOR YOUR NEW PROJECTS: -->

<project name="primemdb" default="deploy" basedir=".">
```

You should not have to change anything else in this file when you reuse this project.

```
<property environment="env"/>
<property name="jboss.home" value="${env.JBOSS_HOME}"/>
<path id="local.classpath">
    <pathelement location="build"/>
    <pathelement location="lib" />
```

Add all JAR files in the `JBOSS/lib` directory to the local CLASSPATH:

```
    <fileset dir="${jboss.home}/lib">
        <include name="*.jar"/>
    </fileset>
    <fileset dir="${jboss.home}/server/default/lib">
        <include name="*.jar"/>
    </fileset>
    <fileset dir="${jboss.home}/server/default/deploy">
        <include name="*.jar"/>
    </fileset>
</path>
```

Unlike the ant build file for XDoclet projects, here you only need to compile all source files in the `src` directory (and subdirectories) and put the resulting compiled class files in the `build` directory:

```
<target name="compile">
    <mkdir dir="build"/>
    <javac destdir="build"
           debug="on"
```

```
            optimize="on"
            classpathref="local.classpath">
        <src path="src"/>
    </javac>
</target>
```

The `dist` ant target copies the `META-INF` directory from the `resources` directory to the `build` directory, creates a `dist` directory, and writes a JAR file to the `dist` directory:

```
<target name="dist" depends="compile">
   <copy todir="build">
      <fileset dir="resources"/>
   </copy>
   <mkdir dir="dist"/>
```

Ant automatically creates a property `ant.project.name` from the project name attribute; you use this name to create a JAR filename:

```
   <jar jarfile="dist/${ant.project.name}.jar"
        basedir="build"/>
</target>

<target name="clean">
   <delete dir="dist"/>
   <delete dir="build"/>
</target>
```

The `deploy` target copies the JAR file from the `dist` directory to the JBoss server deployment directory:

```
<target name="deploy" depends="dist">
   <copy todir="${jboss.home}/server/default/deploy">
      <fileset dir="dist"/>
   </copy>
</target>
```

The `undeploy` ant build target deletes the EJB JAR file from the JBoss server deploy directory—this hot undeploys the EJB:

```
   <target name="undeploy">
      <delete
file="${jboss.home}/server/default/deploy/${ant.project.name}.jar"/>
   </target>

</project>
```

I find the example project files discussed in this section very useful for Message-Driven EJBs; I can create and test a new MDB very quickly using this framework—I hope that it also simplifies your MDB projects. However, for all other types of EJBs, I prefer using XDoclet.

SOLUTION 58

Writing JUnit Test Classes

PROBLEM You like using ant for your Java development process. Now you want to integrate JUnit tests with your ant build processes.

SOLUTION I will show you how to write Java JUnit test classes and how to use these with ant.

The example directory `parts_12_13_src` contains four EJB examples; two of these, stateless session EJBs and container managed persistence EJBs had JUnit tests. After introducing you to JUnit, I will show you these JUnit tests and examples of using JUnit with standalone Java programs and classes. In addition to the JUnit tests in the `parts_12_13_src` directory (found in the `parts_12_13_src.zip` file on the website for this book) the directory `junit_demos` (found in the `junit_demos.zip` file on the website) contains tests for individual classes.

Getting Up to Speed

You already know how to write ant build files, so using JUnit will be simple. There are two steps in writing unit tests with JUnit: adding JUnit test targets to your ant build files and writing test classes that are derived from the JUnit base testing class `junit.framework.TestCase`.

Before starting with a simple example, I want to cover some of the philosophy of test-driven programming and discuss some benefits. Testing should be an integral part of development—no one would argue this point. However, running tests should not be dull repetitive work for developers. With automated testing, it is easier to be flexible and change code rapidly when your boss or customers desire changes. If you break code, you want to know about it sooner rather than later.

In object-oriented design and development, it is difficult to get the design of classes right the first time. A key part of object-oriented development is the ability to easily refactor classes by moving methods, abstracting out common behavior to super classes, etc. Automated testing makes it easier to "do the right thing" and refactor when appropriate. In the long run, you will reduce the costs of development if you take the time to incrementally improve your design. Spending the time to set up automated testing will save time so that you can afford to spend time on iteratively improving design and implementation and adding new features.

Unit Testing Java Classes

Okay, I assume that you are motivated, so I will present a very simple example to get you up to speed on both writing JUnit test classes and the required ant build file test targets. The first example you will look at is in the directory `junit_demos/simple`. The following illustration shows the project directory structure for this first project:

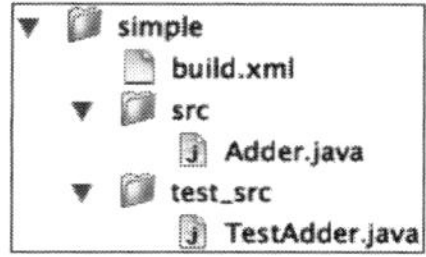

I like to keep the unit test Java source files in a separate directory `test_src`. This illustration shows a clean project directory. Using the ant build targets produces a working directory `build` where compiled class files for both the application classes and the unit test classes are written.

The following code snippet shows the application class that we will be testing:

```
public class Adder {
    public double add(double num1, double num2) {
        return num1 + num2;
    }
    public double add(String n1, String n2) {
        return Double.parseDouble(n1) + Double.parseDouble(n2);
    }
}
```

You will write two separate tests, one for each public method, but you can place them in one test class; the following code snippets show the implementation of the test class `TestAdder`:

```
import junit.framework.TestCase;
```

You derive your test classes from the JUnit `TestCase` base test class. You must call the super class constructor in this class constructor. The ant build file for this project (which you will look at later) expects test classes to start with `Test`.

```
public class TestAdder extends TestCase {
    public TestAdder(String test) {
        super(test);
    }
```

The tests will require an instance of class `Adder`, so you will share one instance among all of the tests:

```
private Adder adder;
```

The JUnit ant task will call the method `setUp()` in your test class before automatically calling each method that starts with `test`. Here, you create an instance of the `Adder` class that is used in the test methods:

```
/** * The fixture set up called before every test method. */
protected void setUp() throws Exception {
    adder = new Adder();
}
```

The `tearDown()` method will be called by the JUnit ant task after all `test` methods are called. This method is empty for this test class, but it is often useful to perform clean-up work here (for example, closing any database connections if a database is used, etc.).

```
/** * The fixture clean up called after every test method. */
protected void tearDown() throws Exception {
}
```

The test methods that you write use JUnit utility classes to check values of calculations and notify the JUnit ant task if unexpected results occur:

```
public void testDouble() throws Exception {
    double answer = adder.add(10, 20.12345);
```

Here you are using the `assertTrue()` method to see if the value of the variable `answer` is equal to 30.12345. Note that sometimes numeric values do not compare exactly, so numeric tests like the following one can be replaced with a test checking that the absolute value of the difference of two numbers is smaller than a very small number. You will look at more JUnit utility methods later that are inherited from the super class.

```
    assertTrue(answer == 30.12345);
}
```

The following test method checks the second method in the `Adder` class:

```
    public void testString() throws Exception {
        double answer = adder.add("10", "20");
        assertTrue(answer == 30);
    }

}
```

The unit tests in this example are fine-grained: each test checks one API call. In the next section, you will see courser-grained testing (integration testing) when you test entire classes and frameworks.

The two test methods use the `assertTrue()` method to check that the test results are correct. Other assert methods inherited from the super class are:

assertEqual() Checks that the arguments are equal.

assertFalse() Checks that the argument is false.

assertTrue() Checks that the argument is true.

assertNotNull() Checks that the argument is not null.

assertNull() Checks that the argument is null.

assertNotSame() Checks that the arguments do not reference the same object in memory.

assertSame() Checks that the arguments reference the same object in memory.

fail() Causes the test to fail returning the string argument as a failure message (this is useful to fail a test if an expected exception is not thrown).

The following code snippets show the contents of the ant build file for this project that includes the use of the JUnit ant task. I assume that you are up to speed on the use of ant now, so I will just comment on the use of JUnit in this ant build file.

```
<?xml version="1.0"?>

<project name="JUnit ant example" default="junit" basedir=".">

  <property name="dir.src" value="src"/>
  <property name="dir.test.src" value="test_src"/>
  <property name="dir.build" value="build"/>
  <property name="dir.build.test" value="build-test"/>
  <property name="dir.dist" value="dist"/>

  <path id="local.classpath">
    <pathelement path="${dir.build}"/>
  </path>

  <target name="prepare">
    <mkdir dir="${dir.build}"/>
  </target>

  <target name="clean">
    <delete dir="${dir.build}"/>
    <delete dir="${dir.build.test}"/>
    <delete dir="${dir.dist}"/>
  </target>
```

I like to separate the building of my application classes from the JUnit test classes; first, compile the application classes:

```
<target name="compile" depends="prepare">
  <javac srcdir="${dir.src}" destdir="${dir.build}">
    <classpath refid="local.classpath"/>
  </javac>
</target>
```

The application classes must be compiled before the JUnit test classes so you make the "compile" build target a dependency of the "compile-tests" target. You should notice that I write the test output class files to a separate build directory: this makes it easier to build an application JAR file without the test classes.

```
<target name="compile-tests" depends="compile">
  <javac srcdir="${dir.test.src}" destdir="${dir.build.test}">
    <classpath refid="local.classpath"/>
  </javac>
</target>
```

The "junit" target uses the junit ant task. This task is available because you installed JUnit with ant in Solution 54.

```
<target name="junit" depends="compile, compile-tests">
```

The junit task does a lot of work: the way I am using it here, it scans the test source directory (and recursively any subdirectories) for files matching the pattern Test*.java and then finds these test classes in the current CLASSPATH and runs them. I set the attribute fork to false so the tests will run in the same JVM as ant; for some test applications, it is useful to spawn another JVM but this slows down testing.

```
<junit printsummary="on" fork="false" showoutput="true"
       haltonfailure="false">

  <classpath refid="local.classpath"/>
  <formatter type="plain" usefile="false"/>
```

The batchtest task runs all available tests in no particular order:

```
<batchtest fork="false" todir="${dir.build}">
  <fileset dir="${dir.test.src}">
```

I want to include all JUnit test classes matching the pattern "Test*.java":

```
        <include name="**/Test*.java"/>
      </fileset>
    </batchtest>
  </junit>
</target>
```

The build-app-jar build target creates a JAR file with the application classes but does not include the JUnit test classes:

```
<target name="build-app-jar" depends="clean, compile">
    <mkdir dir="${dir.dist}"/>
    <jar jarfile="${dir.dist}/adder.jar">
       <fileset dir="build">
           <include name="**/*.class"/>
       </fileset>
```

```
        </jar>
    </target>
</project>
```

The following code snippet shows ant running the `junit` build task. There were no errors during this test. If errors do occur, they would appear in both the program output and the error summary printout.

```
markw% ant junit
Buildfile: build.xml

prepare:
    [mkdir] Created dir: /Users/markw/Content/Java_10_minute_solutions/junit_
demos/simple/build

compile:
    [javac] Compiling 1 source file to /Users/markw/Content/Java_10_minute_
solutions/junit_demos/simple/build

compile-tests:
    [javac] Compiling 1 source file to /Users/markw/Content/Java_10_minute_
solutions/junit_demos/simple/build

junit:
    [junit] Running TestAdder
    [junit] Tests run: 2, Failures: 0, Errors: 0, Time elapsed: 0.032 sec
    [junit] Testsuite: TestAdder
    [junit] Tests run: 2, Failures: 0, Errors: 0, Time elapsed: 0.032 sec

    [junit] Testcase: testDouble took 0.008 sec
    [junit] Testcase: testString took 0 sec

BUILD SUCCESSFUL
Total time: 4 seconds
```

You can also define JUnit test suites that group individual tests. A test suite is a subclass of `junit.framework.TestSuite`. For almost all of my JUnit testing, I use the method in this example: specifying a top-level test directory and using ant to automatically process all tests with the pattern `"Test*.java"`. One advantage of using test suites is that you control the ordering of running tests.

Integration Testing EJBs

JUnit was designed for unit testing. Unit testing is fine-grained testing. However, I also find JUnit to be very useful for coarse-grained automated testing. I will cover integration testing of EJBs in this section. You will use the EJB demo from Solution 50 from the demo directory parts_12_13_src/session in this section. You will recall from Solution 50 that I used separate subdirectories for a test client and JUnit tests:

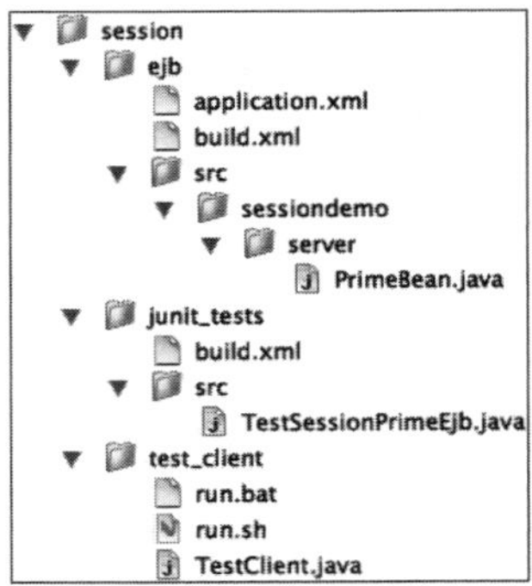

You notice in this illustration that the directory junit_tests has its own ant build file. The ant-based integration testing assumes that both the PrimeBean EJB is built and deployed to a running JBoss server. You will look at the JUnit test class TestSessionPrimeEjb and later at the ant build file:

```
import junit.framework.TestCase;
```

The JUnit test class requires the same EJB-specific support classes that you used for the standalone test client in Solution 50:

```
import javax.naming.InitialContext;
import javax.naming.Context;
import java.util.Hashtable;
```

The test class requires the interfaces automatically created by the XDoclet ant task when building the PrimeBean EJB:

```
import sessiondemo.interfaces.PrimeBean;
import sessiondemo.interfaces.PrimeBeanHome;

public class TestSessionPrimeEjb extends TestCase {
    public TestSessionPrimeEjb(String test) {
        super(test);
    }
```

The setUp() and tearDown() test methods are empty in this example:

```
    /** * The fixture set up called before every test method. */
    protected void setUp() throws Exception {
    }
```

```
    /** * The fixture clean up called after every test method. */
    protected void tearDown() throws Exception {
    }
```

The code in the test method is identical to that in the standalone test client except that you use the JUnit assertTrue() and *assertFalse()* methods to check the results returned from the remote EJB running in the JBoss container:

```
    public void testSomething() throws Exception {

        Hashtable env = new Hashtable();
        env.put(Context.INITIAL_CONTEXT_FACTORY,
                "org.jnp.interfaces.NamingContextFactory");
        env.put(Context.PROVIDER_URL, "localhost:1099");
        env.put("java.naming.factory.url.pkgs",
                "org.jboss.naming:org.jnp.interfaces");
        InitialContext lContext = new InitialContext(env);

        PrimeBeanHome lHome =
           (PrimeBeanHome) lContext.lookup("ejb/PrimeBean");
        PrimeBean primeBean = lHome.create();
```

The checkPrime() method returns a Boolean value, so you use assertTrue() and assertFalse() to make sure that the PrimeBean considers 13 to be a prime number and that 21 is not a prime number:

```
       assertTrue(primeBean.checkPrime(13));
        assertFalse(primeBean.checkPrime(21));
        primeBean.remove();

    }
}
```

Although using JUnit to perform coarse-grained integration testing is a useful technique, I find myself usually using JUnit more often for fine-grained testing for individual APIs as you saw in the last section.

The combination of ant and JUnit is powerful. While you might at first think writing the test classes is too much trouble, once you get used to writing unit tests (and writing these tests very early in your development cycle!), I believe their value will far exceed the time spent writing them.

TIP The www.junit.org website has tutorials and documentation on using JUnit. I have only tried to cover the basics in this solution.

Java Data Objects

SOLUTION 59

Object Persistence with the Hibernate JDO Implementation

PROBLEM You want to automate the mapping between Java objects and their persistent storage in relational databases.

SOLUTION I will show you how to use the open source Hibernate JDO implementation to persist your Java objects.

Java Data Objects (JDO) is a specification for mapping Plain Old Java Objects (POJOs) to rows in database tables. There are several commercial JDO implementations and some open source implementations. Solutions 59 and 60 will use the free open source Hibernate JDO implementation.

TIP JDO is a Sun Java Community Process (JCP) project. More information is available at `www.jcp.org`. The website `www.jdocentral.com` has useful material on JDO.

The goal of the JDO architecture is to provide Java developers with an object-oriented method for persisting data and to abstract away the details of different database servers. Like JDBC, it should be simple to migrate JDO-based Java applications to different database products. The JDO specification defines standard interfaces that are implemented in concrete classes by JDO implementations like Hibernate.

JDO and Container Managed Persistence (CMP) EJBs (see Solution 51) both allow simple mapping between Java data objects and persistent store in a relational or object-oriented database. When do you want to use CMP EJBs and when do you want to use JDO? There is one obvious difference: JDO persisted POJO objects can be used in any Java programs, while CMP EJBs execute in the environment of an EJB container. Another difference is that CMP EJBs provide for remote access, while JDO persisted POJO objects need to be created in the same JVM as the client code.

NOTE The Hibernate JDO implementation can also be used in managed environments. Hibernate development has just become part of the JBoss organization and by the time you read this book, Hibernate might be the default persistence mechanism in JBoss.

Setting Up a Test Database

When you use the Hibernate JDO implementation for the demos in this solution and in Solution 60, you will first use JDBC APIs to create a connection to an existing database "test" and use an existing table "customer". Here is the definition for the table "customer":

```
                Table "customer"

   Column   |       Type        | Modifiers
------------+-------------------+-----------
 customerid | integer           | not null
 name       | character varying |
 address    | character varying |
 email      | character varying |
 phone      | character varying |

Primary key: customerid
```

I am using PostgreSQL for this example, but you can use any database server that you want if you modify the demo programs to change the database URL for your database server (see Solution 34). You should use this SQL statement to create this table:

```
create table customer (customerid integer primary key,
                       name varchar, address varchar,
                       email varchar, phone varchar)
```

One of the demos (the class `TestWrite`) creates several rows in this table, so you will want to execute the SQL command "delete from customer" to clear the table if you rerun the demos.

Getting Started with Hibernate

The ZIP file part14.zip contains the Hibernate examples for this solution and Solution 60. The following illustration shows the project layout for the demo project for both solutions:

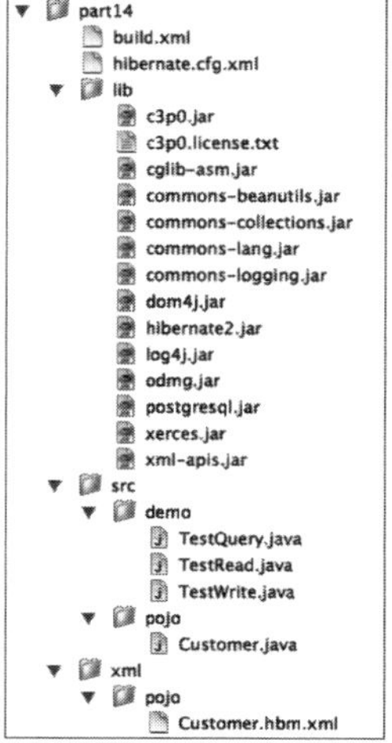

The lib directory contains all JAR files that you will need to both compile the demo programs and to run them; you do not have to download or install Hibernate—these JAR files contain both Hibernate and all required libraries. I used PostgreSQL for the test database, so you may want to replace the postgresql.jar file with a JAR containing JDBC code for your database server. The hibernate.cfg.xml file contains configuration data that you will look at later in this solution. The src directory contains the POJO class Customer and Hibernate demo test programs. The Customer.hbm.xml file contains configuration for the Customer POJO class and should be in the same directory as the file Customer.class at runtime.

NOTE The Hibernate system and supporting libraries included with this example were current as of October 2003—if you start using Hibernate in a production environment, you should get the latest stable version at www.hibernate.org.

Plain Old Java Object Test Class

You need a POJO class for the demo; this class is Customer. A POJO class typically just defines private data and public GET/SET methods to access the private data. The following code snippet shows part of the Customer class implementation (most of the public GET/SET methods are not shown for brevity):

```
package pojo;

public class Customer {
    private int id;
    private String name = "";
    private String address = "";
    private String email = "";
    private String phone = "";

    public String toString() {
        return "Customer: id: " + id + " name: "+name +
               " address: " + address + " email: " +
               email + " phone: " + phone;
    }

    public int getId() {
        return id;
    }

    public void setId(int id) {
        this.id = id;
    }
```

The rest of the class is not listed here but you have the source code in the project directory. The problem that you want to solve is shown in the following illustration: you want to be able to create multiple customer objects in an application and, with the least trouble possible, persist the data in these objects to a database and, at a later time (usually the next time your program runs), restore the transient customer objects from persistent storage.

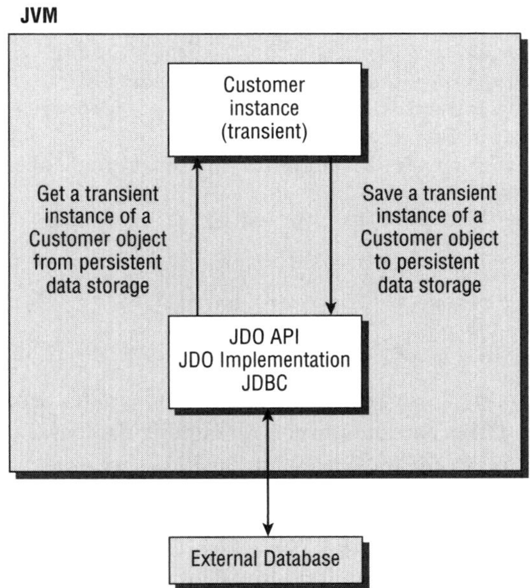

Hibernate Configuration Files

There are three aspects to using the Hibernate JDO implementation: configuring Hibernate, writing a configuration file for each POJO class that you want to persist, and writing the Java code that uses the JDO APIs. In this section, you will look at two configuration files: one for configuring Hibernate and one to specify object to database mappings for the Customer POJO class.

The file `hibernate.cfg.xml` contains general configuration data for running Hibernate. The only changes you have to make for your own projects are setting the data source (that is, the database name) name and the mapping files for your POJO classes (shown here in bold font):

```
<?xml version='1.0' encoding='utf-8'?>
<!DOCTYPE hibernate-configuration PUBLIC
        "-//Hibernate/Hibernate Configuration DTD 2.0//EN"
        "http://hibernate.sourceforge.net/hibernate-configuration-2.0.dtd">
```

```
<hibernate-configuration>
    <!-- a SessionFactory instance listed as /jndi/name -->
    <session-factory
        name="java:comp/env/hibernate/SessionFactory">
        <!-- properties -->
        <property name="connection.datasource">test</property>
        <property
          name="dialect">net.sf.hibernate.dialect.GenericDialect
        </property>
        <property name="show_sql">true</property>
        <property name="use_outer_join">true</property>
        <property name="transaction.factory_
class">net.sf.hibernate.transaction.JTATransactionFactory</property>
        <property
            name="jta.UserTransaction">java:comp/UserTransaction
        </property>
        <!-- mapping files -->
        <mapping resource="Customer.hbm.xml"/>
    </session-factory>
</hibernate-configuration>
```

In the demo programs, I use a database connection created with JDBC so the data source property is ignored. Hibernate supports both generic database support (which you are using here) and specific support for most popular database servers.

For every POJO class that you want to persist in a database, you need a class-specific configuration file. Here is the file for the `Customer` class (things that you are likely to change in your own applications are highlighted in bold font):

```
<?xml version="1.0"?>
<!DOCTYPE hibernate-mapping SYSTEM "http://hibernate.sourceforge.net/hibernate-
mapping-2.0.dtd">

<hibernate-mapping>
```

You need to specify the fully packaged qualified class name and the name of the database table that will be used for persistence:

```
<class name="pojo.Customer" table="customer">
```

The ID element is used to define the class primary key ID name, the Java type for the primary key, and the column name in the table for the primary key in the database. I wanted to explicitly assign the ID to be of type `integer` and use the database column `"customerid"`, so I am using an assigned generator class instead of letting Hibernate generate an ID for me:

```
<id name="id" type="int" column="customerid">
    <generator class="assigned"/>
</id>
```

Besides the primary key, you need to specify the property names to be persisted; for easier configuration, I make these names (class private data) the same names as the associated database column name so it is sufficient to just set the `name` attribute. If you want to map the specified name to a column with a different name, you can also specify a `column` attribute. I did not specify the type for the following properties—Hibernate can determine types by introspection.

```
        <property name="name"/>
        <property name="address"/>
        <property name="email"/>
        <property name="phone"/>
    </class>
</hibernate-mapping>
```

TIP It may look like a bit of a hassle to set up the configuration data for Hibernate and each POJO class that you want to persist, but as long as you do not change database servers or modify the POJO classes, this setup is a one-time process.

Hibernate Demo Programs

You use two demo programs in this section: one for persisting POJOs to a database and the other for restoring objects from the database using primary keys to identify objects. I separated out persisting and restoring objects into separate short example programs. For most applications in which I use Hibernate, I load a set of objects when the program starts, then I use the objects the entire time the program is executing, and then I save modified objects during program shutdown—I am using JDO to access persistent Java objects. An alternative is to simply use JDO as a higher-level abstraction for database access—many short-lived objects are restored from a database, used, discarded, and so on.

NOTE I am going to cover persisting objects to a database and restoring objects from a database in this section. I will cover a database query demo program in Solution 60.

Persisting POJOs to a Database

In this short demo program, I combine Hibernate setup with original object creation, persistence, and so on in one short Java class. You will probably want to separate the setup code and persist code (and the restore code seen in the next section) in different classes in large applications. The following code snippets show the implementation of the `TestWrite` class:

```
package demo;
```

You need to import the following Hibernate classes for this demo:

```
import net.sf.hibernate.cfg.Configuration;
import net.sf.hibernate.MappingException;
import net.sf.hibernate.SessionFactory;
```

```
import net.sf.hibernate.HibernateException;
import net.sf.hibernate.Session;
```

You need two JDBC classes:

```
import java.sql.Connection;
import java.sql.DriverManager;
```

You will be creating instances of class `Customer` and persisting them:

```
import pojo.Customer;

public class TestWrite {
    public static void main(String[] args)
           throws Exception, HibernateException {
```

You need to load a JDBC driver (I am using PostgreSQL—you will have to change this class name if you are using a different database):

```
        Class.forName("org.postgresql.Driver");
```

You need a database connection; change the database URL for your database server type, test database name, and username:

```
        Connection conn =
           DriverManager.getConnection(
           "jdbc:postgresql://localhost:5432/test?user=postgres");
```

You need to create a Hibernate configuration object. The `Configuration` class constructor loads the `hibernate.cfg.xml` file. The `addClass()` method loads the `Customer.hbm.xml` file that contains mapping information for the `Customer` class:

```
        Configuration cfg =
            new Configuration().addClass(Customer.class);
```

You create a Hibernate session factory and then a Hibernate session object using the database connection object:

```
        SessionFactory sessions = cfg.buildSessionFactory();
        Session sess = sessions.openSession(conn);
```

You can create an instance of class `Customer` for testing persistence:

```
        Customer mark = new Customer();
        mark.setId(123);
        mark.setName("Mark");
        mark.setEmail("mark@cc.zzz.com");
        mark.setPhone("111-2222");
```

When you use the Hibernate session object to save this customer instance, the return value is a Java object representing the value of the primary key for the new row in the database. For simple Java types (an `int` in this case), the primary key is wrapped in an object (an `Integer` in this case):

```
        Object obj = sess.save(mark);
        System.out.println("return id from save: " + obj + ", class: " +
                           obj.getClass());
```

Mostly for testing the next two demo programs (one of which is in Solution 60), you want to create several more persisted objects:

```
        for (int i = 1; i < 5; i++) {
            Customer c = new Customer();
            c.setName("name" + i);
            c.setEmail("");
            c.setPhone("" + i + i + i + "-" + i + i + i + i);
            c.setId(i);
            sess.save(c);
        }
```

The `flush()` method will actually write the data to the database:

```
        sess.flush();
```

After you are done with the Hibernate session object, you should close it:

```
        sess.close();
    }
}
```

A Hibernate session maintains a connection to the database, so it is important to close the Hibernate session before your program terminates. I usually leave a Hibernate session while a JDO-based application is running to eliminate the overhead of setting up and closing a session repeatedly. One of the advantages of using a JDO implementation is that you use a simple API for accessing persisted objects while the authors of a JDO implementation worry about efficient database access.

Setting up the Hibernate session is a bit of work, but in a real application you would create one session on program startup and close it when the program terminates. For safety and portability to other JDO implementations, you should use a session object within a single thread and not share it between threads. It is up to you how often you want to save POJOs to the database and flush the session changes. I will discuss flushing sessions in the next section on transactions.

Reading POJOs from a Database

Reading data from a database and recreating POJO objects in memory is simple. The following code snippets are from the test program `TestRead`; most of the Hibernate session setup and creation is not shown because the code is the same as you saw in the last section (I leave out exception handling for brevity):

```
Session sess = sessions.openSession(conn);
Customer cust =
     (Customer) sess.load(Customer.class, new Integer(123));
System.out.println("cust name:" + cust.getName());
```

As you can see, if you know the primary key of an object, it is simple to recreate a POJO. The `load()` method requires two arguments: the POJO class name and the value of a valid primary key in the database table. I chose a simple Java type for the POJO class primary key (an `int`) to drive home a point: Hibernate always expects Java objects for primary key values, so you need to wrap simple Java types as objects.

What do you do if you do not know the primary key for the object you want to restore? Solution 60 introduces the Hibernate query language that lets you find data in a database as you would with SQL select statements.

Using Transactions

You can manually use transactions with JDO by using the following pattern:

```
Session sess = ...
Transaction trans;
try {
    trans = sess.beginTransaction();
    // use JDO APIs here for database updates...
    trans.commit();
} catch (Exception ee) {
    if (trans != null)  trans.rollback();
    ee.printStackTrace();
} finally {
    sess.close();
}
```

You can also set the flush mode for a JDO session. The class `FlushMode` has three static elements that you can use:

AUTO The JDO implementation periodically flushes before query operations to make sure that the cache data and persisted data are synchronized. This is the default flush mode.

COMMIT Useful with transactions: the session is flushed when the transaction `commit()` method is called.

NEVER You have to explicitly call the session's `flush()` method.

You can see what the current flush mode is using:

```
System.out.println("Default flush mode: " +
                   sess.getFlushMode());
```

If you are only reading objects from a database, you can make your code more efficient by calling:

```
sess.setFlushMode(FlushMode.NEVER);
```

TIP The demo directory `part14` contains an ant build file for building and running the examples in this solution and in Solution 60.

SOLUTION 60

Database Queries with Hibernate

PROBLEM You want to be able to search for persisted Java objects based on object fields.

SOLUTION I will show you how to use the Hibernate JDO query facility.

You saw in Solution 59 how persisting Java objects to a database and restoring them is simple using the Hibernate JDO implementation. There is a problem, however: you need to know the primary keys used to store the objects. In this solution, you will look at the Hibernate query language that is similar to SQL but extended to be more object oriented.

The code snippets in this solution are from the class `TestQuery` in the same demo project that I used in Solution 59 (the demo directory `part14`). I will not cover basic use of Hibernate here—I assume that you have read Solution 59. I use the same POJO class `Customer` that I used in Solution 59. The following code snippets show how to perform queries that returns multiple customer objects:

```
Session sess = sessions.openSession(conn);
String s;
```

The following query is similar to an SQL select statement with a few changes: substitute "from" for "select" and use the pattern `in class <Java class name> where <one or more conditions>`. The variable `c` represents a customer and allows conditions to be specified compactly:

```
s = "from c in class Customer where c.id < 3";
System.out.println(s);
Query q = sess.createQuery(s);
```

The `setProperties()` method takes an empty instance of the persisted class and configures the query to fill class instances with the values returned from a matched row in the database. There are other ways to fetch returned values, but I find automatically populating a POJO instance to be the most convenient:

```
q.setProperties(new Customer());
```

The list() method returns a List interface to the fetched data objects:

```
List ll = q.list();
```

You create an iterator from the list to enumerate all customer objects that were fetched by the query:

```
Iterator iter = ll.iterator();
while (iter.hasNext()) {
```

Once you cast the next list item to a `Customer` object, the new object is available for use in any way you want. Remember to persist the object back out to the database if you modify it and want to permanently save the changes (see Solution 59):

```
      Customer c = (Customer)iter.next();
      System.out.println(c.toString());
}
```

The output from this query with the database rows created by the `TestWrite` demo class in Solution 59 is (notice that the ID values are less than 3) as follows:

```
Customer: id: 1 name: name1 address:  email:  phone: 111-1111
Customer: id: 2 name: name2 address:  email:  phone: 222-2222
```

The `www.hibernate.org` website has full documentation on the query language, but I will show you some more example queries to get you started. The following query gets all customer objects from the database where the name field equals "Mark":

```
s = "from c in class Customer where c.name='Mark'";
```

The output from this query with the demo database from Solution 59 is

```
Customer: id: 123 name: Mark address:  email: mark@cc.zzz.com
        phone: 111-2222
```

The following query fetches customer objects where the name field is in the set with members "Mark" and "name4":

```
s = "from c in class Customer where c.name in ('Mark', 'name4')";
```

The output from this query with the demo database from Solution 59 is

```
Customer: id: 123 name: Mark address:  email: mark@cc.zzz.com
          phone: 111-2222
Customer: id: 4 name: name4 address:  email:  phone: 444-4444
```

The following query simply fetches all customers in the database table:

```
s = "from Customer";
```

The output from this query with the demo database from Solution 59 is

```
Customer: id: 123 name: Mark address:  email: mark@cc.zzz.com
          phone: 111-2222
Customer: id: 1 name: name1 address:  email:  phone: 111-1111
Customer: id: 2 name: name2 address:  email:  phone: 222-2222
Customer: id: 3 name: name3 address:  email:  phone: 333-3333
Customer: id: 4 name: name4 address:  email:  phone: 444-4444
```

TIP Remember that only the field `id` is a primary key in this example, so searching on nonindexed fields like name will be slow if the table has many rows. If you are going to be doing many queries on nonprimary key fields, you should manually create database indices for the corresponding table columns.

Index

Note to the Reader: Throughout this index boldfaced page numbers indicate primary discussions of a topic.

A

B

C

D

H

I

J

O

P

Q

R

S

T

U

V

W

X

Z